Contents

Notes on contributors

Daniel Bensaid is a member of the Ligue Communiste Révolutionnaire in France and author, among other works, of *Marx for Our Time*

Paul Blackledge teaches in Leeds and is the author of *Reflections on the Marxist Theory of History*

Joseph Choonara works on *Socialist Worker* and is the author of *Venezuela: Revolution in the 21st Century*

Neil Davidson is the author of *Origins Of Scottish Nationhood*

Charlie Kimber is a journalist on *Socialist Worker* and has written on Africa and the Labour Party in earlier issues of *International Socialism*

Hassan Mahamdallie works for the Arts Council and has previously written in this journal on William Morris (issue 71) and racism in Britain (issue 95)

Andrew Murray works for the Transport and General Workers Union, and is chair of the Stop the War Coalition and a member of the Communist Party of Britain

John Newsinger is the author, most recently, of *The Blood Never Dried: A People's History of the British Empire*

Richard Seymour produces the popular blog Lenin's Tomb

Megan Trudell is doing research on the Italian workers' movement after the First World War

Martin Smith was an activist in the PCS civil servants' union and is author of *The Awkward Squad* and *John Coltrane: Jazz, Racism and Resistance*

The wounded beast

'Mission accomplished' has turned mission bust...the US is facing defeat in Iraq... The longer the US military occupation continues, the already declining US influence in the Middle East will give way to regional extremism and instability—*Zbigniew Brzezinski, architect of US foreign policy for Democratic Party administrations since the mid-1970s*

Stability in Iraq remains illusive and the situation is deteriorating... The ability of the US government to shape outcomes is diminishing. Time is running out... Other countries fear significant violence crossing their borders... Such a broader sectarian conflict could open a Pandora's box of problems—including radicalisation of populations, mass movement of populations and regime changes—that might take decades to play out—*Report of the Iraq Study Group, headed by James Baker, architect of foreign policy under George Bush Senior in the late 1980s*

If you mean by 'military victory' an Iraqi government that can be established and whose writ runs across the whole country, I don't believe that is possible... But a hasty withdrawal from Iraq would have disastrous consequences...for which we would pay for many years—*Henry Kissinger, architect of US foreign policy under Nixon and Reagan*

No, sir—*Reply of Robert Gates, Rumsfeld's replacement, when asked whether the US was winning in Iraq*

The debacle of US policy in Iraq is the central fact of global politics today. The neocons' gambit for to securing 'a New American Century' of global hegemony by occupying Iraq is backfiring with devastating effects for US imperialism—and this can only unleash a political crisis at the heart of the beast. Yet there are still some on the left who fail to understand this.

The seriousness of the situation was spelt out to devastating effect at the beginning of December by one of imperialism's own think tanks, the Iraq Study Group headed by Republican Party heavyweight James Baker and Democratic Party heavyweight Lee Hamilton. It contains language that only deeply worried members of a ruling class would use, bemoaning the loss of 'blood and treasure' with an estimate of the costs to US capitalism of a massive £1,000 billion (equal to seven months output from the British economy). But the worries extend much further than that:

> The global standing of the United States could suffer if Iraq descends further into chaos. Iraq is a major test of, and strain on, US military, diplomatic, and financial capacities. Perceived failure there could diminish America's credibility and influence in a region that is the centre of the Islamic world and vital to the world's energy supply. This loss would reduce America's global influence at a time when pressing issues in North Korea, Iran, and elsewhere demand our full attention and strong US leadership of international alliances.
>
> Continued problems in Iraq could lead to greater polarisation within the United States. Sixty six percent of Americans disapprove of the government's handling of the war, and more than 60 percent feel that there is no clear plan for moving forward. The November elections were largely viewed as a referendum on the progress in Iraq. Arguments about continuing to provide security and assistance to Iraq will fall on deaf ears if Americans become disillusioned with the government that the United States invested so much to create. US foreign policy cannot be successfully sustained without the broad support of the American people.
>
> America's military capacity is stretched thin: we do not have the troops or equipment to make a substantial, sustained increase in our troop presence. Increased deployments to Iraq would also necessarily hamper our ability to provide adequate resources for our efforts in Afghanistan or respond to crises around the world.

No direction out

But even this list of perils does grasp the full depth of the problem. This lies in the inability of US imperialism to see any way to extricate itself from the mess it is in. The contradictions in the report's recommendations are living proof.

It called for negotiations with Iran to stabilise Iraq, but did not indicate how an Iranian government which feels itself to be in a very strong position could be persuaded to accept the US agenda of rebuilding its hegemony over the region. It called on Israel to return the occupied Golan Heights to Syria and to make concession to the Palestinians, but again did not indicate how the Israeli government was going to be persuaded to do these things. It called upon the sectarian political forces the US has put in charge of the Iraqi government to mend their ways, but the inducement it could provide for them to do so was the threat to sink the government (and a key plank of US policy) if they failed to do so.

Above all, it contradicted itself on the central issue, arguing that 'the longer the United States remains in Iraq without progress, the more resentment will grow among Iraqis who believe they are subjects of a repressive American occupation', only to then insist that 'our leaving' would make things 'worse'.

Or, as Lee Hamilton admitted, 'We don't know how it can be turned around, but we have to try.'

No wonder Anthony Cordesman, security adviser to various presidents, says the report should be titled 'The Elephant Gives Birth to a Mouse': 'The US effectively sent a bull to liberate a china shop, and the study group now calls upon the US to threaten to remove the bull if the shop doesn't fix the china'.[1]

Such language shows how deep are the divisions within the US ruling class over what to do. The core group of the US administration around Bush are resistant to giving any ground over Iraq. Their immediate response to the report was to up their pressure on Syria (using the excuse of the assassination of Pierre Gemayal), to press ahead with the call for sanctions against Iran, and to rubbish any talk of pressure on Israel. And they could even find a passage in the Baker report to justify such an approach. It called for the US to maintain a major military presence in Bahrain, Kuwait and Qatar, even if it is forced to withdraw from Iraq, so as 'to deter even more destructive interference in Iraq by Syria and Iran'. As Simon Tisdall of the *Guardian* comments, this is 'an apparent threat of military strikes against the two countries'.[2]

The politics of pending defeat

All this is remarkably similar to previous efforts of imperialist powers to keep their possessions in the face of increasingly successful resistance activities—the British in Ireland in 1920-21, in India in 1946-47 and in Aden in 1967, the French in Algeria in 1958-61 and, of course, the US in Vietnam in 1968-75.

Fear of a loss of global influence led on each occasion to desperate attempts to hang on in the face of mounting losses (and exactly the same warnings of armed forces stretched almost to breaking point). There were agonised debates within cabinets and military high commands, with bitter divisions emerging between those who believed it was possible to 'see things through to the end' and those who saw that was impossible. In each case, those who wanted to hold on prevailed, using the most barbarous means—until suddenly staying was no longer an option and there was a humiliating scramble to get out as quickly as possible.

In the process, they could not only cause devastating chaos in the occupied countries (the partition of Ireland and India), but, in the cases of Algeria and the US, political crises at home (the series of attempted military coups in France, the huge anti-war movement and the Watergate affair in the US).[3]

The Christian fundamenalists in the White House and the secular capitalists who back them will be haunted by the biblical tag, 'A house divided against itself cannot stand.' The US ruling class is caught between the fear that the 'Saigon moment' of complete defeat is approaching and the fear of the consequences of admitting it. This is true of the Republican administration, weakened by the congressional election results. But it is also true of the Democratic Party, whose leaders went along with the war. They are jubilant because they managed to do well in the November elections, getting large numbers of people who want the US troops out of Iraq to vote for candidates who are for keeping them there (as Hillary Clinton made absolutely clear on prime time television). Their only difference with Bush's policy, that of wanting a 'multilateral' policy of bringing on board the French and German governments, does not provide a way forward, since the point has long been reached where the combined efforts of the European and American governments are no more likely to bring stability than the efforts of the US government alone.

The whole American political establishment is faced with a problem that it cannot solve easily and which is not going to go away. This makes further splits within it—within both its parties—inevitable as its members row with each other about the way out. The consequences will be felt not only in the Middle East, but throughout the world as well—including in the US itself. When the ruling class cannot continue in the old way, there is hope for all those who want to fight against it.

Causes and consequences

There has been a powerful current of feeling on the left to the effect that imperialism is all-powerful. This can sometimes be an understandable reaction to those pretend left wingers (the Hallidays and Hitchens) who see the US as somehow able to bring civilisation and 'human rights' to the rest of the world (see Richard Seymour's account of their twists and turns later in this issue). But it is an overreaction that contains dangers of its own. For, if US imperialism is too powerful for resistance to succeed against it, the logic can be for its opponents to 'self-limit' their resistance in the hope of not provoking an onslaught from it. What seems like a very 'leftist' analysis of imperialism ends up collapsing into the mildest reformism, if not complete passivity and miserablism.

That is why we have debated these issues in this journal over the last three and a half years (see, for instance, the debate between Alex Callinicos on the one hand and Leo Panitch and Sam Gindin on the other, in issues 107, 108 and 109 of *International Socialism*). It was this which led us to assert, in the immediate aftermath of the US taking of Baghdad in 2003:

> The determination of the Bush gang to hammer home the US's global military hegemony by going to war without allies (apart from Britain) ensured they blitzkrieged their way to Baghdad without establishing the prerequisites for the quick establishment of a stable new pro-US regime. In the aftermath they are faced with the choice between staying for a very long period of time or putting in Iraqi clients who may not be able to keep control of the country as a whole... This choice was causing splits within the Bush administration's 'unilateralist' war camp the very day after the conquest of Baghdad... The US triumphant remains the US weak. The splits with the other powers will continue, even though they will alternate between defiant gestures and grovelling actions. There will also be recurrent splits within the US political establishment and ruling class as the Bush magic fails to transmute military self-glorification into the humdrum business of making bigger profits.[4]

The only fault with our analysis was that we underestimated how quickly Iraqi resistance would cause devastating problems for the US. It is these problems which will ricochet around the world—and probably wreak havoc within US domestic politics—in the period ahead.

War seemed a logical policy in 2001 and 2003 for members of a ruling class whose huge military power stands in marked contrast to the relative weakening of their economic power over the last half century. The US accounts for 45 percent of world military spending but only around 20 percent of world GNP—and is now the world's biggest debtor (see the graphs in the article 'Snapshots of Capitalism' later in this journal). And bombs can be deployed to 'persuade' others to toe the line even if troops are not available. The temptation to have another go may well be too great for sectors of the American ruling class to resist.

US imperialism cannot take defeat in Iraq lying down. It will try to hit out to restore its position, as it did last summer by backing the Israeli attack on Lebanon. But it will do so from a position of weakness, and can easily miscalculate—as it did in that war.

This is no time for the anti-war movement to wind down. We have to be prepared not only for a continuation of the carnage in Iraq, but also for sudden military confrontations elsewhere. For these reasons it is scandalous that a party like Rifondazione Comunista in Italy, whose leaders campaigned against the wars on Afghanistan and Iraq in 2001-2003, is now prepared to vote through support for the sending of troops to Afghanistan and Lebanon (see Megan Trudell's article in this journal). Not only is the carnage in Afghanistan and Lebanon as horrific as the continuing carnage in Iraq, but the impact of defeat for US and British imperialism (and for their Italian, French and German NATO allies) can further weaken the forces of an already damaged imperialism. We have a duty to fight against the carnage—and in doing so, increase the possibilities of victories against imperialism everywhere in the world.

NOTES

1: Quoted in *Financial Times*, 7 December 2006.

2: *Guardian*, 8 December 2006.

3: For more on this see Chris Harman, *Socialist Review*, November 2006.

4: Chris Harman, 'Analysing Imperialism', *International Socialism* 99 (Summer 2003).

In the name of decency: the contortions of the pro-war left

Richard Seymour

In January 2005, following the torture and murder of the Iraqi trade unionist Hadi Saleh, 'Labour Friends of Iraq' issued an open letter demanding the Stop the War Coalition condemn the murder (which it already had[1]), and drop its support for the right of Iraqis to resist the occupation. Among the signatories were former members of the *New Left Review* editorial board Branka Magas, Quintin Hoare, Norman Geras and Chris Bertram. Columnists Nick Cohen and David Aaronovitch, as well as Paul Anderson of the Labour left *Tribune*, also signed. Not all of the signatories were in favour of the war on Iraq, but all were agreed that support for the anti-imperialist resistance was out of question.[2]

This was the first of a series of initiatives in which left wing supporters of the 'war on terror' sought an alliance with those of its opponents who had no principled objection to imperialism. Later initiatives such as Unite Against Terror and the Euston Manifesto confirmed this alliance, gaining the support of such figures as Christopher Hitchens, one time International Socialist. Indeed, many of the pro-war left's most strident adherents were both anti-imperialists and revolutionaries in the past. For a variety of reasons, these people are now united by the conviction that in the current geopolitical realities, support for imperialism is a left wing position. In this, they are allied with liberals and social democrats who have a history of support for imperialism.

After 9/11, the deluge

Within weeks of the attacks on New York and Washington a small number of liberal and left wing pundits were rushing to offer their services. The implicit promise in their declarations was that they could police the left, while persuading left wing readers that there would be something in the 'war on terror' for them. 'Can there be a Decent Left?', wondered *Dissent*'s Michael Walzer in 2002. He observed that 'most leftists had criticised the invasion of Afghanistan while providing no clear alternative of their own and 'without any visible concern about preventing future terrorist attacks'.[3] Marc Cooper berated the left for 'self hatred', unable to see fellow citizens as having been the victims on this occasion.[4] Christopher Hitchens, with inspiring biliousness, averred that the left was guilty of 'fascist sympathies'.[5] He angrily disaffiliated from the left and ceased writing for American left liberal magazine *The Nation*.[6] John Lloyd described a struggle between 'the decent left, which is on the side of those willing to fight Islamic fascism, and the rigidly anti-American left'.[7] He blamed Noam Chomsky and the 'anti-globalisation' movement that he so despises for spreading 'anti-Americanism',[8] and eventually ceased writing for the *New Statesman*.[9] Martin Amis, with characteristic loquacity, attacked Chomsky with the bruising assessment that 'the moral equivalence line just didn't work. Anti-Americanism doesn't impress me as a very rational position'.[10]

Norman Geras, a sometime 'liberal Marxist' and an admirer of Michael Walzer's theses about 'Just and Unjust Wars', compared the left's assertion that the 9/11 attacks were caused in part by US foreign policy with German historian Ernst Nolte's claim that the Nazi Holocaust had to be understood as a 'pre-emptive' anticipation of a threat from the Soviet Union.[11] This raises the hitherto unheard of possibility that Norman Geras has a vivid imagination. David Aaronovitch accused the left of 'political cretinism' for having allegedly hinted that there was 'some kind of relationship between a Mandela and a Bin Laden'.[12] Whatever else can be said about such a rebuke, it is neither precise nor to the point. Aaronovitch, of course, is not paid well because he writes well, but because he reflects the prejudices of a segment of liberal opinion. Michael Ignatieff declared that 'either we fight evil with evil or we succumb'. 'Terrorist movements like Al Qaida or Hamas are death cults', he added, in another theme that has become ubiquitous.[13] Paul Berman explained that the left should support the bombing of Afghanistan, and the spreading of 'liberty and democracy'. The left should simply 'behave correctly under the circumstances'.[14]

Behaving correctly is precisely what the pro-war left does best. And increasingly hysterical demands on others to behave well ensued in the five years after 9/11, especially once the invasion of Iraq had become widely recognised as a catastrophe for the purportedly liberated populace.

In 2005, following the 7 July tube bombings, a statement called 'United Against Terror' was launched, organised by Jane Ashworth of 'Labour Friends of Iraq', formerly of the Alliance for Workers' Liberty.[15] The statement is very selective about which terror it opposes. It opposes that carried out by a variety of groups inspired by a reactionary kind of Political Islam. It doesn't oppose that carried out by far right Colombian militias. It doesn't show any solidarity with trade unionists and peasants being murdered by those terrorists. It doesn't oppose the terrorism of states against civilian populations: the targeting of civilians by the Russian government in Chechnya; the massacre in Fallujah; the use of death squads in the 'new Iraq'; the repeated assaults on Palestinians. About these, it is wordless—and culpably so. It also insists that Western foreign policy shares no responsibility for the attacks it addresses, and invites readers to endorse a two-state settlement for Palestine and condemn 'terrorism' there—not Israeli terrorism, but the resistance of the Palestinians.

A new initiative called 'The Euston Manifesto' was launched by the same confederacy of bloggers and commentators from the soft left in April 2006.[16] Its pioneers formulated their creed in a pub in Euston, and it shows. The introduction, co-written by Nick Cohen and Norman Geras, dispenses a series of stern charges against the anti-war left—anti-Semitism, anti-Americanism, apologetics for totalitarianism and fanaticism etc—and complains, without a trace of irony, about those who devote 'most...energy to criticism of political opponents at home'. It contains the proposition that a racist state that has come into existence through ethnic cleansing and theft and sustained itself through war and expansion must perpetuate itself: 'There can be no reasonable resolution of the Israeli-Palestinian conflict that subordinates or eliminates the legitimate rights and interests of one of the sides to the dispute.' Its proposed solution negates the legitimate rights and interests of Palestinians, while upholding an entirely illegitimate and spurious claim by Zionists based on biblical exegesis and racial domination.

These people profess to oppose racism and religious fundamentalism, by the way. Its authors espouse 'universal principles, for the establishment of which the democratic countries themselves, and in particular the United States of America, bear the greater part of the historical credit'. If one supports 'humanitarian intervention' and 'liberation' by imperialist states as a socialist or a liberal, one must see such states as the bearers of one's values. As Scott McLemee rightly remarked, 'The Eustonians seem to be issuing blank moral checks for whatever excellent adventures George Bush and Tony Blair decide to undertake'.[17]

Afghanistan: a successful example of what could happen to Iraq

The invasion of Afghanistan was justified in several ways: as an attempt to capture Al Qaida leaders; as an overthrow of a state that housed them; and as liberation for the people of Afghanistan. All of these were cited as benefits of the invasion by Christopher Hitchens and others.[18] New Labour MP Ben Bradshaw asserted the official position, which was that the war was only 'against bin Laden, the Al Qaida network and those who protect him, to bring those to justice who are responsible for 11 September'.[19] These excuses were contemptible enough. The US has a well-known history of sponsoring overseas terrorist movements that have killed tens of thousands—in El Salvador, Nicaragua, Cuba, etc. It has recently released from custody a notorious terrorist leader named Luis Posada Carriles, a former CIA affiliate who carried out aeroplane and hotel bombings in Cuba, despite requests for his extradition.[20] None of the apologists for the bombing of Afghanistan have ever suggested that the US or any of its military installations or governmental facilities be bombed, or that any military penalty be applied in any shape or form. The implication is the racist one, that the death of several thousand civilians in Afghanistan is acceptable, but not even the slightest offence to the US.

The excuses for invasion were entirely bogus. What in fact happened was that the US bombed Afghanistan, dislodged a regime with a tenuous grip on power, replaced a largely Pashtun elite with a largely Uzbek elite, and caught no significant Al Qaida leaders. Alec Station, the CIA unit assigned to hunt down Bin Laden and his confederates, has since been quietly dismantled.[21] Bush remarked shortly after the topple of the Taliban that 'I don't know where Bin Laden is. I have no idea and really don't care'.[22] Catching those alleged to be responsible was not a top priority for the Bush administration. It was not, in fact, necessary for the US to bomb Afghanistan if they had simply wanted to capture those they alleged were responsible for the attacks. The Taliban had offered to hand over Bin Laden, a proposal that was not pursued.[23] If the US had wished to dislodge the Taliban and the networks they housed, there was an internal oppositional movement that was working to bring down the Taliban—but it was opposed to the US bombing.[24]

Those who argued that 'liberation' would be a beneficial side-effect of the occupation were mistaken. Those who thought that this was what the US *intended* were purblind. The UNHCR had warned that 'we are facing a humanitarian crisis of epic proportions in Afghanistan with 7.5 million short of food and at risk of starvation.' The response of the United States to that crisis had been to demand the 'elimination of truck convoys that provide much of the food and other supplies to Afghanistan's civilian population'.[25] Whatever else could be said about such a decision, it was not taken with the interests of those 7.5 million civilians at heart. Although the catastrophe was avoided, up to 10,000 civilians died as an immediate result of the bombing.[26] Many supporters of the war cited the return of refugees to Afghanistan as evidence of liberation—yet, at the height of the Taliban's authority, in 1998, the UNHCR was helping 107,000 refugees to return to Afghanistan,[27] and a large number of those refugees who did return after 2001 did so because they were forced back by the British and neighbouring states, despite their extreme reluctance to return.[28] Kate Allen of Amnesty International wrote that 'with two thirds of the country unstable and covered in up to 10 million unexploded bombs and landmines', Afghanistan was not a safe country for those being forced to return.[29]

Since the overthrow of the Taliban, a government has been installed comprising war criminals such as General Abdul Rashid Dostum, and headed by Hamid Karzai, a former Taliban supporter with no social base in Afghanistan.[30] A network of bribed warlords[31] as well as like figures, 'implicated in murder, torture, intimidation, bribery and interfering with investigations into misconduct by officers directly under his control', help hold Afghanistan together for the occupiers, while repeated and bloody war crimes have been inflicted on the civilian population by the US forces.[32] The condition of women in Afghanistan doesn't quite match the glowing pre-war rhetoric: stonings, child marriage, massive physical, mental and sexual violence all continue.[33] From their base in Kabul the occupiers have run a series of torture prisons,[34] while extending courtesies to Uzbekistan, a dictatorship across the border every bit as vicious as the Taliban. You would think that Bush's attempt to kill the War Crimes Act could be related to his administration's conduct, and that this would be important.[35] Yet among the pro-war left little attention is paid, except to note those atrocities that are attributable to the Taliban while steadfastly ignoring those committed by the occupiers and their surrogates. Our Boys are only ever associated with things like protecting schools for girls.[36]

And a remarkable thing has begun to happen. The Taliban, five years ago a discredited and marginal political force in Afghanistan, are making a come-back in the south of the country. Lieutenant-General David Richards recently explained that 'we need to realise we could actually fail here'.[37] This is not because the Taliban have an appealing political programme, but rather because of the failure of the occupation to resemble anything close to 'liberation', because of mass starvation, and because of the ongoing and intensifying attacks by the occupiers on civilians.[38] None of the apologists spotted the cruel humour when Donald Rumsfeld remarked that Afghanistan was 'a breathtaking accomplishment' and 'a successful model of what could happen to Iraq'.[39]

Iraq: laptops and liberation

The episode of the 'war on terror' that has generated the most opposition also produced the most rhetorical frenzy from the pro-war left. Nick Cohen, who had opposed the war on Afghanistan,[40] was converted to the cause of imperialism during the build-up to the attack on Iraq because he was convinced that the Iraqi National Congress wanted to 'replace minority rule with a multiracial, devolved democracy which stands up for human rights'.[41] Indeed, Cohen was eager to see 'how Noam Chomsky and John Pilger manage to oppose a war which would end the sanctions they claim have slaughtered hundreds of thousands of children who otherwise would have had happy, healthy lives in a prison state'.[42] Those are lines that ought to shame him, but the pro-war left's attitude to murder at the hands of Western states is astonishingly blasé. Cohen cites, as the key influence in changing his attitude to the 'war on terror', Paul Berman's slender polemic *Terror and Liberalism*. The book brought on a minor epiphany: 'He convinced me I'd wasted a great deal of time looking through the wrong end of the telescope. I was going to have to turn it round and see the world afresh.' Berman belongs to something Cohen calls the 'anti-totalitarian left' and the 'central point' of his book 'is that Islamism and Baathism are continuations of Nazism and communism, not only in their fine points... but in their fundamentals'.[43] And so Cohen is resisting 'totalitarianism'. Christopher Hitchens claims that he was anxious for war with Iraq following a ride in a jeep with some pro-Bush Kurds back in 1991.[44] His old friend Dennis Perrin points out that this is false:

> I spent time with him in the period he mentions, and he never stopped criticising Bush's 'mad contest' with Saddam... As late as 2002, when I asked him directly if he did indeed favour a US invasion, he waffled and said that W would have to convince him on 'about a zillion fronts' before he could sign on.[45]

In fact, in October 2002, he told *Salon*, 'I don't favour an invasion of Iraq. But I favour a confrontation with Saddam Hussein'.[46] Then, he decided, there would be no war deserving the name, the attack would be 'dazzling' and would be greeted as an 'emancipation', and so 'bring it on'.[47]

Hitchens threw caution to the wind when he introduced a set of essays written during the war with a monograph entitled 'Twenty-Twenty Foresight'.[48] In what did this foresight consist? Well, for example, following a series of surgical strikes, 'a massive landing will bring food, medicine and laptop computers to a surging crowd of thankful and relieved Iraqis and Kurds'.[49] You heard the man—*laptops*. Further, 'Will an Iraq war make our Al Qaida problem worse? Not likely'.[50] As for WMDs, he still anticipates their discovery. He asked *The Nation*'s David Corn during a debate, 'Doesn't anything ever strike you as odd,' he asked Corn, 'about the figure of zero for [WMD] deposits found in Iraq?... Doesn't that suggest a crime scene that has been pretty well dusted in advance, the fingerprints wiped? Well, it does to me.' Corn remarks, 'Hitchens was saying that the fact that *no* weapons had been uncovered in Iraq (after nearly three years of searching) was evidence that there had been weapons'.[51] He continues to insist on the Baghdad-Bin Laden connection (via Zarqawi), despite ample refutation.[52]

David Aaronovitch cut a deal with his readers on WMDs: 'If nothing is eventually found, I—as a supporter of the war—will never believe another thing that I am told by our government or that of the US ever again'.[53] However, like Johann Hari,[54] he did not base his support for the war on the claims about mass destruction or on the putative Al Qaida connection, but rather on 'humanitarianism'. Unlike Hari he did not recant once the appalling consequences made a mockery of the moralistic basis of his support for it.[55] Francis Wheen, an early signatory to the Euston Manifesto, also supported the war 'kind of, sort of, a little bit'[56] on humanitarian grounds. Norman Geras is rather impatient with the discussion about the absence of WMDs, mordantly attributing such talk to a 'global intelligence failure'.[57] He argued that the war had 'brought to an end the brutalising and murder' of Iraqis, which even as early as mid-2003 took some denial.[58] By the same method and principle, one assumes Geras will argue for a coalition to militarily overthrow the United States government, whose prolonged career in global murder and torture has actually racked up considerably more bodies than Saddam Hussein: more Iraqi bodies.

However, this is a step in the logic of 'humanitarian intervention' that no one ever takes. The logic doesn't apply to 'us'. One thing never properly engaged with by the pro-war left is the matter of agency—that is, the capacities and propensities of the institutions that they are relying upon to deliver 'liberation'. Norman Geras has defended Rosa Luxemburg's insistence that socialism could only come through the self-education and activity of the working class.[59] But he is happy to en trust the 'liberation' of oppressed people to state actors whose record gives him no right to invest such trust in them. As David Chandler writes, the ideology of 'humanitarian intervention' is deeply conservative doctrine. Given humanity's availability for venality and violence, the logic runs, the more states can do to constrain it, the better. This is how Lord Ashdown ran things in Bosnia, and how Bernard Kouchner operated in Kosovo, as 'benign' dictatorships.[60] The doctrine can mean 'good' states restraining 'bad' states—it can also involve 'good' states restraining 'bad' people, so that: 'If the Iraqis were to elect either a Sunni or Shia Taliban, we would not let them take power'.[61]

The quality of their mercy

Christopher Hitchens told David Horowitz's *Front Page* magazine in 2003 of his 'exhilaration' at watching 'the towers fall in New York, with civilians incinerated on the planes and in the buildings' because it offered the prospect of 'a war to the finish between everything I love and everything I hate'.[62] He elsewhere asserted that bin Laden had done Americans 'a service' in attacking the twin towers because now they could have their 'war on terror'.[63] The good cheer continued when Hitchens was asked about the use of cluster bombs in Afghanistan:

> It's pretty good because those steel pellets will go straight through somebody and out the other side and through somebody else. And if they're bearing a Koran over their heart, it'll go straight through that, too. So they won't be able to say, 'Ah, I was bearing a Koran over my heart and guess what, the missile stopped halfway through'. They'll be dead, in other words.[64]

Elsewhere Hitchens remarked that cluster bombs had a 'heartening effect'. This eliminationist fantasy is one he meditates on often. 'We can't live on the same planet as them' he said of those he referred to as 'Islamofascists'. 'I don't want to breathe the same air as these psychopaths and murders [sic] and rapists and torturers and child abusers. It's them or me. It's a duty and a responsibility to defeat them. But it's also a pleasure. I don't regard it as a grim task at all'.[65] When Fallujah was destroyed, Hitchens complained that 'the death toll is not nearly high enough...too many [jihadists] have escaped'.[66] It isn't as if this was his first chuckle over mass murder. About the genocide of Native Americans and pre civil war slavery, Hitchens, channelling Harry Lime, has written that it is 'the way that history is made, and to complain about it is as empty as complaint about climatic, geological or tectonic shift'.[67] Let's give Saddam Hussein some credit—even he could invent a better excuse for genocide and slavery than that. The one virtue of Hitchens's cheerful obscenities is that he at least expresses openly what his confederates tend to corset in moralising and disavowal—that the lives of those in non-Western states are worth less than those of Americans and Europeans.

The 'heartening effect' of cluster bombs is to disperse into thousands of bomblets over wide areas and detonate, sending out sheets of white hot shards that tear apart the flesh and organs of anyone within range. Recent studies have shown that 98 percent of victims of cluster bombs are civilians.[68] The problem is deeper and broader than the use of particular weapons. Martin Shaw, a sociologist who occasionally embeds himself with the pro-war left, describes the tendency towards 'degenerate' war in which civilian populations increasingly bear the brunt of attacks, especially where they provide a community of support and encouragement for oppositional movements.

It was this form of 'degenerate' war that manifested itself in the discovery of rape and torture at Abu Ghraib. One victim, Manadel al-Jamadi, had died by a method known in Israel as 'Palestinian hanging', in which a prisoner has his arms tied behind his back, and is then hung from the wrists. His chest was crushed and he slowly suffocated as blood poured from his mouth and nose. His corpse appears in pictures with specialists Charles Graner and Sabrina Harman smiling over him with thumbs up.[69] The same logic obtained when the 'Salvador Option' was floated in the press, suggesting that the US would make sympathisers with the Iraqi resistance 'pay a price' at the hands of kidnappers and assassins.[70] Subsequently, reporters have found blood-splattered torture chambers in the CIA-constructed interior ministry, and the US itself was obliged to reveal and close down one chamber in which 173 people had been held and tortured, some having skin ripped off their bodies,[71] a method not unknown from the US-sponsored terror regime in El Salvador in the 1980s.[72] The Brussels Tribunal found that '92 percent of the 3,498 bodies found in different regions of Iraq have been arrested by officials of the Ministry of Interior'.[73]

You would scour the publications, columns and blogs of the pro-war left in vain for a hint of this. Only Abu Ghraib arrested their attention, briefly. Any serious attempt to grasp the scale of the catastrophe that has befallen Iraq is either ignored or dismissed. Hitchens advertises that he pays no attention to the casualty figures (is oblivious to the evidence in other words), yet becomes hysterical the second anyone mentions the *Lancet* report, describing 100,000 excess deaths as of October 2004. He has described it as 'politicised hack-work', a 'crazed' fabrication, whose conclusions had been 'conclusively and absolutely shown to be false'.[74] This extensively peer-reviewed study, which won the approbation of many independent peers,[75] told the world that the occupation was worse than the combined effect of Saddam Hussein and sanctions—100,000 worse, and growing. For this excellent reason, of course, Geras ignored it, as did Cohen and, initially, Johann Hari. David Aaronovitch would only be drawn to explain to the editors of Media Lens that 'I have a feeling...it may be a dud'.[76] In March 2006 one of the authors of the report, Les Roberts, estimated that it would by then be as high as 300,000 on a conservative estimate. In October 2006 a new study was released by the Johns Hopkins University's Bloomberg School of Public Health, which estimated that 655,000 Iraqis had died as a result of the invasion and occupation.[77] Geras responded that he could not comment on the figures, but it was obvious that too many had died. He added that if he had been able to foresee such results, 'I would have withheld support for the war without giving my voice to the opposition to it'.[78] This is a curious stance indeed for someone who has devoted so much scrutiny to those who stand by in the face of catastrophe.

While Hitchens was rather cheerful about the massacre in Fallujah, Norman Geras was able to write four separates entries for his website about the brutal killings of security contractors in the city, but not one about the ensuing sieges that brutally killed thousands of civilians, subjected others to chemical weapons, and destroyed homes and the infrastructure.[79] Aaronovitch was present in Iraq before the April 2004 assault on Fallujah, and had his sleep disturbed by the thought of 'swarming' insurgents,[80] but later conceded blandly that it 'may be disappointing' that Blair wouldn't condemn the US actions there.[81] About the November attack on the city, he would only mention that he was sick to death of conspiracy theories.[82] Nick Cohen did not mention the slaughter. William Shawcross, a sycophant of both the Queen and her crown-in-parliament, denounced the 'Saddamites, Islamist terrorists and the murderers of Fallujah',[83] but about the US murdering sprees would only say that 'there is no easy answer—either you appear brutal or you appear weak'.[84] Only Johann Hari,[85] by then moving away from his explicit identification with the pro-war left, eventually got round to mentioning the topic.

For a tendency that collectively complains in the Euston Manifesto of 'tactful silences', this is strange indeed.

Resistance and pacifism

The pro-war left often claims that the anti-war movement is not really anti-war, but *for the other side*. This is because many in the anti-war movement vocally support the right of people in occupied countries to defend themselves. Most of us are not pacifists. The historically determined capacity for organised killing cannot be undone overnight. The best that can be said is that we may eventually abolish those social structures that generate and direct the use of such violence, and in the meantime restrain the agents of it as far as is we realistically can. A little realism suggests that such restraints will themselves often take the form of violence, and this is fundamentally what characterises the Iraqi resistance, the resistance of Aristide's followers to the multilateral destruction of Haitian democracy, and the Lebanese resistance to the recent failed Israeli invasion.

Are we not supposed to notice that when, for instance, Saddam Hussein was raping, killing, imprisoning and torturing Iraqis, resistance was deemed entirely legitimate, and yet when the present dictators of Iraq do the same, resistance is derided by the pro-war left? Is it supposed to escape our attention that the pro-war left in fact favour pacifism for the weak and militarism for the strong?

Among Hitchens's expostulations on the topic is his suggestion that 'where it is not augmented by depraved Bin Ladenist imports, the leadership and structure of the Iraqi "insurgency" is formed from the elements of an already fallen regime, detested in its own country and universally condemned'. Norman Geras takes a similar line on the 'murderous "insurgency"',[86] as does Jeff Weintraub of *Dissent*, who describes the resistance as an attempt 'to restore fascist dictatorship (or an Islamist replacement)'.[87] The Cohen and Geras-penned preamble to the Euston Manifesto derides support for the 'gangs of jihadist and Baathist thugs of the Iraqi so-called resistance'.

This portrayal is largely fantasy. For sure, there is a restorationist wing in the resistance, and there is a salafist wing. There is also, unfortunately, a civil war dynamic unfolding in Iraq, encouraged by the sectarian policies of the occupiers. But the arresting fact about this is that the bulk of the resistance is neither Baathist nor salafist, nor does it, on the whole, target civilians. In repeated studies and figures released by think-tanks, the US department of defence, the CIA, the press, independent analysts and the 'coalition' military authorities in Iraq, the picture that emerges is of a resistance dominated by local, decentralised, disarticulated groups who *overwhelmingly* attack military and not civilian targets. Indeed, it is widely acknowledged that the nationalist resistance has been disciplining the salafist elements whose actions have hindered rather than helped the effort to evict the occupiers.[88]

This is perhaps one reason why support for the resistance has been growing, so that now fully 60 percent of Iraqis (including Kurds) support attacks on troops.[89] The pro-war left, in amplifying the role of Zarqawi and people like him, may have been unwitting vectors for a propaganda campaign mounted by the US military.[90] However, the acceptance of this propaganda is extremely comforting for those who still wish to believe that there is some form of 'liberation' going on in Iraq—even if it is not a 'liberation' they would choose for themselves, or one that Iraqis are inclined to accept.[91]

Lebanon: 'Signed, the State of Israel'

Radio broadcasts, and leaflets dropped on south Lebanese towns and villages, warned residents to flee or face slaughter. They always signed off 'The State of Israel' so that no one could doubt that the threat was genuine.[92] As Israel's invasion advanced on the territory south and east of the Litani River, the population was repeatedly instructed to evacuate, while Israel prepared for a 'civil administration'[93] in the conquered part of Lebanon. This war, planned at least one year in advance,[94] was launched with the avowed aim of recovering two soldiers kidnapped by Hizbollah fighters close to the Lebanese border, but it targeted the civilian infrastructure and population centres,[95] killing up to 1,300 civilians[96] and displacing almost a million people.[97] Israel's pathetic excuse was that Hizbollah was using civilians as human shields,[98] a claim dismissed by Human Rights Watch monitors.[99] By contrast, the Israeli human rights organisation B'Tselem confirmed that Israel was using human shields in Gaza.[100] The evident aim was to conquer Lebanon as a preliminary strike in a proxy war against Syria and Iran, and the south of the country was to be annexed in the process.

Michael Walzer's verdict: 'War Fair'.[101] Israel's wars never cease to be fair for Walzer, but in this case he relied on a simple reversal: if the capture of two soldiers was an act of war, then an act of war in return could not be considered illegitimate. The paucity of 'just war' theory is thus summarised: one could equally say that Israel, having kidnapped thousands of Palestinians and Lebanese in expansionist aggression, had no right to complain of similar actions. Without a materialist analysis, instead bruiting an abstract set of moral codes for war, one can find legitimacy in almost any atrocity, even as one regrets its excesses.

Norman Geras preferred to say, 'Israel does have just cause. This I don't argue for, I merely assert...no other country on the planet would be thought to be obliged to endure missile attacks on its population from a neighbouring country'.[102] Indeed, asserting but not arguing things is a method of his, but he may have forgotten that missile attacks on Israel's population started *after* the Israeli invasion began. Nick Cohen, reluctant to defend Israel, thought it was an opportunity to complain about the demise of interventionism, perhaps not noticing that Israel was indeed intervening in Lebanon and that the US and UK were intervening on behalf of Israel.[103] Christopher Hitchens signalled his reappraisal of Zionism, hallucinating that while Israeli right-wingers admitted 'that Israeli colonisation of Arabs is demographically impossible and morally wrong', Syria and Iran were using proxies to attack Israel. He didn't like the war's 'lack of proportion', but nevertheless blamed Hamas and Hizbollah for it.[104] Such obtuse formulae! Israel has never sought to colonise the Arabs—instead it has tried to liquidate the very idea of Palestine and to *expel and dispossess* the Arabs. And Israel's 'lack of proportion', its deliberate attacks on civilians, its attempt to ethnically cleanse the south of Lebanon, its use of chemical weapons, its bombing of households and fleeing cars—did none of this indicate that perhaps the war was not the defensive venture that Hitchens took it to be? The cognitive dissonance involved in supporting American aggression while trying to retain some pro-Palestinian credentials evidently could not be sustained for very long: how does one oppose in Lebanon what one supported in Iraq, especially when the same scheming enemies lurk?

Totalitarianism, Islam and Enlightenment

Neoconservatives and the pro-war left are not only united on their purblind support for imperialism: they share a vocabulary, and a conceptual apparatus. This was perhaps first expressed in a statement signed by 60 academics including such diverse figures as Michael Walzer, Francis Fukuyama and Samuel Huntington, in which the new wave of American militarism was explained as an affirmation of 'fundamental truths' including the wisdom that all human beings are born free and equal, seek rational inquiry, need freedom of conscience and shouldn't murder in the name of god.[105]

Totalitarianism and the Enlightenment are among the favourite themes of the pro-war left. Increasingly, so is Islam. Eustonite Alan Johnson avers that every generation 'has to re-discover anti-totalitarianism for itself'.[106] Jeffrey Herf et al signed the manifesto because 'radical Islamism' is 'the third major form of totalitarian ideology of the last century, after fascism and Nazism, on the one hand, and Communism, on the other'.[107] Francis Wheen embraces a fetishism of unproblematised Enlightenment, and he has taken the trouble to upbraid Adorno and Horkheimer for having blamed all of modernity's ills on the Enlightenment and not understanding its contribution to notions of human freedom. Evidently, he did not get all the way through the first page of *Dialectic of Enlightenment*, in which the authors write that 'social freedom is inseparable from enlightened thought'.[108] For Hitchens, it is the Enlightenment that Al Qaida is after: in a phrase, they hate our scientific enquiry. This, he describes as 'theocratic totalitarianism'.[109] The Euston Manifesto similarly defends what signatory Eve Garrard calls 'Enlightenment values',[110] and among other glittering generalities echoes the 'great rallying calls of the democratic revolutions of the 18th century'.[111] The problem with this isn't, as John Gray imagines, that Enlightenment values had a 'seamy side', or that the zealous pursuit of such values can undermine the prospects for a *modus vivendi* because these values can issue incompatible demands.[112] It is that their invocation is in this instance platitudinous and unmaterialist.

Martin Amis, like his friend Hitchens, makes the link between Enlightenment and his hostility to Islam explicit. In his memoir *Experience*, Amis remarks at least twice that he thinks about Israel 'with the blood'. He adds that he will 'never be entirely reasonable about her'. Blood comes up quite a bit: he pines for a lost love who has gone to 'give blood' for Israel. To openly declare that one will never be rational about a defining political issue of the day advertises a sort of fanaticism. Yet the mysticism of blood and soil, the giving of life's fluid back to the land itself, is converted into a liberal apologia for Zionism. He is still 'thinking with the blood' when he encounters a gatekeeper at the Holy Mosque in the Arab Quarter of Jerusalem and declares, 'I saw in his eyes the assertion that he could do *anything* to me, to my wife, to my children, to my mother, and that this would only validate his rectitude'.[113]

Sam Harris, in a book purportedly celebrating the values of Enlightenment against religion, singles out Islam for particular opprobrium. He writes of Islam that 'the basic thrust of the doctrine is undeniable: convert, subjugate, or kill unbelievers; kill apostates; and conquer the world'. Further, the West is at 'war with Islam...with precisely the vision of life that is prescribed to all Muslims in the Koran'. Writing about the Danish 'cartoons' controversy, he wrote:

> 'Muslim extremism' is not extreme among Muslims. Mainstream Islam itself represents an extremist rejection of intellectual honesty, gender equality, secular politics and genuine pluralism... Muslims intentionally murder noncombatants, while we and the Israelis (as a rule) seek to avoid doing so...the people who speak most sensibly about the threat that Islam poses to Europe are actually fascists.

With a billion Muslims in the world, the wonder is that only 19 of them have so far launched an attack in the United States and that the vast preponderance of Muslims has thus far decided against converting, subjugating, killing unbelievers and apostates.

Nevertheless, it is because of the omnipresent threat of Islam that Harris supports the war on Iraq and the use of torture against prisoners (citing arguments developed by Alan Dershowitz).[114]

The present obsession with Islam is an artefact of the racist hysteria generated to support the current strategies of imperialism, and the integration of

Islam into the 'totalitarianism' thesis is a crude update of Cold War doctrine.

It was, of course, the collapse of that 'anti-totalitarian' consensus brought about by mass opposition to the Vietnam War that produced the neo-conservative reaction, whose patron saint, the right wing Democrat Henry Jackson, is still a hero for today's liberal imperialism. The collapse of the revolutionary left in the 1970s also led many activists to embrace 'anti-totalitarianism' and support NATO—particularly in France, where ultra-left critiques of the PCF gradually lent themselves to lesser-evilism and accommodation with the Socialist Party, under hysterical anti-Marxist crusades led by Francois Furet and Andre Glucksmann.[115] Among descendants of the Maoist left to embrace humanitarian imperialism was Bernard Kouchner, who founded Medicins Sans Frontiers, served in the Mitterrand government in 1992-93, went on to become the UN's proconsul in Kosovo, and argued in favour of war on Iraq.[116] Kouchner is Paul Berman's hero, exemplifying the 'anti-totalitarian' politics that he espouses.

What is totalitarianism? To Jeane Kirkpatrick, a prominent neo-conservative and US Ambassador to the United Nations under Reagan, 'totalitarianism' was what distinguished the dictatorships the US opposed from those it supported, which were merely 'authoritarian'.[117]

In the hands of Paul Berman, the 'liberal hawk', 'totalitarian' is whoever might be considered an enemy of the US today. He complains that it took the 9/11 attacks to 'reopen the public discussion of totalitarianism in the Muslim world', which includes Ba'athism and 'Islamic fundamentalism', but not imperialism or Zionism, for instance. Ironically, Berman cites Hannah Arendt's *The Origins of Totalitarianism*, without noticing that a substantial part of the book argued that imperialism was a crucial ingredient in 20th century totalitarianism, or that she had been repelled by the 'totalitarian methods' of Zionism against the Palestinians.[118]

One of the weaknesses of the totalitarianism thesis has always been its availability for manipulation: it is, as Domenico Losurdo writes, a category possessing several distinct meanings. It refers to ideologies, movements, states—whatever you like—and can embrace a critique of imperialism, or not. It can even be a criticism of *anti*-imperialism—hence John Lloyd complains about the 'totalising critique' of US imperialism.[119] If the term can therefore be stretched to cover Arab nationalist regimes and various forms of political Islam, it is perhaps beyond being useful except as a catch-all expression for the targets of American wars. Norman Geras back in the 1980s noticed the tendency to cite 'a concept of "totalitarianism" in its familiar Cold War sense' among ex-Marxists complaining that they seemed 'to forget' 'what they once knew...that the evolution of ideas has a social and material context'.[120] Hitchens mocked the use of the notion by neo-conservatives to give 'watery notions of the strength of concrete' and 'petrify' political opponents.[121] Yet 'totalitarianism' has proven too useful for such converts to imperialism to ditch.

Life behind the iron curtain

Why are democratic and egalitarian ideals pressed into the service of imperialism by both right and left? Ellen Meiksins Wood offers a few suggestions. In the first instance, capitalism does not need formal political inequalities—rather domination and class rule are expressed as rights, specifically as property rights. Initially, these were explicitly asserted by the English in Ireland as the right to seize occupied land if it was not being put to profitable use, and you can still find this claim in Zionist apologias about how the settlers 'made the desert bloom'. However, modern imperialism finds this less useful, instead seeking to sustain relations of domination through market transactions, guaranteed by an orderly global system of disciplined nation-states. The American empire seeks an ideology that legitimises constant, open-ended interventions, requiring an level of intervention and military build-up.

The available ideological resources are narrowed by capital's formal disavowal of principles of inequality, so imperialism's supporters are obliged to draw on democratic and egalitarian ideologies, which are supposedly threatened. The specifically American interpretation of democracy, as Wood has it, is extremely useful since it is an impoverished notion, offering many strategies for insulating the public from the state.[122] One can see this happening in Iraq, where formal elections are allowed to take place (after considerable pressure), but where the state is effectively controlled by networks of patronage, unelected 'reconstruction' bodies, and unaccountable bodies. 'Advisers' from the massive American Embassy penetrate every ministry, while the basic political framework has been determined at every step by the coalition and its surrogates.[123] Yet the belief that the US represents the prototype for democracy is supposed to give it the right to Americanise any regime it does not like.

Availing themselves of this ideology, the pro-war left exist in an almost impregnable moral fortress, from which they permit themselves to see only the empire's immense charity and benevolence. Hence, nervous and bloodied from their support of the calamitous invasion of Iraq, they plead with Western states to perform merciful feats in Sudan. Predictably, the fate of Darfur is reduced to 'Islamism' and 'totalitarianism' in the hands of the pro-war left.[124] In their calls for intervention there, however, they may find some supporters among liberal leftists who opposed the Iraq war. Jonathan

Freedland[125] and David Clark,[126] for instance, have both argued that an invasion of Sudan would be a good instance of intervention. Both supported the war on Yugoslavia. In the US liberal commentators like Todd Gitlin,[127] formerly of Students for a Democratic Society, have derided Bush for 'inaction' in Darfur, while glitterati like George Clooney and Don Cheadle have made much the same point.[128] It is the segment of people represented by such commentators who the pro-war left hope to win over through such initiatives as the Euston Manifesto. In response to such initiatives, the anti-imperialist left has to argue that the state is not the bearer of the interests which liberals hope to advance, and must insist on a minimally realistic account of US strategy in the world.

The US has an iron curtain of military bases extending from Greenland, through Europe via the Balkans, into the Arab world and Africa and right through Central Asia, many of them established through violent military interventions. They aren't there to provide creche facilities for the locals. Having got its hands on the oil spigot in Iraq, the US continues to pump thousands of barrels a day out of the Niger delta through Chevron, which is accused of murdering civilians. The State Department's International Military Education and Training programme and similar programmes offer training to 70 percent of the world's armies, and America's arms industries carefully direct weapons to surrogate armies such as the warlords in Somalia and the death squads in Colombia.[129] It now sustains a network of stasi-style secret prisons. Such an empire is to 'liberation' what Madame Guillotine was to respiration. Whether living behind America's iron curtain or Israel's iron wall, the empire's fanciers are blind to what the whole world can see. Something similar could once be said of Stalin's admirers—and that is strange, for a tendency that sees itself as upholding 'anti-totalitarianism'.

NOTES

1: Sami Ramadani, letter to *Independent*, 7 January 2005; www.stopwar.org.uk/Conference2005.htm

2: Labour Friends of Iraq, 'The murder of Hadi Saleh—why are you silent? An open letter to the leaders of the Stop the War Coalition', 26 January 2005, http://www.labourfriendsofiraq.org.uk/archives/000167.html

3: *Dissent*, vol 49, no 2 (Spring 2002).

4: *Los Angeles Times*, 14 October 2001.

5: *Spectator*, 29 September 2001.

6: *New York Times*, 26 September 2002.

7: *New Statesman*, 11 March 2002.

8: *Observer*, 17 March 2002.

9: *Guardian*, 11 April 2003.

10: Cited in above.

11: In 'Marxism, the Holocaust and September 11: An Interview with Norman Geras', *Imprints*, vol 6, no 3 (2002).

12: *Independent*, 16 October 2001.

13: M Ignatieff, *The Lesser Evil: Political Ethics in an Age of Terror* (Edinburgh University Press, 2004).

14: P Berman, 'Terror and Liberalism', *The American Prospect*, vol I, issue 18 (22 October 2001).

15: http://www.unite-against-terror.com/

16: http://eustonmanifesto.org/joomla/

17: S McLemee, 'Euston... We Have a Problem', *Inside Higher Ed*, 24 May 2006.

18: Hitchens argued this case in 'The War on Terror: Is There an Alternative?', *London Review of Books* debate, Institute of Education, London, 15 May 2002.

19: K O'Brien, 'Anthrax may be a new terrorist weapon', *Australian Broadcasting Corporation*, 9 October 2001.

20: The announcement was actually made on 11 September 2006, the fifth anniversary of the 9/11 attacks, suggesting that someone in the US legal system has a sense of humour.

21: 'Al Qaeda's Inner Circle', *New York Review of Books*, 19 October 2006.

22: 'President Bush Holds Press Conference', White House, 13 March 2002, http://www.whitehouse.gov/news/releases/2002/03/20020313-8.html

23: P Bishop, 'Pakistan Blocks Bin Laden Trial', The Daily Telegraph, 4 October 2001.

24: B Bearak, 'Peshawar Gathering', *New York Times*, 25 October 2001 and A Haq, 'US Bombs Are Boosting the Taliban', *Guardian*, 2 November 2001, cited in N Chomsky, *Hegemony or Survival: America's Quest for Global Dominance* (Hamish Hamilton, 2003), p201.

25: Cited in N Chomsky, 'The Afghanistan Food Crisis', ZNet, 4 September 2005.

26: A A Benini and L H Molton, 'Civilian Victims in an Asymmetrical Conflict: Operation Enduring Freedom', *Journal of Peace Research*, vol 41, no 4, 2004; Prof M W Herold, 'A Dossier on Civilian Victims of United States' Aerial Bombing of Afghanistan: A Comprehensive Accounting', http://www.cursor.org/stories/civilian_deaths.htm

27: Amnesty International, 'Refugees from Afghanistan: The World's Largest Single Refugee Group', 1 November 1999.

28: UNHCR, 'Feature: Afghan refugees who are reluctant to return', Reliefweb, 6

October 2003.

29: K Allen, Letter in *Amnesty International News*, 23 June 2003.

30: 'Afghan power brokers: International fundraiser in chief', *Christian Science Monitor*, 10 June, 2002.

31: 'Afghanistan's civilian deaths mount', BBC, 3 January, 2002; 'Afghan leader says US bombed civilians', BBC, 3 February 2002; K Connolly and R McCarthy, 'New film accuses US of war crimes', *Guardian*, 13 June, 2002; 'Afghan: US bomb hits wedding party', CNN, 1 July 2002; M Herold, 'Attempts to Hide the Number of Afghan Civilians Killed by US Bombs Are An Affront To Justice', 8 August 2002; B Dehghanpisheh, J Barry and R Gutman, 'The Death Convoy of Afghanistan', *Newsweek*, 26 August 2002; 'US bombing kills Afghan children', BBC, 7 December 2003; 'Afghans understand deaths—US', CNN, 7 December 2003; P Constable, 'US troops shot at Afghans after crash: Military says soldiers fired in self-defense', *Washington Post*, 1 June 2006.

32: 'Afghanistan: Reject Known Abusers as Police Chiefs, Time for President Karzai to Show He Is a Genuine Reformer', *Human Rights Watch*, 4 May 2006.

33: 'Afghanistan woman stoned to death', BBC News, 23 April 2005; Lailuma Sadid, 'Suicide an option for desperate war-widows, UNIFEM Survey revealed: '65 percent of the 50,000 widows in Kabul see suicide the only option to get rid of their miseries and desolation'', *Indo Asian News Service*, 14 August 2006; Haroon Najafi Zada, 'Attack of Police' to Girl's Dormitory in Balkh', BBC Persian (Translated by RAWA), 5 June 2006 (http://www.rawa.org/balkh.htm); Human Rights Watch, *The Status of Women in Afghanistan*, October 2004; 'Gulbar is Burnt by Her Husband', RAWA report, 26 January 2006 (http://www.rawa.org/burning_p.htm); J Huggler, 'Women's lives "no better" in the new Afghanistan', *Independent*, 1 November 2006.

34: D Campbell and S Goldenberg, 'Afghan detainees routinely tortured and humiliated by US troops', *Guardian*, 23 June 2004.

35: J Brecher and B Smith, 'Senate Vote Advances President's Effort to Kill War Crimes Act', *The Nation*, 22 September 2006.

36: For instance, see D Aaronovitch, 'All the greatest missions have crept spectacularly. This is no exception', *Times*, 3 July 2006; N Geras, 'Girls out of school', *Normblog*, 13 July 2006; C Hitchens, 'Let the Afghan Poppies Bloom: How the drug war is undermining the war on terrorism', *Slate*, 13 December 2004.

37: M K Bhadrakumar, 'Afghanistan: Why NATO cannot win', *Asia Times*, 30 September 2006.

38: K Sengupta, 'Afghanistan: Campaign against Taliban "causes misery and hunger"', *Independent*, 6 September 2006; A Jones, 'Why It's Not Working in Afghanistan', *TomDispatch*, September 2006.

39: Quoted in C Lamb, 'Death Trap', *Sunday Times review*, 9 July 2006.

40: N Cohen, *Observer*, 4 November 2001.

41: N Cohen, *Observer*, 14 April 2002.

42: N Cohen, *Observer*, 10 March 2002.

43: 'Writer's Choice 5: Nick Cohen', *Normblog*, 5 July 2005.

44: Labour Friends of Iraq, 'Christopher Hitchens and Others Debate Iraq on Start the Week 30 May 2005', 31 May 2005.

45: D Perrin, 'Punchy', *Red State Son*, 2 June 2005.

46: E W Lempinen, 'How the Left Became

Irrelevant', *Salon*, 29 October 2002.

47: Quoted in 'Cakewalk', *Salon*, 28 March 2003.

48: C Hitchens, *A Long Short War: The Postponed Liberation of Iraq* (Plume, 2003).

49: C Hitchens, 'What Happens Next in Iraq', *Mirror*, 26 February 2003.

50: C Hitchens, *A Long Short War*, as above, pp60-62. Unfortunately: BBC News, 'Iraq War "Increased Terror Threat"', 2 February 2004; A Grice, 'Iraq War Increased the Threat of Attacks, Says Major', *Independent*, 26 July 2005; B Bender, 'Study Cites Seeds of Terror in Iraq', *Boston Globe*, 17 July 2005.

51: D Corn, 'Sorry, Hitch–You're Wrong About Niger, Plus: Christopher Hitchens responds', *Salon*, 26 September 2006.

52: C Hitchens, 'In Front of Your Nose', *Slate*, 25 October 2005; 'Powell Claims Iraq Is Harboring Al Qaeda Terrorists, But Leaves Out Evidence Implicating US Allies; We Hear Responses From Baghdad, France and Cameroon', *Democracy Now!* (6 February 2003). D Van Natta, Jr, 'Portrait of a Terror Suspect: Is He the Qaeda Link to Iraq?' *International Herald Tribune*, 10 February 2003. C Simpson and S Swanson, 'Prisoner Casts Doubt on Iraq Tie to Al Qaeda', *Chicago Tribune*, 11 February 2003. 'Mullah Krekar Interview,' *Insight TV* (http://www.insightnewstv.com/d80/). International Crisis Group, 'Radical Islam In Iraqi Kurdistan: The Mouse That Roared?', *Middle East Briefing*, no 4, 7 February 2003. Indeed, much of the 'evidence' linking Ansar al-Islam to Al Qaeda appears to come from PUK sources, or their prisoners: C Taylor, 'Taliban-style Group Grows in Iraq', *Christian Science Monitor*, 15 March 2002. For information on the Al Qaeda-Zarqawi disputes, see J Burke, *Al-Qaeda: The True Story of Radical Islam* (Penguin Books, 2004). For more on the Zarqawi myth, see L Napoleoni, *Insurgent Iraq: Al-Zarqawi and the New Generation* (Seven Stories Press, 2005). Suffice to note that like every other bogey man of the US imperialist imaginary, Zarqawi was Hitler: 'Rumsfeld: Zarqawi Like Hitler,' CBS, 26 May 2005. This according to Donald Rumseld who, unlike Zarqawi, actually did meet Saddam and did exchange weapons of mass destruction in the process.

53: D Aaronovitch, *Guardian*, 29 April 2003.

54: J Hari, 'WMD are Irrelevant; Iraqis Wanted the War', *Independent*, 11 July 2003.

55: J Hari, 'Was I Wrong about Iraq? Doubts and Dreams', *Independent*, 14 April 2004; J Hari, 'Abdul's grandparents are trapped in Fal lujah. What do I say to him? Uncertainty', *Independent*, 8 November 2004; J Hari 'After three years, after 150,000 dead, why I was wrong about Iraq: A melancholic mea culpa', *Independent*, 18 March 2006.

56: B O'Neill, interview with Francis Wheen, *Spiked*, 26 May 2004.

57: N Geras, 'Global Intelligence Failure', *Normblog*, 12 July 2004.

58: N Geras, talk given to a Workers' Liberty summer school in London, 21 June 2003, reprinted in T Cushman (ed), *A Matter of Principle: Humanitarian Arguments for War in Iraq* (University of California Press, 2005).

59: N Geras, 'Democracy and the Ends of Marxism', *New Left Review*, I/203, January-February 1994.

60: D Chandler, *From Kosovo to Kabul: Human Rights and International Intervention* (Pluto Press, 2002).

61: Christopher Hitchens explaining to an Iraqi dinner guest, as reported by liberal American gossip columnist Michael Totten, 'Drinking with Christopher Hitchens and the Iraqis', *MichaelTotten.com*, 6 February 2005.

62: J Glazov, 'Frontpage Interview: Christopher Hitchens', *FrontPagemagazine.com*, 10 December 2003.

63: C Hitchens, 'A War to Be Proud of', *Weekly Standard* 10.47, 5-12 September 2005.

64: A Shatz, 'The Left and 9/11', *The Nation*, 23 September 2002.

65: 'An Interview with Christopher Hitchens ('Moral and Political Collapse' of the Left in the US)', *WashingtonPrism.org*, 16 June 2005.

66: M Ludders, 'Columnist Hitchens Lectures on Political Dissent', *The Kenyon Collegian*, 18 November 2004.

67: C Hitchens, 'Minority Report', *The Nation*, 19 October 1992.

68: B S Klapper, 'Red Cross calls for end to cluster bombs', *Associated Press*, 6 November 2006.

69: D Filkins, 'Testimony ties key officer to cover-up of Iraqi death', *New York Times*, 25 June 2004.

70: M Hirsh and J Barry, '"The Salvador Option": The Pentagon may put Special-Forces-led assassination or kidnapping teams in Iraq', *Newsweek*, 14 January 2005.

71: 'US "troubled" by Iraq abuse claim', BBC News, 16 November 2005.

72: Annual Report Of The Inter-American Commission On Human Rights 1989-1990, Resolution No 26/89, Case No 179, El Salvador, 28 September 1989.

73: http://www.brusselstribunal.org/IraqUNHRC.htm

74: Debate at Baruch College, New York, hosted by Amy Goodman, 14 September 2005.

75: Epidemiologists in the press quoted extensively in 'Burying the Lancet–Part 1', *Media Lens*, 5 September 2005.

76: As above.

77: G Burnham, S Doocy, E Dzeng, R Lafta and L Roberts, 'The Human Cost of War in Iraq: A Mortality Study 2002-2006', Bloomberg School of Public Health, Johns Hopkins University, Baltimore, Maryland and School of Medicine, Al Mustansir Mustansiriya University Baghdad, Iraq in cooperation with the Center for International Studies, Massachusetts Institute of Technology, Cambridge, Massachusetts (http://web.mit.edu/CIS/pdf/Human_Cost_of_War.pdf); D Brown, 'Study Claims Iraq's "Excess" Death Toll Has Reached 655,000', *Washington Post*, 11 October 2006.

78: N Geras, 'Failure in Iraq', *Normblog*, 15 October 2006.

79: N Geras, 'Today in Falluja', *Normblog*, 31 March 2004; N Geras, 'Falluja 2', Normblog, 2 April 2004; N Geras, 'Falluja 3', Normblog, 2 April 2004; N Geras, 'Falluja 4', Normblog, 4 April 2004.

80: D Aaronovitch, 'So this is Free Baghdad', *Guardian*, 9 April 2004.

81: D Aaronovitch, 'It's diplomacy, actually', *Observer*, 18 April 2004.

82: D Aaronovitch, 'Why I hate the madness of these conspiracy theories', *Observer*, 21 November 2004.

83: W Shawcross, 'Nurture the seeds of civil society in Iraq', *Financial Times*, 5 April 2004.

84: W Shawcross, 'We're not Bush's poodles: we're fighting on the right side of history', *Times Online*, 17 April 2004.

85: J Hari, 'The use of chemical weapons in Fallujah: War crimes and silence', *JohannHari.com* 15 November 2005.

86: N Geras, 'Out of Tune', *Normblog*, 19 March 2005.

87: J Weintraub, 'Some thoughts on the terrorist strategy of the Iraqi 'insurgency'', *Normblog*, 15 March 2005.

88: W Pincus, 'CIA Studies Provide Glimpse of Insurgents in Iraq,' *Washington Post*, 6 February 2005; M Schwartz, 'Schwartz on Why the Military Is Failing in Iraq', *TomDispatch*, 5 March 2005; You can consult the graphics at http://www.lefthook.org/Charts/CSIS.jpg and http://www.lefthook.org/Charts/NYTimes.jpg. M Junaid Alam, 'Does the Resistance Target Civilians? According to US Intel, Not Really', *LeftHook*, 16 April 2005; F Kaplan, 'Western Targets: The Iraqi insurgency is still primarily an anti-occupation effort', *Slate*, 9 February 2006; 'Iraq violence: Facts and figures', BBC, 17 August 2006; A S Hashim, *Insurgency and Counter-Insurgency in Iraq* (Cornell University Press, 2006); L Napoleoni, *Insurgent Iraq: Al-Zarqawi and the New Generation* (Constable & Robinson, 2005); Z Chehab, *Iraq Ablaze: Inside the Insurgency* (IB Tauris, 2006).

89: 'New Poll Says Majority of Iraqis Approve of Attacks on US Forces: An Overwhelming Majority Think US Forces Are Provoking Conflict', *ABC News*, 27 September 2006.

90: See briefing slides from military commanders boasting about propaganda successes, reprinted in 'Leverage Xenophobia', *Washington Post*, 10 April 2006. Among the tactics discussed are: 'Eliminate Popular Support for a Potentially Sympathetic Insurgency; Deny Ability of Insurgency to "Take Root" Among the People', and 'Villainize Zarqawi/leverage xenophobic response'.

91: 'Iraq violence: Facts and figures', *BBC News*, 26 October 2006.

92: C Chassay, 'Info war goes personal with voicemail and text message', *Guardian*, 24 July 2006.

93: A Pfeffer, 'IDF prepares for civil administration in Lebanon', *Jerusalem Post*, 23 July 2006.

94: M Kalman, 'Israel set war plan more than a year ago: Strategy was put in motion as Hizbollah began increasing its military strength', *San Francisco Chronicle*, 21 July 2006.

95: L Ohrstrum, 'Latest targets of air blitz: milk and medicine', *Lebanon Daily Star*, 19 July 2006; '"Many dead" in Israeli raids', *ABC Australia News*, 19 July 2006; 'Israel pounds Lebanon again', *Sydney Morning Herald*, 20 July 2006; E O'Loughlin, 'Grim proof ordinary folk are dying in the killing zone', *Sydney Morning Herald*, 20 July 2006.

96: R Fisk, 'Lebanon's pain grows by the hour as death toll hits 1,300', *Independent*, 17 August 2006.

97: H Hendawi, 'Day 22: Bloodiest Day for Israel...1 Million Displaced in Lebanon So Far...', *Associated Press*, 3 August 2006.

98: 'Statement by Ambassador Dan Gillerman, Permanent Representative during the open debate on "The Situation in the Middle East"', United Nations Security Council, New York, 30 July 2006.

99: Human Rights Watch, 'Fatal Strikes: Israel's Indiscriminate Attacks Against Civilians in Lebanon,' vol 18, no 3(E) (August 2006), p3.

100: 'Israeli soldiers use civilians as human shields in Beit Hanun', *B'Tselem*, 20 July 2006.

101: M Walzer, 'The Ethics of Battle: War Fair', *The New Republic*, 31 July 2006.

102: N Geras, 'The rights and wrongs of Israel's military action', *Normblog*, 26 July 2006.

103: N Cohen, 'Once we believed in intervention. Now, to our shame, we turn away', *Observer*, 23 July 2006.

104: C Hitchens, 'The Politics of Sabotage', *Wall Street Journal*, 18 July 2006.

105: 'What We're Fighting For: A Letter from America', 13 February 2002: http://www.yale.edu/lawweb/avalon/sept_11/letter_002.htm

106: A Johnson, 'No One Left Behind: Euston and the renewal of Social Democracy', *Normblog*, 1 June 2006.

107: J Herf et al, 'American Liberalism and the Euston Manifesto', *Euston Manifesto*, 12 September 2006.

108: F Wheen, *How Mumbo-jumbo Conquered the World: A Short History of Modern Delusions* (Fourth Estate, 2004); T W Adorno and M Horkheimer, *Dialectic of Enlightenment* (Verso, 2002).

109: C Hitchens, 'Against Rationalization: Minority Report', *The Nation*, 8 October 2001; '"Don't Cross Over if You Have Any Intention of Going Back": Politics and Literature in the Mind of Christopher Hitchens', *The Common Review*, vol 4, no 1 (2005).

110: E Garrard, 'Lipstick and Enlightenment', *Normblog*, 18 June 2006.

111: 'Statement of Principles', *Euston Manifesto*, 29 March 2006.

112: J Gray, 'Ideas: Beyond good and evil', *New Statesman*, 19 June 2006; J Gray, *Two Faces of Liberalism* (Polity, 2000).

113: M Amis, *Experience: A Memoir* (Vintage, 2000), pp256-265.

114: S Harris, *The End of Faith: Religion, Terror and the Future of Reason* (Norton, 2004); S Harris, 'In Defense of Torture', *The Huffington Post*, 17 October 2005; 'Sam Harris on The Reality of Islam', *Truthdig*, 7 February 2006; S Harris, 'Head-in-the-Sand Liberals: Western civilization really is at risk from Muslim extremists', *Los Angeles Times*, 18 September 2006.

115: See, for instance, M S Christofferson, *French Intellectuals Against the Left: The Antitotalitarian Moment of the 1970s* (Berghahn Books, 2004).

116: A Powell, 'Kouchner: Iraqi voices remain unheard: People are the silent players amid all the talk', *Harvard University Gazette*, 20 March 2003.

117: J J Kirkpatrick, 'Dictatorship and Double Standards', *Commentary Magazine*, vol 68, no 5 (November 1979).

118: P Berman, *Power and the Idealists* (Soft Skull Press, 2005); H Arendt, *The Origins of Totalitarianism* (Harvest Books, 1971). For a discussion of this, see D Losurdo, 'Towards a Critique of the Category of Totalitarianism', *Historical Materialism* 12.1 (April 2004).

119: J Lloyd, 'How anti-Americanism betrays the left', *Observer*, 17 March 2002.

120: N Geras, 'Post-Marxism?', *New Left Review* I/163 (May-June 1987).

121: C Hitchens, 'How Neo-Conservatives Perish', as above.

122: E Meiksins Wood, 'Democracy as Ideology of Empire' in Colin Mooers (ed), *The New Imperialists: Ideologies of Empire* (Oneworld, 2006).

123: For a discussion of this, see E Herring and G Rangwala, *Iraq in Fragments: The Occupation And Its Legacy* (Hurst, 2006).

124: See, for instance, C Hitchens, 'Realism in Darfur: Consider the horrors of peace', *Slate*, 7 November 2005; N Cohen, 'How the UN lets genocidal states get away with murder', *Observer*, 29 October 2006.

125: J Freedland, 'How to stop Hotel Darfur', *Guardian*, 30 March 2005.

126: D Clark, 'Why both Blair and the left have been silent on Sudan', *Guardian*, 2 July 2004.

127: T Gitlin, 'More on Puncturing the SOTU Balloon', *TPM Café*, 31 January 2006.

128: D Cheadle and J Prendergast, '"Never Again"—again', *USA Today*, 31 January 2005.

129: See C Johnson, *The Sorrows of Empire: Militarism, Secrecy and the End of the Republic* (Verso, 2004).

Rifondazione votes for war

Megan Trudell

Many supporters of Italy's Rifondazione Comunista party are shocked and disoriented. Three years ago it put itself at the front of Europe's anti-capitalist movement. It spearheaded massive mobilisations after paramilitary police had attacked the Genoa demonstration against the G8, and then kept the momentum going through to the 1 million-strong finale to the Florence European Social Forum and the three million or more who took the streets against the Iraq war and against the Berlusconi government's neoliberal policies. But its deputies and senators have now voted to refinance Italian troops in Afghanistan and send Italian troops to Lebanon as a result of choosing to join the centre-left government of Romano Prodi, alongside the social democrats of the Democrat Left and a section of the Christian Democrats.

Rifondazione has justified its participation in a bourgeois government as a necessary next step for the movement, as a natural growing over from protest to a government which it claims can be held to a left course.

The strategy is a flawed and dangerous one for the future of the Italian movement, as can be seen from looking at the situation in Italy and at a historical precedent for the party's action, the 'historic compromise' of the 1970s.

The left, the right and the Prodi government

In April 2006 the Prodi's Unione coalition beat Silvio Berlusconi's right wing Casa della Libertà coalition by the slenderest of margins. The Unione government has since been in a position of extreme weakness in parliamentary terms. It has only one more member of the senate than Berlusconi's supporters, despite having a majority in the Chamber of Deputies—and both houses have equal weight. This weakness has been used by Rifondazione's leadership as an excuse to prevent any of its parliamentary representatives, even those on the far left, from voting down the sort of measures it used to denounce vociferously.

Rifondazione's decision to join the Unione coalition goes back to September 2004. Fausto Bertinotti, the party's national secretary, drew up 15 theses describing the overriding priority as 'the urgent need to defeat the Berlusconi government' through 'programmatic agreement among all the forces that are today in opposition' to that government.[1] Bertinotti was a key figure during the election campaign in presenting the Unione as the logical conclusion of the growth of the movement and its 'capacity to impact on the sphere of political decisions'.[2] His performance contributed in part to the high vote for Rifondazione. The party received 2.5 million votes in the election for the Senate (7.4 percent of the total) and 2.2 million (5.8 percent) for the Chamber of Deputies.[3] 'A government programme', he wrote in 2004, 'must have as its defining characteristics a break in the continuity of the politics of the Berlusconi government, the construction of itself as a real alternative and the opening of a way for the independence of the movements and the class struggle to win new spaces for the transformation of society'.[4]

The reality of the Unione in government in a few short months has differed greatly from this ideal picture. There is already more continuity than break with Berlusconi's government in domestic and foreign policy alike. An initial statement on withdrawing troops from Iraq has been watered down to a phased withdrawal, which had already been agreed between Bush and Berlusconi, and Italian troops have gone to Afghanistan and Lebanon. The government's proposed budget offers change only in that it aims at making Italian capitalism more efficient and profitable than Berlusconi was able to.

The economic situation that the Prodi government has inherited is a poor one. The Italian economy has been on the decline since its high point in 1987, when Italy's GDP surpassed that of Britain. The country's growth has been the slowest in the European Union for 15 years, averaging below 1.5 percent between 1990 and 2004.[5] Under Berlusconi, Italy's budget surplus fell to 0.6 percent of GDP from 3.4 percent in 2001, and Italy's public debt rose for the first time since the early 1990s.[6]

The *Economist* describes the seriousness of the situation:

> Italian companies, especially the small, family-owned firms that have been the backbone of the economy, are under ever-increasing pressure. Costs have

> risen, but productivity has remained flat or even declined. Membership of the euro, Europe's single currency, now rules out devaluation, which for many years acted as a safety-valve for Italian business. Italy's competitiveness is deteriorating fast, and its shares of world exports and foreign direct investment are very low... The economy has also proved highly vulnerable to Asian competition because so many small Italian firms specialise in such areas as textiles, shoes, furniture and white goods, which are taking the brunt of China's export assault.[7]

The Italian ruling class desperately wants growth and profits, which Berlusconi—despite appearances—did not deliver. The president of the Confindustria employers' federation, Luca Cordero di Montezemolo, could not be clearer: 'We want this country to grow, to create affluence, to create wealth. To redistribute wealth we must first create it'.[8] The ruling class desires major 'reform' involving deep cuts—and there has already been furore at Prodi's limitations in delivering this—with many of its members preferring a 'grand coalition' government involving sections of the right.

The pressures of increased costs and competition on family firms is a major cause of middle class bitterness, and is exacerbated by rising housing costs and the increased cost of living since Italy joined the euro. Many middle and working class Italians are having to cut back on holidays and household consumption in an increasing struggle to make ends meet. In 2005, 40 percent of adults between 30 and 34 still lived with their parents, unable to afford a place of their own thanks to rising house prices, low wages, unemployment—especially high among young people and in the south—or an inefficient, bureaucratic education system that often results in students not getting degrees until they are well into their thirties.[9] The lack of opportunities for graduates simply increases the frustration.

Such a cocktail of pressures is expressed politically, as elsewhere in Europe, in a degeneration of social democracy, producing increased polarisation—a process reflected in the relatively high vote for Rifondazione in the election, but also in the high votes for the 'post-fascist' Alleanza Nazionale and Berlusconi's Forza Italia.

This is the situation in which the Prodi government submitted its budget in September—a serious attack on living standards masquerading as redistribution. All the signs at the time of writing are that Rifondazione deputies will not obstruct its parliamentary approval. The budget includes 20 billion worth of spending cuts: €3 billion worth of cuts in healthcare, €4.6 billion in local authority provision and €9.5 billion from pensions.[10]

Early budget proposals were to raise €13 billion by increasing taxes for those earning over €70,000 and lower them for those on less than €40,000. These caused an uproar. Employers and the European financial press attacked the measures. Berlusconi and the right, far from being cowed by Prodi's victory, went on the offensive and organised a demonstration of tens of thousands in Rome in October in response to what they regard as a left wing attack on the middle class. Forza Italia vice-chairman Paolo Romani said, 'The communist parties have Prodi in a stranglehold. Rifondazione is intent on revenge. The middle class is being asked to pick up the tab, because the old communists are outraged by the fact of wealthy citizens'.[11]

Matteo Colannino, head of the young businessmen's section at Confindustria, concurred: 'The government's reformist wing is submitting to the influence of the extreme left. Italy doesn't need new taxes, but to create an atmosphere more favourable to business'.[12] As a result of this pressure, Prodi made concessions to small businesses over the most contentious issue—they will not have to transfer severance pay funds into the state pension scheme, although big businesses and banks have agreed to, in return for compensation.

This may all be to Prodi's advantage. As the *Economist* pointed out, the outcry 'helps to comfort the powerful left of Mr Prodi's heterogeneous administration, and may even give him enough leeway to pass other liberalising reforms'.[13] In other words, the tax-raising proposals in the budget may well get whittled away in order to win the parliamentary vote. This can be blamed on the resistance of the right—while the left concedes the budget cuts affecting those who voted for it.

The budget signals Prodi's intention to continue the privatisation of public industries, and attacks on wages and conditions of public sector workers, like those at the national airline Alitalia and on the railways, and to revive Berlusconi's attacks on pension rights, including raising the retirement age. These moves, described by finance minister Tommaso Padoa-Schioppa as merely 'an hors d'oeuvre', provide 'a welcome whiff of liberalism', according to the *Economist*, which the right and the employers have interpreted as a signal to push hard at the open door. Their protests are aimed at forcing the government to drop any concessions to its coalition partners and follow a full-blooded neoliberal course. For workers it means a continuation of falling living standards, price rises and increasing unemployment and job insecurity. Yet the main CGIL union federation has so far fallen in line with the government; it has, for example, called off proposed national action over job cuts at Alitalia.

Confindustria, which opposed Berlusconi's re-election but preferred a 'grand coalition' of the centre-right to Prodi, complained that the cuts were not sufficient. 'We expected courageous cuts, more courage,' said Cordero di Montezemolo recently.[14] In this, Italy's bosses are not alone. In October, two credit rating agencies downgraded Italian government debt to the same level as that of Botswana, concerned that Prodi is just 'muddling through', and not taking strong enough action to cut public spending and raise productivity.[15] The IMF has stated that Italy should commit itself to a 'credible path' of debt and deficit reductions, and a staff mission was planned in November to examine the budget.[16]

Unsurprisingly, government popularity has plummeted: a poll in *La Repubblica* newspaper in October found that 45 percent trusted the government, down from 57 percent the previous month.[17] Rifondazione is part of a coalition that has so far had very little to do with delivering reforms for the improvement of workers' lives or with constructing a real alternative to neoliberalism.

Bertinotti declared in an interview in this journal in spring 2004 that the twin principles on which an alternative left capable of challenging the 'moderate left' and the right could be built in Italy were 'the general rejection of war, especially imperialist war' and 'opposition to, and an exit strategy from, neoliberal politics'.[18] Yet when Prodi called two confidence votes over the refinancing of Italy's mission in Afghanistan, where it has 1,300 soldiers as part of the NATO force, Rifondazione deputies and senators—including one from the left inside Rifondazione, Sinistra Critica (Critical Left), which said it was against the mission—nevertheless backed the funding by refusing to oppose the confidence vote.

Another, more symbolic, example of the speed with which the Rifondazione leadership has shifted rightward was the newspaper photograph of Bertinotti embracing Gianfranco Fini of the 'post-fascist' Alleanza Nazionale while sharing a platform with him at the annual conference of that party's youth wing at which the Rifondazione leader spoke of the need to 'build bridges between the different traditions'.

This dramatic shift to the right has confused and disoriented many activists politicised by the movement since Seattle, especially Rifondazione's own members. The early impact on the movement in Italy has been nothing short of disastrous. Two years ago 1 million marched in Rome against the Iraq war but a recent anti-war demonstration in Rome mustered only a thousand people.

Rifondazione's political itinerary

For many, Rifondazione's behaviour is history repeating itself. It held the balance of power as part of the Olive Tree coalition that governed between 1996 and 1998, also led by Prodi, after receiving over 3 million votes. On that occasion it refused government positions but was under great pressure not to bring down the first centre-left government in 50 years and was understandably desperate not to risk the return of Berlusconi. The party faced a contradictory situation two years later when it did eventually leave the coalition, causing the government to fall. It had been electorally damaged by its association with Prodi's cuts (its vote fell in local elections in 1997 and it has never regained 1996 levels nationally). But it was also attacked by the rest of the coalition parties and lost a lot of members to a split to the right.

There is, however, a major difference between Italy in 1996 and 2006. The intervening decade witnessed the birth and development of the anti-capitalist movement, at its strongest and most dynamic in Italy, and the international movement against the Iraq war. Rifondazione has played an important role in that movement and has been seen as a powerful force within it. As Fabio Ruggiero has described it, Rifondazione's 'actions in the movement enhanced its reputation in the eyes of the many thousands of people, not only in Italy but all over Europe, for whom hope had revived that another world is possible'.[19] There was a deeply held conviction among the Rifondazione leadership that the movement 'had anti-capitalist potential' necessitating a fundamental shift in the party. For Bertinotti, it was the birth of the movement that laid the 'material and subjective building blocks for a "refoundation" [of a new communist party]'.[20]

Unfortunately, a genuine identification and engagement with the movement as it was on the rise also disguised contradictions in the party's approach that have not been resolved, predisposing it to lurches to the left and to the right. It had never developed a theoretical tradition within its ranks capable of analysing the trajectories of international neoliberalism and imperialism. It had not acknowledged and learnt the lessons from the behaviour of its forerunner, the Italian Communist Party (PCI). And in 'making the turn to the movement, it absorbed many of the autonomist ideas'.[21]

There was a failure to challenge the notion within anti-capitalism that the movement should be 'non-ideological'. This had a negative impact on the Italian movement. It meant, for example, that there was no systematic discussion of imperialism and the importance of a coherent, nationally coordinated anti-war movement. The lack of theoretical clarity over such issues as the UN has made it easier for deputies and senators to justify their actions in voting for Italian involvement in Lebanon under the UN flag and to support the government over Afghanistan. The disparate nature of anti-war activity has made it more difficult for the movement to hold them to account. The anti-war movement is much weaker as a result.[22]

Resistance within Rifondazione to theoretical discussion of parts of the old Italian Communist Party's past goes back to the time of its formation in 1991. It emerged out of the minority in that party who opposed its transformation into the social democratic Democratic Left (DS) after the collapse of the Soviet Union. There were early internal struggles within Rifondazione between those like Bertinotti's predecessor, Sergio Garavini, who criticised Stalinism, seeing the need to learn the lessons of the collapse of the Soviet Union and the need for a new form of communist party, and those representing the Stalinist right, led by Armando Cossutta (who eventually split in 1998). Garavini's resignation in 1993 led to discussion in the party becoming 'focused entirely on institutional issues...specifically on the issue of the party's involvement in electoral pacts, and subsequently, membership of an actual government'.[23]

An emphasis on electoralism and a close relationship with the Democratic Left led to a major split in the party leadership in 1995 when Rifondazione deputies voted, against party policy, for the caretaker Dini government, which was continuing the attacks of the first Berlusconi government after a general strike had forced him from office. Then came the experience of the first Prodi government in 1996, the subsequent break in 1998, and Berlusconi's re-election as Rifondazione leader in 2001.

A post-Genoa document to the Rifondazione conference of that year suggested that lessons had been learned from this cycle. It linked the necessity of a break from the party's Stalinist past with a break from the centre-left in electoral terms, regarding both as key to the 'refoundation' of communism: 'The rupture with the centre-left and the exit of the majority who supported the Prodi government was one of these acts of refoundation, a rupture also with the prevalent culture of the leaders of the Italian Communist Party'.[24]

However, even in the aftermath of Genoa, when the party was making a serious turn to the movement, there was no discussion of the period of 'historic compromise' in the 1970s and the impact of the actions of the Italian Communist Party on the trajectory of a previous mass movement. A proposed conference on the subject under Garavini was dropped and never resurfaced.[25]

That absence of a serious theoretical consideration of its history has made easier the resurrection of electoralism within the party, now that the breach with the 'centre-left' (the DS) has been papered over. One result of under-theorising the past (and the present) is that the divisions in the movement are being replicated within Rifondazione's membership, which is increasingly influenced by a mixture of reformist faith in Rifondazione in government, and autonomism. It is therefore ill equipped to challenge the compromises of its leadership.

Clearly, Rifondazione is not the same as the pre-1991 Italian Communist Party. Most of its members joined in the 1990s or after Genoa. There is, nonetheless, continuity. Many among the leadership were members of the old party and Rifondazione claims to stand in its tradition, especially regarding its role in the liberation of Italy from fascism. Going over the history of the Communist Party's role in the last mass movement in Italian history, that of the 1970s, remains relevant.

The historic compromise

The period from 1967 to 1976 was one of tremendous struggle and turmoil in Italian society as massive student protests burst out, radicalising a generation and igniting an explosion of workers' struggle.

Italian society at the beginning of that period was dominated by the political influence of the Christian Democrat Party, which had governed since the end of the war. Its successive governments were increasingly unstable because of deep corruption and infighting between interest groups within the party. In the mid-1960s the Socialist Party had entered government and also been sucked into the clientilist political machine.

The Italian Communist Party was the largest communist party in the West. It had 1.5 million members in 1968, a loyal membership and deep roots in Italian society through the trade unions, cooperatives and cultural associations attached to it. It was, however, excluded from government.

Protests among university students in Pisa, Trento and Venice in 1967 quickly spread to affect most of Italy's universities by the beginning of 1968. Radicalisation also spread fast. The protests were initially non-violent, but turned to active resistance following police attacks. Students' political ideas were influenced by the Vietnamese liberation struggle against the US, the Maoism of the Chinese Cultural Revolution and the May events in France, but not by the Italian Communist Party, which declared itself opposed to 'extremist and anarchist positions that have appeared in the student movement'.[26]

The Italian student movement sparked a 'massive rebellion amongst the factory workers of Northern Italy in 1968-69 which shook the power of the bosses for at least a decade'.[27] These strikes were largely spontaneous and involved young workers, often semi-skilled emigrants from the South, fighting against speed-ups, repression and the discriminatory conditions in the factories.

Strikers battled with police in the Veneto in April 1968, and at Montedison near Venice in June the first assemblies of workers were set up, bypassing the union apparatus. More spontaneous strikes broke out at Pirelli in Milan. It was 'symptomatic of the earthquake in Italian society that the workers, like the students of the previous year, did not look to the PCI for leadership'.[28] The leaders were often to join the revolutionary left groups, Lotta Continua, Avanguardia Operaia and Potere Operaia.[29] In March 1969 workers at Italy's largest factory, Fiat's Mirafiori plant in Turin, struck for 50 days. City-wide workers' and students' assemblies were established in June, and by September Italy's 'hot autumn' of strikes had spread across the country: 'Five and a half million Italian workers, more than a quarter of the entire labour force, were involved in strikes that autumn... On 19 November 1969, 20 million Italians joined a general strike that forced the government to reform the pensions system'.[30]

Union membership rose dramatically with the strikes—from 4.5 million in 1968 to 6 million in 1973—and the PCI, through its influence in the largest union federation, the CGIL, encouraged the development of factory councils to run the strikes. The party argued it was extending democratic organisation, expanding and institutionalising the system of spontaneous organisation that had developed in the course of the movement. But over time the union bureaucracy came to dominate the councils, allowing the PCI to exercise restraint over the strikes.

Social upheaval increased the polarisation in Italian society. The fascist MSI nearly doubled their vote from 5.8 percent in 1968 to 10.7 in 1970. The Christian Democrats moved further right in turn in an attempt to preserve their base and the Socialist Party was pushed aside in the 1972 election. The outcome was a reactionary Christian Democrat government under Fanfani that went on the offensive against the workers' movement—and was met by resistance.[31] The movement had fractured the Christian Democrat domination of national institutions, while the migration of rural workers to the cities weakened the hold of its allies in the Catholic Church on millions of people. Then at the end of 1973 soaring oil price rises triggered severe economic recession and made the situation immeasurably worse for Italy's rulers.

Against this background of a right wing government losing control in the face of economic crisis and profound social rebellion, the Communist Party stepped in to prop up Italian capitalism. Its leader, Enrico Berlinguer, used the recent military coup against Salvador Allende to justify a party bid to share power with the Christian Democrats in the autumn of 1973. 'Chile, Berlinguer argued, showed that a country polarised between right and left was in danger of civil wars and military coups. The answer was a "historic compromise" between the parties which would guarantee stability while the reforms desired by most advanced sections of capital were pushed through'.[32] He talked of 'connecting and uniting the more radical tendencies to the movement of the broad masses, creating a fusion of revolutionaries, progressives and democrats'. What this meant in practice was a 'strategy of class alliances derived from the legacy of the Popular Front of the 1930s'.[33]

Increasingly, another justification for a concord between the Christian Democrats and the Communist Party was the 'strategy of tension'. Sections of the Italian police and military were alarmed by the strength and militancy of the workers' movement, the breakdown of ideas of 'order' and declining obedience to church and state. They harked back to the fascist era and conspired with right wing terrorist groups. 'Black' terrorist bombings killed 16 people in Milan in 1969, 12 on the Florence-Bologna train in 1974, and a further 84 at Bologna station in 1980. The terrorists were rarely arrested. Instead the outrages were blamed on the left, and police persecuted revolutionaries, militant workers and anarchists.

The Communist Party fell in line with the strategy of tension. Desperate to keep pace with the Christian Democrats and the possibility of shared government alive, it argued hard with its supporters that there was no alternative to the historic compromise in order to stop the right. 'An organic entente with Christian Democracy, reassuring the propertied and middle classes, was supposed to isolate and neutralise the neo-fascist fanatics in the wings of the political scene, by denying them the climate of social fear in which they might thrive'.[34] This was disingenuous and dangerous in the extreme. As Toby Abse explains, 'Neo-fascism has never been a force clearly separable from the structures of the Italian state that emerged...after the Second World War.' Christian Democrat politicians who had presided over the state ever since, 'honeycombing it with their party's appointees', could not be unaware of right wing conspiracies even if they were not directly implicated.[35] Collusion with the party that was implicated in the conspiracies could in no way combat the growth of the right. The Communists' move to the right to forge a great coalition for stability did nothing to resolve the tensions in Italian society. In 1975 the government was forced to concede the scala mobile (increasing wages along with inflation) and the 'crisis of the institutions' deepened.

The Communist Party benefited electorally from the expectations born from eight years of tremendous struggles and, paradoxically, from its failure to enter the government—despite its refusal to side with the movement to unseat it. In the 1976 election it won 32.4 percent of the vote as the only party untainted by public office. The Christian Democrats were still the strongest party but were unable to form a government without Communist support, making the realisation of the historic compromise appear inevitable. However, much of the ruling class and the United States would not countenance communists in government . The party agreed, instead, to support the

DC government of 'National Solidarity' led by Giulio Andreotti without holding any seats in it and did so from August 1976 to the beginning of 1979. The aim of National Solidarity was to solve the 'emergency' of economic crisis and restore the viability and stability of Italian capitalism.

The PCI was crucial to winning workers' acceptance of an austerity package of deflationary measures proposed by the IMF. Berlinguer argued for 'austerity' as a moral virtue intrinsic to the labour movement. The workers' movement had forced government to pass a statute of workers' rights in 1970 and the scala mobile five years later. In contrast, not a single significant reform was granted under the National Solidarity government. 'The political consequences for the country were disastrous. For inevitably not all the forces set in motion by the earthquake of the late 1960s would suffer and be still. Ultimately the price of a blocked political system was a spiralling dialectic of violence and repression that ended in the lunacy of terrorism'.[36]

One year into National Solidarity a new student movement broke out in 1977. It was born into economic depression, expressing the despair and frustration of young people at their predicament and at the seeming impossibility of change. This time the movement remained isolated from the organised working class. The ideas of autonomism quickly gained hold in the absence of the revolutionary left, which had largely collapsed as the movement of 1968-9 gave way to historic compromise, and in the face of PCI hostility.

Autonomia Operaia, a group around Toni Negri, had reversed their 'workerist' emphasis on factory workers in the early 1960s for a rejection of the 'privileged' organised working class. It now regarded students, the unemployed and marginalised members of society as 'social workers', the key forces for change in society, and believed street violence was central to the victory of the movement through 'autonomous' struggle. Ultimately this stress on violence against police resulted in increased repression and, catastrophically, gave oxygen to 'left' terrorists like the Red Brigades, notorious for the kidnapping and murder of Christian Democrat politician Aldo Moro in 1978.[37] Such 'red' terrorism attracted many who were disillusioned by the collapse of the revolutionary left and embittered by the Communist Party's betrayal and police repression, while leading the party to support increased police repression and the arrest of many revolutionaries.

The party left the National Solidarity government in 1979 to bargain for seats that it still did not get—and lost votes in the subsequent election. Nevertheless it continued to support the principle of the historic compromise. The smashing of the movement of 1977 had been one outcome; the breaking of the workers' movement was the other. In 1979 Fiat bosses launched a counter-offensive after a decade of being on the defensive and sacked 61 workers. The Communist Party refused to support the victimised militants, claiming they were 'red' terrorists. Then in 1980 a key strike to oppose massive job cuts was supported by the party and the unions but resulted in a decisive defeat for the Italian working class, with a political impact similar to that of the miners' defeat in Britain in 1985.

The party's announcement in 1979 that it was turning its back on the strategy of National Solidarity and returning to opposition 'was accompanied by no self-criticism of the political errors of the Historic Compromise, or its costs'.[38] As Lucio Magri of the left wing Il Manifesto group warned at the time, faced with a mass movement the right turn of the PCI served to 'complicate and delay the construction of an anti-capitalist alternative'.[39]

Confusions and possibilities

There are obvious parallels between the 1970s and today but there are also significant differences. Most importantly, the attitude of Rifondazione to the movement has not been one of hostility and suspicion, but of active support and involvement. However, with the decline of the movement from its 2001-03 highpoint, the party's largely uncritical acceptance of the language of autonomism and its ideological confusion have allowed Bertinotti to present the Prodi government as the political expression of the movement. This strategy has been largely accepted among activists because of the failure of the movement to dislodge Berlusconi. Also important is the fact that the party has not abandoned support for all extra-parliamentary action. It was central to the recent 200,000-strong demonstration against 'precarious' jobs and for workers' rights, using the success to argue that there is no contradiction between government and the movement:

> As for the chorus which holds forth...on the impossibility of our being a party of struggle and a party of government, we say to all of them... did you see the streets of Rome yesterday? It was full of politics, of the desire for a new politics. Whoever cares, as we do, about the quality of the Prodi government knows that it is here, among these people, this youth, among this strong symbolic representation of a new workers' movement, that the key to future success lies.[40]

The protest was unquestionably significant in demonstrating that the movement has not disappeared in Italy and that the potential to pose a real alternative to Prodi's government is there. But Rifondazione—despite the fine words—insisted the demonstration was not opposed to the government, and refused to connect the feeling against job insecurity with action against the budget. As with the votes supporting funds for Afghanistan, the central danger of Rifondazione's strategy is that its presence in government causes it to blunt the militancy of forces opposed to cuts, insecurity and war.

Despite the argument that Rifondazione has to be 'in it to win it' as part of a government fighting for reform, the reality of the 1970s was that significant structural reform eluded the Italian Communist Party. All the major gains for workers, from improved contracts to the scala mobile, were a direct result of the rebellion in the factories.

Building expectations of Prodi can also strengthen the right. The imperative to stop the right was a central argument for joining the government, and the continued justification for pacifying resistance to Prodi's policies is that the right could win the next election if the government falls. Rifondazione argues that the ruling class wants a grand coalition of the centre-right and that the only way to prevent the Prodi wing moving in this direction is to exercise a pull from the left. The reality is that the tacit agreement of the left to neoliberal policies can only strengthen the right, just as the support of Berlinguer for the Christian Democrat National Solidarity government of the late 1970s did. Another lesson from the 1970s is that leaving a space to the left can result in the increased influence of autonomist ideas, as those wanting to register a protest against policies of privatisation and war and frustrated with Rifondazione's compromises can turn to autonomism's rejection of political parties and the organised working class.

At the moment the effect of the main political party associated with the movement taking a right turn has been to pull many autonomists, like the disobbedienti, behind Rifondazione, as the electoral strategy seems to have worked in ousting Berlusconi. At the same time within the party the concession to autonomist ideas and language has increased its influence, especially in the youth section—some of whom have reacted to entry into government by arguing against the need for a party! If, however, as things unfold, Rifondazione is complicit in continued attacks on its supporters, this 'unity' can unravel and autonomism can appear more radical to many who will be on the sharp end.

Joining the Prodi government was not the logical extension of a strong movement. Rifondazione could have focused on building a movement outside parliament that posed a genuine alternative to Berlusconi—and on fighting within it for political clarity. It could have been part of a united electoral list to oppose the right but refused to enter the government. Paradoxically, if had not thrown its all into the election, it could have generated more enthusiasm for evicting Berlusconi and creating a meaningful alternative to Prodi. It would have reinvigorated the anti-war movement if its deputies had refused to bow to imperialism.

Rather than 'opening a path for the movement to create an alternative world', the Prodi government shuts the door on the movement's goals and Rifondazione support for it can only damage the movement. It is a strategy that risks disillusioning those who thought they were members of a new kind of party and can lead to passivity and acceptance of the reformist agenda.

It is, of course, far from inevitable that Prodi will succeed in his attacks, regardless of the complexion of the government. November's demonstration proves that the anger, imagination and combativity of the movement have not disappeared. The mass presence of FIOM on the demonstration raises the possibility of union resistance to the proposed budget onslaught. The election results showed that a great many Italians wanted an alternative to Berlusconi, but that there was a significant lack of enthusiasm for Prodi. A large part of support for the Unione was clearly for the left within it.

Rifondazione's history and its continued connection to the movement suggest the possibility that the party can break with Prodi—it is quite capable of lurching back to the left at some point. However, it is essential for there to be a strong left opposition to the current right turn within Rifondazione's ranks if the movement and the party are not to succumb to autonomism, reformism or a combination of the two. Sadly, the revolutionary left within Rifondazione has made serious mistakes, which make this task increasingly difficult. Most damagingly, a Sinistra Critica member was among those Rifondazione deputies and senators who voted to support the government over Afghanistan. The problem for the left is that it did not build a strong pole of attraction within Rifondazione and its recent collapse over the confidence votes stems in part from the resulting isolation, with the fear of marginalisation if it refuses to fall into line at crucial moments. The pressures that Rifondazione faces within the Unione coalition are reproduced for the left within Rifondazione.

The task of building a genuine alternative to Prodi necessitates taking a clear line against his budget and against continued support for imperialism, together with resistance to the notion that 'practical politics' means supporting the neoliberal agenda and attacks on workers. For the revolutionary left to weld together a genuine opposition within Rifondazione entails a continued political critique of the party's entry into a bourgeois government—and a commitment to act accordingly.

NOTES

I am grateful to Chris Bambery, Tom Behan and Chris Harman for comments on an earlier draft.

1: Fausto Bertinotti, '15 Tesi per il Congresso di Rifondazione Comunista', September 2004, quoted in *International Socialism* 105 (Winter 2005), p132.

2: Quoted in Fabio Ruggiero, 'Rifondazione's U-turn', *International Socialism* 105 (Winter 2005), p128.

3: http://electionresources.org/it

4: Fausto Bertinotti, '15 Tesi per il congresso di Rifondazione Comunista', no 12, September 2004. Available at www.rifondazione.it

5: *Economist* online, www.economist.com, 24 November 2005.

6: *Financial Times*, 20 October, 2006.

7: *Economist* online, 24 November 2005, as above.

8: *Business Week*, 23 October 2006.

9: *Economist* online, 24 November 2005, as above.

10: Steve Scherer and Alessandra Migliaccio, 'Prodi Budget Raises Tax on High Income, Trims Deficit', 30 September 2006, www.bloomberg.com.

11: Quoted in Marianne Arens, 'Prodi Government Submits Austerity Budget', 7 October 2006, www.wsws.org.

12: *Financial Times*, 26 October 2006.

13: *Economist*, 19 October 2006.

14: Quoted in Marianne Arens, as above.

15: *Financial Times*, 23 October 2006.

16: Reuters news agency, 19 October, 2006. www.reuters.com.

17: *La Repubblica*, 18 October 2006.

18: Fausto Bertinotti interviewed by Tom Behan, 'Refounding Further', *International Socialism* 102 (Spring 2004), p104.

19: Fabio Ruggiero, 'Rifondazione's U-turn', *International Socialism* 105 (Winter 2005), p126.

20: Fausto Bertinotti interviewed by Tom Behan, as above, pp94-95.

21: Chris Harman, 'Anti-capitalism Five Years After Seattle', *International Socialism* 104 (Autumn 2004), p18. See also Tom Behan, 'The Return of Italian Communism', *International Socialism* 85, Winter 1999, and Chris Bambery, 'How Long Can the Party Last?', *Socialist Review*, May 2006.

22: I am grateful to Chris Bambery for this point.

23: R Mordenti, *La Rivoluzione. La Nuova via al Comunismo Italiano* (Milan, 2003), quoted in Tom Behan, unpublished manuscript.

24: Draft resolution to PRC conference, 2001. Available in English on www.internationalviewpoint.org

25: An unpublished manuscript by Tom Behan has contributed greatly to my understanding of Rifondazione's early development.

26: Tobias Abse, 'Judging the PCI', *New Left Review* 153, September-October 1985, p15.

27: As above, pp10-11.

28: As above, p11.

29: For more discussion of the revolutionary left in this period, see Chris Harman, *The Fire Last Time: 1968 and After* (London 1988), pp202, 205.

30: Tobias Abse, 'Judging the PCI', as above, p12.

31: Chris Harman, as above, p198.

32: As above, p200.

33: Tobias Abse, 'Judging the PCI', as above, p16.

34: As above, p18.

35: As above, p19.

36: As above, p28.

37: As above, p31.

38: As above, p36.

39: Lucio Magri, 'Italian Communism in the Sixties', *New Left Review* 66, March-April, 1971, p52.

40: Rina Gagliardi, 'Avete Capito Cosa Vuol Dire Fare Politica?', *Liberazione*, 6 November, 2006.

The shape of the working class

Martin Smith

'There was a time when one in four of the world's big ships were built on the Clyde and more than 1 million of the UK's workers were coal miners. Today the supermarket giant Tesco's employs just over 250,000 workers—making it the biggest private sector employer'.[1] So began a report on BBC 2's *Newsnight*. The programme took for granted the 'common sense' argument that the traditional working class in Britain is in terminal decline and is being replaced by a low paid, unorganised, part time, casualised workforce based in the service sector.

These conclusions are drawn from two main assumptions. The first is the decline in all major capitalist countries of manufacturing industries. The second argument, and one promoted by the likes of New Labour, Polly Toynbee and Will Hutton, is that the majority of people in Britain are now home owning, white collar and middle class. They cite the huge expansion of white collar jobs in teaching, local government, the civil service, design and technology, which were regarded as middle class professions, as proof that the majority of people are middle class.

They believe the country's workforce looks something like an hourglass, with a large glass bowl at the top, containing around 70 percent of the population, which is doing very well or reasonably well. The bottom glass bowl contains the other 30 percent—the poor (unemployed, part time workers) and low paid service sector workers. Toynbee believes that the growth of the service sector means workers do not have the economic power or the industrial muscle that their forefathers had. The politics underpinning this assumption is Margaret Thatcher's and subsequently Tony Blair's belief that we live in a 'classless society'.

Yet arguments about the death of the working class are nothing new. Over the past 50 years they have regularly been resurrected. For instance, in the 1950s academics claimed that workers in the motor industry had become 'embourgeoisified' because they could afford fridges, cars and holidays abroad. French theorist Andre Gorz declared in an article written in early 1968 that 'in the foreseeable future there will be no crisis of European capitalism so dramatic as to drive the mass of workers to revolutionary general strikes', and the historian Eric Hobsbawn made a series of assertions that the working class was in terminal decline in the1980s.[2]

Are we all middle class now? What does the working class look like in Britain today? Are the trade unions finished? These are the questions I want to attempt to answer. I also want to refute the notion that the working class is in decline, arguing instead that it is becoming larger and more diverse in its make up.

Who is working class?

Before we look at who makes up the working class in Britain today, it is important to define what makes someone working class.

Marx argued that under capitalism there are those who own the means of production, the factories, offices, railways etc—the ruling class; and the working class who sell their labour power in order to survive. In the *Communist Manifesto* he argued that the ruling class has developed 'a class of labourers, who must sell themselves piecemeal, are a commodity, like every other article of commerce, and are consequently exposed to all the vicissitudes of competition, to all the fluctuations of the market'.[3] In other words, class is a social relationship.

The Marxist historian G E M de Ste Croix put it the following way:

> Class (essentially a relationship) is the collective social expression of the fact of exploitation, the way in which exploitation is embodied in a social structure. By exploitation I mean the appropriation of part of the product of the labour of others: in a commodity-producing society this is what Marx called 'surplus value'.
>
> A class (a particular class) is a group of persons in a community identified by their position in the whole system of social production, defined above all according to their relationship (primarily in terms of the degree of ownership or control) to the conditions of production (that is to say, the means and labour of production) and to other classes.[4]

However, today the structure of capitalist society is more complicated than simply being divided into two diametrically opposed classes—the ruling class and the working class. There is a substantial 'middle class' in Britain. Sociologists claim it represents about 15 to 20 percent of the population—foremen, low grade managers, doctors, head teachers, etc. These people face contradictory pressures. On the one hand, their wealth and social position mean that they buy into the system; on the other hand, because they sell their labour power they too can find themselves in conflict with the system and look to a collective response. The class forces around them shape their reaction to events.

It is interesting to note that a growing number of people describe themselves as 'working class'. In 1994 51 percent of those surveyed by Mori described themselves as working class; by 2002 it had risen to 68 percent.[5]

But Marxists reject the popular notion that what defines your class background has something to do with your lifestyle, income, accent or how you feel about your class position.

In the early 1980s I worked as a civil servant in the London Passport Office. One member of staff used to come to work wearing a three piece suit, bowler hat, briefcase and a copy of the *Financial Times* under his arm. From his appearance you would have assumed that he was a top civil servant—he was in fact a filing clerk! Likewise the stereotypical view of an airport check-in worker is of a 'corporatised glamorous woman'. Yet it was these women, in the summer of 2005, who brought British Airways to its knees when they organised an unofficial sit-in. When their working conditions were under attack they were forced to act collectively—in fact they went further than that: they adopted militant tactics associated with car workers in the 1930s or Glasgow shipyard workers in the 1970s.

So it is important to understand that being working class is an objective relationship; the actual class position of individuals depends not on what they feel about which class they belong to, but whether they are forced to sell their labour power or not. Class position is not the same as class consciousness. Workers are still workers even if they vote Tory, own shares or buy their council houses.

There are those who view the working class through the prism of what it looked like in the 1950s. They therefore conclude that because the number of miners in Britain in the 1950s was 600,000 and today it stands at less than 4,000 the working class is in decline.

Capitalism is characterised by the constant revolutionising of the means of production. This means that from its earliest inception one of its key features has been restructuring: once-dynamic industries go into decline and new ones spring up. Alongside these grow newly developed towns and regions, and new working methods. Most importantly, this means that the working class is also constantly changing. This process of the constant revolutionising of the means of production was recorded by Marx. He wrote, 'All old established national industries have been destroyed or are daily being destroyed. They are dislodged by new industries, whose introduction becomes a life and death question'.[6]

This process is as old as capitalism itself. The basis of much of the Industrial Revolution was the textile industry. As the century wore on, coal and heavy industry became the backbone of British capitalism. These mainly male blue collar workers are what shape many people's vision of what a worker should look like. It is not true that these workers were automatically militant and pro-union. I once saw an exhibition at the now closed Labour History Museum in east London. It had a display of two photographs of a boilermaker in east London. In one photograph taken in 1886 he is standing there surrounded by apprentices, looking like a 'middle class gentleman'. In the second, dated 1900, he is wearing a boiler suit with a union badge pinned on it, surrounded by a dozen men who look just like him. The transformation was down to two things, the deskilling of his job and the New Unionism strike wave that hit the country in 1889.

Again in the1930s Britain experienced the growth of new industries such as car manufacturing and light manufacturing goods. If you look at the car industry, much of it developed on new greenfield sites like Dagenham, Coventry and Oxford in the 1920s and 1930s. These factories were state of the art and hostile to trade unions. There were many at the time who said that it was impossible to organise in them because the workers had been bought off. Similar things are said about bank workers, IT workers and media workers today. By the 1950s car workers were regarded as one of the best-organised and most militant sections of the working class. The experience of work and collective organisation and struggle brought about those changes.

Socialists have to understand the conditions that create the working class as what Marx termed a 'class in itself', and how that class can develop revolutionary ideas and become capable of making a revolution, become a 'class for itself'.[7]

Manufacturing

The 2006 UK Social Trends survey notes:

> It is well known that the UK economy has experienced structural change since the end of the Second World War with a decline in the manufacturing sector and an increase in the service sector. Jobs in the service industries have

increased by 45 percent, from 14.8 million in 1978 to 21.5 million in 2005, while those in manufacturing have fallen 54 percent from 6.9 million to 3.2 million over the same period.[8]

Figure 1 reveals this trend.

This decline in the numbers of workers involved in manufacturing was going on throughout the 20th century as the table demonstrates. At the same time we have seen a steady rise in the numbers of people working in the white collar jobs and the service sector. Today white collar and service sector workers are the majority. This trend also shows no signs of being reversed.

However, manufacturing workers are still a large and powerful section of the working class. To put it into perspective, one out of seven of the British workforce is employed in the manufacturing sector. These workers often work in large and well-organised workplaces like engineering, car manufacturing and food production. Although their numbers have fallen, those workers who are still employed have become more and more productive and in some senses more powerful. Take, for instance, the UK car industry. Over the last 30 years there has been a huge fall in the numbers of workers employed in the industry. However, car production has barely fallen. At the height of UK car production in the 1970s Britain produced about 1.7 million cars a year. By 2005 it had only fallen to 1.6 million a year. New technology means that one car worker can produce eight times what their predecessors could 30 years before.[9] Polycell, the wallpaper paste and DIY products manufacturer, has seen productivity rise by nearly 300 percent in the last 25 years. This is despite the fact that the workforce has halved over the same period.[10] Each worker is more productive and consequently more powerful.

Numerically, union membership is fairly evenly split between the private and the public sector, with 47 percent of union members employed in the private sector and 53 percent employed in the public sector. However, union density in the public sector is 59 percent and only 19 percent in the private. The difference in density is explained by the fact that there are more people working in the private sector (ie around three quarters of all workers). Union density in sections of manufacturing remains very high (see Figure 2).

White collar workers

When I started work as a civil servant at the London Passport Office 22 years ago I made the terrible mistake of believing I was going up in the world. I arrived at work wearing my best suit (in fact it was my only suit). I

Figure 1: Jobs by sex and industries

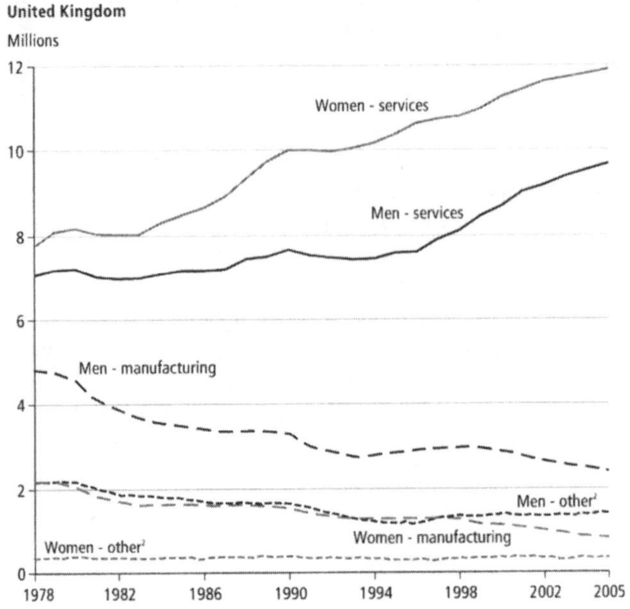

United Kingdom
Millions
12
10
8
6
4
2
0
Women - services
Men - services
Men - manufacturing
Men - other[2]
Women - manufacturing
Women - other[2]
1978
1982
1986
1990
1994
1998
2002
2005

1 At June each year.
2 Includes agriculture, construction, energy and water.

Source: Short-term Turnover and Employment Survey, Office for National Statistics

Figure 2: Union density by industry

Agriculture, fishing
9%
Utilities, mining etc.
44%
Manufacturing
27%
Construction
19%
Retail, hotels, catering
10%
Transport, communics
42%
Finance, business services
16%
Public admin, health, educ
51%
Other services
21%
0%
20%
40%
60%

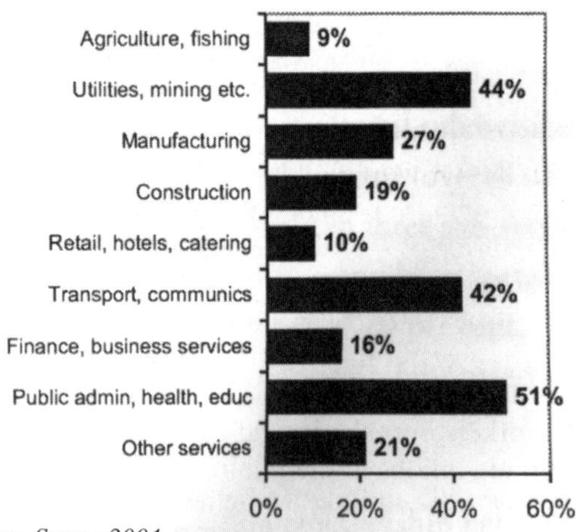

Source: Labour Force Survey 2001

got the shock of my life: everyone else was wearing jeans. I ended up being assigned to a huge office, where half the people opened letters all day and the others stuffed envelopes. My job was to stamp the passports with a huge brass embossing machine all day long. I was part of a clerical production line.

The nature of white collar jobs has changed massively over the last 100 years. Clerical workers in the 19th century were regarded as middle class. Their pay, status and even dress made them more akin to managers. A clerical post was seen as a prized job and was usually a lifetime post. It was also a job that required a high level of skill. Very few clerical workers see themselves as that today.

The growth of white collar jobs throughout the last century has been accompanied by a huge growth in the number of women workers. Over the last 40 years office work has become increasingly deskilled and dependent on machinery. Work has become boring and repetitive. The introduction of costly technology (computers, faxes and photocopiers) has changed the pattern of work inside the office. A similar process has gone on in education, banking and local government.

One council housing worker described the drudgery of his work.

> We don't have to clock in and out like my dad did when he worked in a factory. We now have a computer—I call it the hidden foreman. It is used by management to record and monitor how much work we do. It knows what time I start work, what time I finish, how long it takes me to have a piss. It monitors the number of telephone calls I answer and at a flick of a switch a supervisor can increase the pace of our work.[11]

Investment in machines means that white collar jobs are no longer nine to five. White collar workers are expected to do shift work. Many offices are now open 24 hours a day. Certainly, in terms of pay, a routine clerical worker is part of the working class. A low-grade civil servant earns around £17,000 a year—no more than a manual car worker at Fords does. The growth of a large layer of middle management has accompanied this growth in white collar jobs.

Today the myth that white collar workers are not part of the working class remains as strong as ever. Yet unionisation levels and strikes in this sector refute this myth. The drive to attack the working conditions, skills levels and pay of white collar workers over the last 30 to 40 years has been accompanied by a growth of trade unions in the public sector. Figure 3 below shows the gross weekly pay scales of public sector workers. It demonstrates that the majority of white collar workers' wages are comparable to manual workers'

Figure 3: Public sector pay levels by gender

Distribution of gross weekly earnings for full-time female employees, April 2005

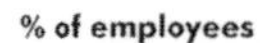

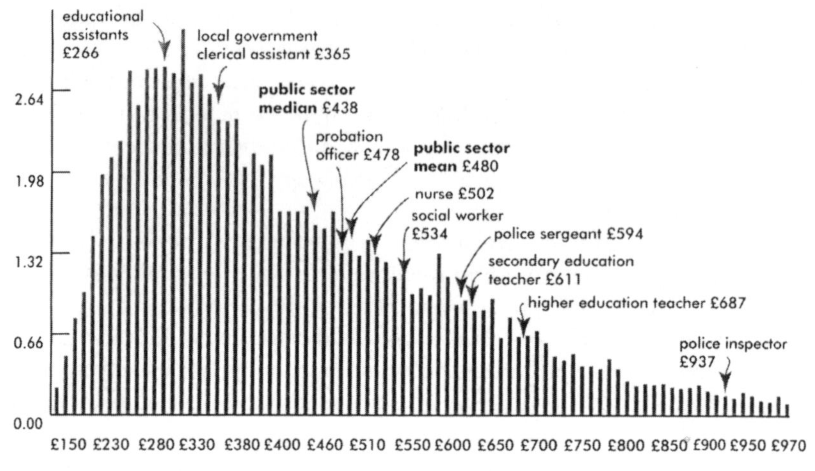

Distribution of gross weekly earnings for full-time male employees, April 2005

% of employees

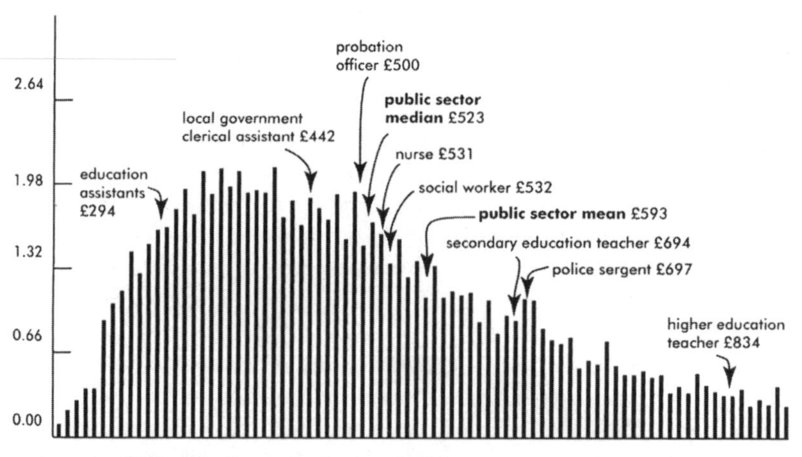

Source: Incomes Data Services

wages. It also demonstrates that women workers are predominantly found in the lower paid jobs.[12]

White collar workers such as office workers, many council workers and teachers make up a large section of Britain's workforce. Today, they are some of the best-organised workers in the country (see Figure 2 above). Just as with their forefathers and mothers in the cotton mills, the mines and car plants, the growth of trade unionism in the white collar sector came about over a relatively long period and as a result of a number of disputes, strikes and campaigns.

Over the past 20 years Britain has witnessed a huge growth in call centres, there are approximately 850,000 workers currently employed in them. Some studies describe the workers in these centres as white collar workers and others as part of the service economy. But they are also commonly described as the new coal miners of the 21st century.[13] If you read most reports in the media you would assume that these workers are completely atomised, have no power and face the constant fear of having their work outsourced to India or Romania. But again that is not a true picture. A series of recent studies shows that most of the companies which run these operations expect the number to keep on growing over the next few years, though not at quite the rate of a few years back. For every story about outsourcing to India, there is one about a new call centre being built in Britain, mostly ignored by the press.[14] In fact a recent report in the *Guardian* notes that companies like Kwik-Fit Insurance and Powergen, who had outsourced their work to India, are now relocating back to the UK because they can't find enough staff with the right level of technical skills and knowledge. Ironically, ICICI OneSource, a Mumbai-based outsourcing company, said it was building a new 1,000 person call centre in Belfast because of 'its highly skilled workforce and relatively cheap property prices'.[15]

Again expanding job opportunities and skills shortages in the industry are giving call centre workers the confidence to demand higher wages and better conditions. Last year I spoke to a call worker from Newcastle. He told me:

> There are five call centres on our industrial park. All of them are constantly advertising for trained staff. You end up meeting workers from other call centres in your lunch break in local cafes and pubs. Of course you find out who has the best hours and who gets the best rates of pay. All you have to do is ask your supervisor for a pay rise or a change in conditions. If they say no you just move to the next call centre across the road. There is a natural levelling up. It's good old fashioned economics of supply and demand.[16]

It's also become clear that unions like the CWU, Amicus and Unison are now organising in some of these centres.

The service sector

The increase in white collar jobs has gone alongside the rise in service jobs. The image painted of the service sector is of low paid, part time McDonald's type jobs, but the reality is somewhat different. Many service workers are in what would be considered 'old working class jobs'. Hospital ancillary workers, dockers, lorry drivers, bus and train drivers and postal workers all work in the service sector. These can hardly be described as 'new' jobs: they have been an integral part of the UK workforce for a considerable length of time. And over the past ten years post and rail workers have been some of the most militant groups of workers. And are their jobs much different from those in manufacturing? What's the difference between someone who makes a clutch or mends or replaces a clutch? Likewise there is very little difference between a worker in a large fast food restaurant and a worker who works in a food processing plant.

In fact the pressure on sectors of the service industry is to centralise and create powerful hubs. This leaves them open to worker pressure and organisation based on new groups of workers.

Look at supermarket distribution. Tesco is now the biggest private sector employer in the UK. It has concentrated all its distribution of food and goods in half a dozen massive warehouses across the country. It also employs 'just in time' methods of distribution. The warehouses are staffed by several hundred 'pickers'—forklift truck drivers and support staff. If they withdraw their labour the whole system comes crashing down. This was demonstrated in the summer of 2005 when Asda distribution workers struck at a distribution centre in the north east.[17]

McDonald's is one of the biggest corporations in the world. In what sense can those workers do any less useful or less real jobs than a worker making a tank or a Barbie doll?

There are those who argue that the growth of the service sector has brought with it greater levels of job insecurity, and part time and temporary working. It is of course true that neoliberalism has brought with it more flexible working but it has not brought about a radical overhaul of working life in Britain. According to *Social Trends* over a quarter of workers were working part time in the spring of 2005; around four in five part time workers were women.[18] The levels of temporary work did increase during the mid-1990s, but have declined in recent years. In 1992 6 percent of workers in the UK worked on a temporary basis and by 1997 it had peaked at 7.5 percent; it has since fallen to 5.5 percent.[19] The vast majority of workers have permanent jobs. In 1984 82.8 percent of the workforce had a permanent job. By 1999 that had fallen by 1.1 percent to 81.7 percent. It is also worth noting that a further 3 million people had joined the workforce.

Women workers

On Tuesday 28 March 2006 nearly 1.5 million workers struck over pensions in the biggest show of unity since the General Strike of 1926. It was the biggest ever one-day strike by women workers in Britain, and it was the most ethnically diverse. The strike smashed the myth that women can never be organised in a way that male workers have traditionally been.

More and more women are taking a central role inside the working class. Today 13 million women work, 49 percent of the total workforce. Women are now more likely to be union members than men. That is one of the findings of a report by the Department of Trade and Industry. The report, based on figures from the Labour Force Survey conducted in 2005, shows that for the second year running, the rate of female union membership has outpaced that for male employees. Over the 12 months to autumn 2005 union density levels among women rose by 0.9 percent to 29.9 percent, while the figure for men fell by 0.3 percent to 28.2 percent (see Figure 4a).[20]

But women still earn less than their male counterparts. The most recent figures available show that average hourly earnings, excluding overtime, for full time women workers are £10.56, compared to £12.88 for men. A government commission on women and work stated that the average pay gap between women and men was 17 percent in 2006. For average weekly earnings, the gap is wider—at 24.6 percent—partly because men are more likely to receive extra payments such as overtime, shift pay and bonus payments. The Equal Opportunities Commission estimates that, over a lifetime women's gross individual income is on average 51 percent less than men's.

You cannot talk about the growth of part time work without talking about women. Women make up the bulk of part time workers—and the vast majority are mothers or wives (the proportion of women involved in part time work is 44 percent compared to 8 percent of men[21]). Their jobs fit around their family commitments and very often around the demands of childcare. Many part time jobs are permanent and crucial to the economy. Today part time working accounts for just over a quarter of all paid jobs.[22] The percentage of women part time workers in trade unions or staff associations is 22 percent, while for men it is just 12 percent.[23] The one point you can make is that it is possible to unionise part time workers—the only thing required is for unions to organise serious recruitment drives among them.

Figure 4a: Union density by sector and gender, autumn 2005

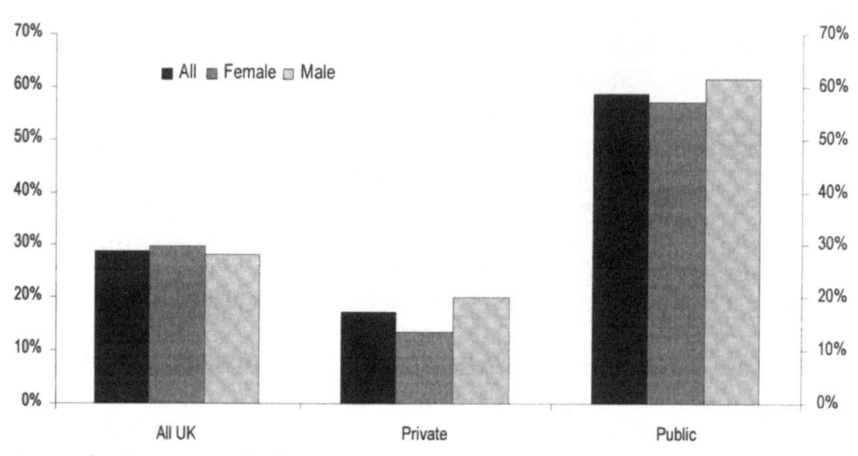

Source: Labour Force Survey, Office for National Statistics

Figure 4b: Union density by gender, 1995 to 2005

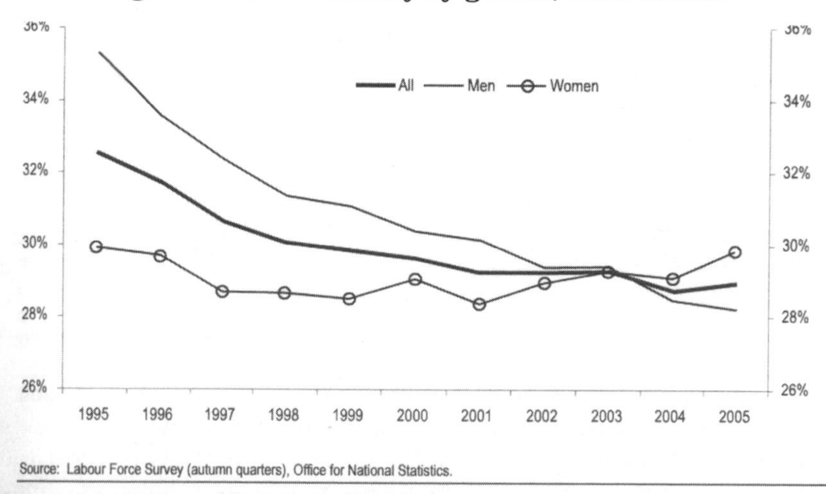

Source: Labour Force Survey, Office for National Statistics

Migrant workers

Low paid cleaners and their supporters stormed and occupied the central London offices of the global investment bank Goldman Sachs last November. They carried placards that read 'Goldman Sucks!'[24] Wealthy bankers, who usually ignore those who clean their offices, were forced to take notice for a change. It could have been a scene from Ken Loach's film *Bread and Roses*. But it wasn't Los Angeles; it was London. The protest was part of a campaign for decent pay by cleaners employed by the ISS who clean the offices of some of the world's most powerful and profitable companies. The TGWU union official involved in the dispute claimed that the workforce was made up mainly of migrant workers.

There seem only to be two stories concerning migrants in the British press—criminal activity and sponging off the state. There are a large number of migrant workers who are forced to work illegally in Britain. For obvious reasons these people eke out a living and find themselves on the fringes of society. Estimates vary that there are between 500,000 and 2 million illegal workers in Britain. The government suggests that 13 percent of UK GDP can be accounted for by the so-called black economy. Many of these poor people find themselves working in terrible conditions without any protection and in fear of being deported. The tragic death of the Chinese cockle pickers in Morecambe Bay is the most obvious example of the dangers and conditions many of these people face.[25]

But migrants have been active in the labour movement since the beginning. Irish labour was a prominent feature of the Industrial Revolution and the trade union movement. Irish names can be found in the list of strikers in the Bryant and May match workers' strike in 1888. Following the Second World War migrants from Italy and Eastern Europe joined those from the Commonwealth in plugging gaps in the labour force.

The pattern of migration since the 1950s has produced a number of distinct ethnic minority populations in the UK. In 2001 the majority of the population in Britain were white British (88 percent). The remaining 6.7 million people (or 11.8 percent of the population) belonged to other ethnic groups. Of these smaller ethnic populations, 'White Other' was the largest (2.5 percent—this is bigger now with the addition of at least 600,000 Eastern Europeans), followed by Indians (1.8 percent), Pakistanis (1.3 percent), those of mixed ethnic backgrounds (1.2 percent), Black Caribbeans (1 percent), Black Africans (0.8 percent), Bangladeshis (0.5 percent) and the remaining minority groups accounting for less than 0.5 percent of the population.[26]

People born outside the UK now make up more than 12 percent of the workforce.[27] But even that doesn't give the complete picture. The proportion of ethnic minorities and migrant workers in the workplace is even greater. There is an obvious reason for this. Most people uprooting and moving to another country tend to be young and certainly of working age (government statistics show that Black Caribbeans have the largest proportion of people aged 65 or over, reflecting their earlier migration to this country).[28]

The impact of migrant workers is much greater in some areas and some industries than others. A third of all the people living in London were born outside of Britain.[29] According to the Greater London Authority, 300 languages are spoken in London.[30] The CWU union membership department claims that two major London sorting offices have workforces that are made up of 60 percent non UK born workers.[31]

The percentage of migrant workers is growing rapidly. According to official figurers published by the Home Office 427,095 migrants from new European Union countries came to Britain to work between May 2004 and September 2005 under the Worker Registration Scheme.[32] For a breakdown of their country of origin see Figure 5.[33] Figure 6 shows that migrant workers are found in many areas of the country and not just London and the South East.[34] One of the many myths surrounding these migrant workers is that they only work in low paid and low skilled jobs. Of course many do and those jobs are vital to the economy, and as a Home Office press statement made clear they have no impact on the rate of unemployment. But also, as Figure 7 shows, many work in key well-organised sections of the working class.[35]

Overall, black and Asian employees are slightly less likely to be in trade unions (black and Asian density stands at 26 percent) compared to white workers (density of 29 percent). However, that comparison really does not capture the wide range of union densities found among different ethnic groups, ranging from a high of 35 percent (black African women) to a low of 18 percent (Pakistani men). The table below sets out the union densities for different ethnic groups and is also broken down by gender.[36] A less detailed survey was conducted by the DTI in 2005 and it also found that black or British black employees had the highest union density and union membership rates were lowest among Asian or British Asian employees—it is worth noting that this gap is decreasing.[37]

Finally, we are also witnessing a number of strikes by migrant workers or in defence of migrant workers. A few years back there were several strikes and union organisation drives in companies like Price Check, Noons and JJ Fast Foods. More recently we have seen a dispute over parity pay rates for Polish ground staff at Luton airport, which was successful. Unions representing construction workers on the 2012 Olympic site in east London have signed a deal that guarantees conditions and pay for all workers regardless of nationality.

Figure 5: Country of origin of East European workers in the UK

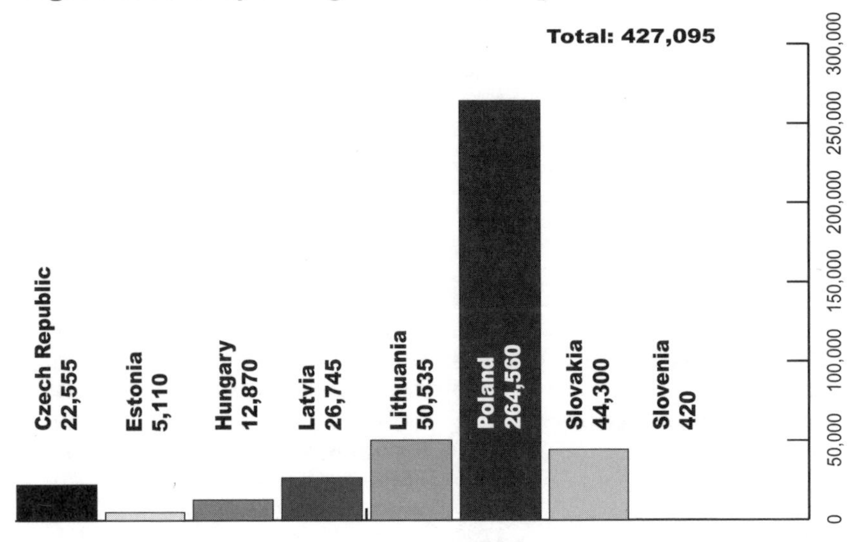

Source: Home Office figures, table compiled by the ***Daily Mirror****, 23 August 2006.*

Figure 6: Where they are working in the UK

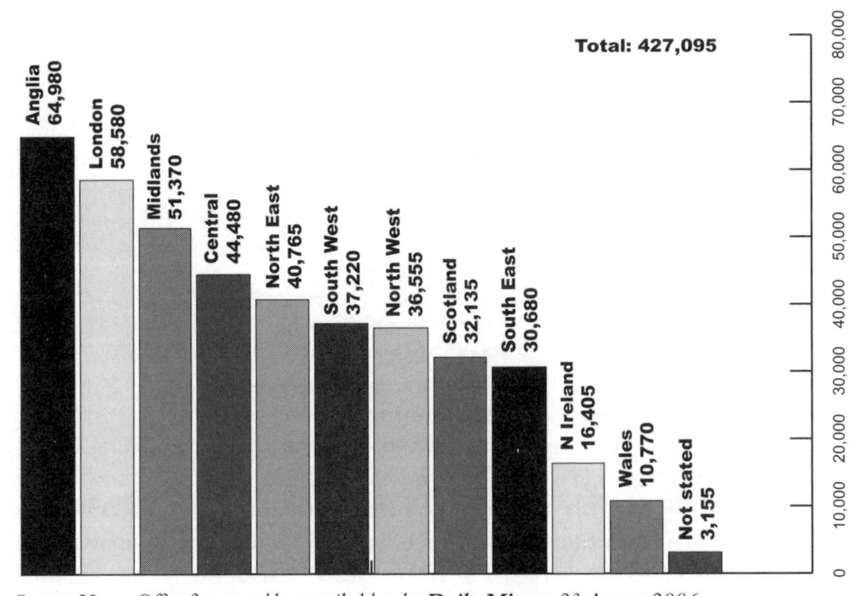

Source: Home Office figures, table compiled by the ***Daily Mirror****, 23 August 2006.*

Figure 7: Occupations of East European workers in the UK

Administrator, general	**3,600**
Administrator, office	1,430
Agricultural machinery operator	**945**
Airport staff	160
Animal husbandry	**495**
Baker	1,695
Bar staff	**6,030**
Bricklayer/mason	945
Butcher/meat cutter	**1,545**
Call centre	480
Care assistants, home carers	**12,610**
Carpenter	2,355
Cashier/check-out operator	**1,255**
Chef	5,470
Childminders	**835**
Cleaner	20,430
Crop harvester	**8,020**
Deliveryman	305
Dental Nurse	**250**
Dentist	310
Doctor (hospital)	**410**
Driver, bus	2,245
Driver, delivery van	**2,695**
Driver, HGV	3,620
Electrician	**390**
Factory worker	99,140
Farm worker	**18,105**
Fishmonger	695
Flower picker	**860**
Food processing (fruit/veg)	6,295
Food processing (meat)	**5,030**
Fruit picker (farming)	3,580
Gardener	**1,305**
GP	80
Handyman	**1,300**
Hotel porter	2,435
Kitchen assistants	**24,090**
Labourer building	10,525
Leisure/theme park attendants	**1,700**
Maid/Room attendant (hotel)	13,835
Mechanic	**1,505**
Packer	24,130
Painter and decorator	**770**
Plasterer	195
Playgroup worker	**175**
Plumber, heating and ventilating engineer	190
Receptionist, office	**785**
Receptionist, hotel	1,230
Refuse and salvage	**540**
Retailer	310
Road sweeper	**335**
Roofer, roof tiler and slater	85
Sales and retail assistants	**10,535**
Security Guard	1,205
Shelf stacker	**265**
Site manager/supervisor (construction)	215
Skilled machine operator (construction)	**675**
Skilled machinery operator (extraction)	320
Skilled vehicle operator (construction)	**80**
Slaughterer, meat	220
Sports and leisure assistants	**525**
Supervisor, production	285
Teacher	**355**
Teacher's assistant	495
Waiter, waitress	**15,840**
Warehouse manager	145
Warehouse worker	**25,215**
Welder	2,275
Window cleaner	**90**
Not Stated	9,865
TOTAL	**388,265**

Source: Home Office figures, table compiled by the ***Daily Mirror****, 23 August 2006.*

Figure 8: Union density by ethnic group and gender 2001

	All employees	Men	Women
white	29%	30%	28%
black & Asian	26%	24%	28%
Asian/Asian British	25%	25%	26%
Indian	29%	30%	27%
Pakistani	20%	18%	25%
Bangladeshi	*	*	*
another Asian background	26%	27%	25%
black/black British	30%	27%	33%
black Caribbean	32%	31%	33%
black African	29%	24%	35%
another black background	*	*	*
Chinese	*	*	*
mixed	25%	22%	27%
other ethnic group	24%	22%	26%

Note: *denotes that sample size is too small to provide reliable estimate

Source: Labour Force Survey 2001, Office for National Statistics

There has been a series of strikes and protests by migrant workers in the fruit picking industry in East Anglia, and protests by low paid cleaners in the City of London and Canary Wharf.[38]

A class in itself

The first part of this article has demonstrated that the working class is going through a period of transformation. It is worth repeating that this is not a new phenomenon. I also believe that the working class in Britain has lost none of its essential characteristics—it is far from being the sort of flexible workforce predicted by many. The numbers who work in manufacturing industries may have shrunk, but those who remain still represent an important and powerful sector of the economy. Secondly, the working class has been supplemented by the massive expansion of the white collar and service sectors. The people who work in these sectors are just as working class as any manual worker. They are forced to sell their labour, and suffer the hardships that manufacturing workers face. They have also created their own organisations to defend themselves—they have joined unions and taken strike action.

Finally, the working class in Britain is being enriched with greater numbers of women workers, workers from ethnic minorities and a new wave of migrant workers who are also entering the workforce. Far from representing a threat to 'traditional' working class organisation they are playing a more central role in trade union life. There are no objective reasons as to why the unions have to a greater or lesser extent failed to stop the neoliberal assault being pursued by the bosses and the New Labour government. The problems are subjective. Overcoming them is the key test for socialists and the trade union movement.

Life in Blair's Britain

Soon after Labour's 1997 election victory Peter Mandelson, now the EU's trade commissioner, said New Labour was 'intensely relaxed about people getting filthy rich'.[39] Never a truer word has been spoken by a New Labour minister. Under a Labour government the gap between rich and poor continues to grow at a shocking rate. The poorest 10 percent of the population in Britain receives the lowest share of national income in Europe, while the richest 1 percent owns nearly a quarter of marketable assets, a higher share than almost anywhere else in Europe. As many as 7 million workers in the UK earn less than £6.50 an hour and a third have no pension provision. Two in five workers work more than 40 hours a week (twice as high as all major European countries). And three out of five workers fear losing their jobs. Insecurity, long hours and low pay are endemic in British society.

The picture of resistance inside the working class is a complex one. On one hand, there is a very high level of political radicalisation in Britain. The Stop the War Coalition has created one of the most powerful mass movements this country has ever seen. You can't measure the impact of the anti-war movement on trade unions in terms of industrial militancy. The key impact has been the radicalisation of the political culture inside the union movement. It has also had the effect of galvanising the opposition to Tony Blair and posing the question of the need for a socialist alternative to Labour. So far two of Britain's smaller unions, the RMT and FBU, have disaffiliated from Labour. Even the pro-Labour union Unison withheld its financial donations to the Labour Party in the run up to the elections last May.

This political radicalisation was also demonstrated in November last year when around a thousand trade unionists attended an unofficial rank and file conference hosted by Respect. Delegates debated the question of political representation in the unions, and the need to link up the different campaigns resisting Labour's attacks, and agreed to organise a series of regional 'Fight Back' rallies linking up the various struggles.

On the other hand, unions are still attempting to recover from the huge haemorrhaging of members and strength that took place under Thatcher in the 1980s. The latest figures show that trade union membership stood at 6.8 million in the autumn of 2004, a decrease of 36,000 (0.5 percent) on the previous year. Between 1995 and 2004 the number of male union members fell by 13 percent, whereas over the same period female membership rose by 7 percent. This was mainly as a result of the decline of manufacturing jobs that has hit male workers harder.[40]

Likewise the level of class struggle remains very low. In 2004 there were 905,000 strike days in the UK, twice the number in 2003 (499,000).[41] The 2004 total is higher than the average number of strike days in the 1990s (660,000), but considerably lower than the average for both the 1980s (7.2 million) and the 1970s (12.9 million). In my pamphlet *The Awkward Squad* I wrote:

> The pattern of industrial disputes over the past few years has been shaped by both the new militancy and a lack of confidence which is a product of years of defeat. So on one hand we have seen explosions of anger, some of which have generalised widespread support inside the working class—Rover and the firefighters' dispute are two obvious examples. This has been followed by periods of relative quiet.[42]

I believe the picture I painted then still remains true today. You can now add the dispute at Gate Gourmet and the public sector one-day pensions strike last March to that list. Without wishing to overstate the fact, many of the industrial ballots that take place show that a large proportion of members are prepared to take strike action and when and if those disputes materialise they are very well supported by the rank and file. There is also a whiff of the anti-capitalist mood around many of these disputes—the cleaners' lightning protests and the NHS campaigns being obvious examples.

There are several other problems facing the union movement. The trade union leaderships today are too male, pale and stale.[43] Women and ethnic minorities make up a large proportion of today's trade union movement. Yet you can count the number of women and ethnic minorities running unions on the fingers of one hand. Women workers now make up something approaching two thirds of the membership of unions like Unison and the PCS. Over the coming years I predict we are going to see a growing number of unions run by women general secretaries.

But the biggest problem facing any recovery of the working class is the trade union bureaucracy. Their timidity in the face of employers' attacks is depressing. Several years ago things looked like they might be changing.

Union general secretary elections saw a new generation of younger officials winning major posts. They supported left wing movements and by and large supported a more robust form of trade unionism. They named themselves the 'Awkward Squad'. However, after several industrial defeats—the firefighters' dispute and the pensions debacle being the most obvious—the Awkward Squad is no more. The timidity of the union leaders in the face of employers still remains a major problem.

All that said, the trade union leaders find themselves in a tight spot. Of course the bureaucracy remain wedded to the Labour Party, for they fear the only alternative is the return of David Cameron and the Tories. Yet at the same time it is a Labour government that is implementing vicious neo-liberal policies. Many in the union movement hoped that the removal of Blair would spell out the end of Blairism. But instead Blair's legacy will continue under the leadership of Brown. Brown is, after all, the economic architect of Blair's policies and as far as the war in Iraq goes it is very much business as usual. That creates anger and bitterness in the rank and file. The heckling of Blair when he spoke at this year's TUC conference shows how deep that goes.

I think we are entering an interesting and possibly exciting period. In the last few months there have been dozens of marches involving close to 100,000 people against the cuts the government wants to impose on the NHS. From Truro to Carlisle we have seen a coalition of trade unionists, health campaigners and patients take to the streets. Billy Hayes, the general secretary of the post workers' union the CWU, said, 'It feels like the poll tax rebellion.' An exaggeration maybe, but I think the sentiment is right. Health unions are planning on calling a national demonstration in March 2007.

The PCS is launching a discontinuous strike ballot involving 250,000 workers in defence of their pensions. On top of this there have been a number of strikes on buses, and the pay campaign for low paid cleaners is picking up steam. All of these disputes will involve large numbers of women and ethnic minority workers. It is pointless trying to predict the outcome of these strikes, or their ability to break through and generalise. The key is for socialists to get involved and support them.

Today the low level of class struggle means that shop stewards and reps generally do not have the confidence to go on the offensive. The recovery that is taking place inside the union movement has everything to do with the political situation and the anti-war movement. Socialists and trade union militants need to practise a form of political trade unionism. By generalising from the political, socialists and trade union militants are beginning to gather around them the best political activists. These groups can become the nucleus of any fightback that might take place in industry in the future.

The question being posed is how do the unions recover? Just approaching the trade union question from the level of class struggle will not do. There are many who judge the revival in trade unions purely on the basis of the number of strikes, membership levels and density of membership. These statistics are an important tool, but they present a static and two-dimensional view of what is going on.

I wrote in this journal:

> Any debate about the nature of class struggle today in Britain has not only to discuss the economic situation but also look at the political and ideological dimensions of the struggle. There are many on the left who argue that an industrial upturn will come about out of a slow rising tide of trade union militancy. Industrial relations academics in Britain often cite the development of trade unions in car plants from the mid-1950s until the mid-1970s as an example of this. Of course this is one model of how an upturn has taken place, and of course this could happen again. But most industrial upturns have not developed this way. For example the upswing of class struggle in Britain in 1889 and 1910, the sitdown strikes in the US in 1934-36, the May events in France in 1968 and the Italian hot summer of 1969 were a product of sudden explosions of anger.[44]

In most cases these revolts were led by groups of workers who had until that point failed to show their potential strength. It is in the process of huge political and industrial struggles that the working class can begin to transform itself from a class in itself to a class for itself. This time round the working class is enriched by its greater diversity and by the deepest political radicalisation seen in society for decades. The working class is still the only social force in society that has the potential to challenge capitalism and bring about lasting change.

NOTES

1: *Newsnight*, 15 November 2005.

2: A Gortz, 'Reform or Revolution', in R Milliband and J Saville, *Socialist Register* 1968, p111. Also see Eric Hobsbawm, *The Age of Extremes*, (London, 1994), pp413-415.

3: Karl Marx and Fredrick Engels, *Manifesto of the Communist Party* (Beijing, 1988), p41.

4: G E M de Ste Croix, *The Class Struggle in the ancient World* (London, 1981), p43.

5: Mori finding on numbers agreeing with statement, 'At the end of the day, I am working class and proud of it', 16 August 2002, at http://www.mori.com/mmr/2002/c020818.shtml

6: *Manifesto of the Communist Party*, as above, p36.

7: 'The Poverty of Philosophy', in Karl Marx, *Collected Works* vol 1 (Moscow, 1977), pp210-211.

8: Office for National Statistics, *Social Trends 2006*, p57.

9: 'What Happened to the Car Industry?', BBC News, 21 March 2002, and for the most recent figures for car production go to www.ukinvest.gov.uk/2/d/10191/en/GB/1.0.html

10: Author's interview with GMB shop steward in June 2006.

11: Interview with housing worker in central London, May 2006.

12: IDS, *Pay in the Public Services* (London, 2006), p21.

13: There is a brilliant website called call centreconfidential.com. It is a diary of a call centre worker and gives a superb account of the drudgery, monitoring and management bullying that take place in one of Britain's biggest call centres.

14: *Socialist Review*, December 2003.

15: *Guardian*, 30 June 2006, p29.

16: Interview with the author at Marxism 2005.

17: 'Asda Distribution Workers Strike Over Pay', *Socialist Worker*, 6 August 2006.

18: *Social Trends* 36 (2006 edition), p50.

19: Employment Relations Research Series, no 56, *How Have Employees Fared? Recent UK Trends* (2006), p7. Available at www.dti.gov.uk/publications

20: As above, p4.

21: 'Today's Trade Unionist', Trade Union Trends Analysis of the 2001 Labour Force Survey, p7.

22: Employment Relations Research Series, no 56, as above.

23: 'Today's Trade Unionist', as above, pp6-7.

24: *Financial Times*, 29 November 2006.

25: For a moving and sympathetic account of the Morecambe tragedy and illegal working in Britain you can do no better than read Hsiao-Hung Pai and David Leigh's account in the *Guardian*, 13 January 2004.

26: Census 2001, Office for National Statistics; Census 2001, General Registar Office for Scotland.

27: *Social Trends*, no 36, 2006 edition, p12.

28: As above, p13.

29: *Evening Standard London Lite*, 13 November 2006.

30: This figure comes from a survey of 850,000 children in London schools carried out by LEAs in 1998-99.

31: Information given to author by the CWU press office. An interesting survey was conducted by the Working Lives Research Institute on the London Bus Industry.

32: Figurers released by the Home Office, 22 August 2006.

33: Breakdown of country of origin of Eastern European workers gaining entry to work in Britain under the worker registration scheme. Home Office figures and table compiled by the *Daily Mirror*, 23 August 2006.

34: As above.

35: As above

36: 'Today's Trade Unionists', as above, p9.

37: DTI, *Employment Market Analysis and Research*, March 2006, p10.

38: For accounts of these disputes see the *Socialist Worker* archive at www.socialist worker.co.uk

39: Andrew Rawnsley, *Sunday Observer*, 17 September 2000.

40: *Social Trends* no 36, 2006 edition, p64.

41: As above, p66.

42: M Smith, *The Awkward Squad* (SWP, 2003), p12.

43: I wish I had thought of this little saying, but alas I did not—it is borrowed from Gregor Gall, who I am sure will be very happy that I use it!

44: Trade Union Struggles in Britain Today: a debate, *International Socialism* 105 (Winter 2004), p113.

Livingstone—the last reformist?

Charlie Kimber

London's *Evening Standard* newspaper recently ran the front page headline 'Ken Backs Terrorist on the Tube'. Most of the capital's 7 million inhabitants will have been in no doubt who 'Ken' was. Almost uniquely among British politicians, London Mayor Ken Livingstone has achieved the status of being recognisable from his first name alone. But the headline relied on more than that. It rested on the readers' supposed awareness that Ken, with his left wing background and reputation for outrageous statements, was just the sort of man who might defend the employment of terrorists on the tube.[1]

Livingstone has been mayor for six years and has retained a certain popularity in limited circles. It is not the genuine popularity engendered by, for example, Tony Benn, but given that most Labour Party members who are in office are actively disliked by very many people, Livingstone is a bit unusual.

Yet even Livingstone's greatest admirer would be hard pushed to say he has brought great change or improvements in London. There are some more buses, there is (temporarily) less traffic in central London, and there are some excellent anti-racist initiatives. But what people generally like is more a tone, a sense that Livingstone is not another Labour clone, that he is a bit rebellious and ready to step out of line if he feels he needs to.

Such a reputation is greatly overdone. Livingstone has proved a good friend of the government and far less of a problem that any of Labour's leaders predicted. He is the embodiment of how very small reforms can sometimes give someone a lustre well beyond what they deserve if there is no alternative that both criticises the existing forces and points to a credible alternative.

Reformism thrives on the fact that small improvements are still possible, and that these loom large until something better becomes real to most people.

He is full of contradictions, a man who sometimes talks radical but mostly delivers exactly what the rich and powerful desire.

It is important to stress that Livingstone also retains a level of popularity because he has always been on the right side on the central issue of domestic and global politics, the war on Iraq. In this he differed sharply from 1999, when during the NATO assault on Yugoslavia Livingstone urged on the Western powers' assault. He compared Serbian leader Milosevic to Hitler, warned of the dangers of what he called genocide, and praised foreign secretary Jack Straw for taking 'the first steps to creating a global resolve that those with power are not allowed to abuse it with impunity'.[2]

But there has never been a shred of backing for bombs on Iraq. Livingstone was on the great anti-war march of 15 February 2003, where he told protesters, 'Let everyone recognise what has happened here today: that Britain does not support this war for oil. The British people will not tolerate being used to prop up the most corrupt and racist American administration in over 80 years.'

He said earlier:

> There is now a growing and powerful international consensus that a war against Iraq must not happen. I am pleased to be adding my voice to the international consensus against this war by speaking at the Stop the War rally, and I would urge Londoners to add their voices too by joining the march.[3]

Livingstone has not been afraid to tear into the US president, saying just after the war began that:

> George Bush is just about everything that is repellent in politics. He is not a legitimate president. This really is a completely unsupportable government and I look forward to it being overthrown as much as I looked forward to Saddam Hussein being overthrown.[4]

When Bush came on an official visit to London, Livingstone brushed aside US requests for protests to be outlawed and told would-be demonstrators:

> You have the moral high ground. You are protesting against an illegal war and occupation. Some US journalist came up to me and said, 'How can you say this about President Bush?' Well, I think what I said then was quite mild. I actually think that Bush is the greatest threat to life on this planet that we've

most probably ever seen.[5]

Livingstone also defended Muslims against the recent wave of demonisation. Speaking at the launch of the first ever report into Muslims living in London, Livingstone said much of the ongoing debate about Muslim dress implied the community was 'somehow at fault' for being at the centre of the storm.

He said the 'vast amount of verbiage' about the issue had been 'quite breathtaking' and that very little was said about barriers the community faces in Britain, such as the 'systematic pattern of discrimination against Muslims in employment':

> It is quite clear that the problems we have in Britain are not because Muslims wish to be separate. I think the entire debate has been totally lopsided as though Muslims were somehow at fault for this. That echoes very much the demonology of Nazi Germany when Hitler said it was the Jews' fault and the problems were brought upon themselves.[6]

But that is not nearly enough to make him an alternative focus to New Labour. This is also the man who has denounced anti-capitalist protesters, called on workers to cross picket lines to break strikes, campaigned for even the most right wing Labour candidates at elections, achieved a good working relationship with Tony Blair, produced a pro-business plan for London and backed the police who murdered Jean Charles de Menezes.

Livingstone is reputed to be a thorn in New Labour's side, yet in November 2006 the government published a bill proposing an enhanced package of powers for the Mayor of London and the London Assembly—building on its 'success to date'.

He also lets taxis drive in the bus lanes—sometimes it's the little things that get to you.

The birth of 'Red Ken'

Born in 1945, Livingstone joined the Labour Party in the late 1960s, a time when the party was haemorrhaging members due to the betrayals of the Harold Wilson government. He rose rapidly through the ranks, winning election to local councils and then the Greater London Council (GLC). He showed a willingness to champion left wing causes and oppose spending cuts, combined with a quick sense of where the best chance for furthering his career lay. The GLC election of 1981 saw a revolt against the national Thatcher government and the London regime of Tory Horace 'Cuts' Cutler.

The Labour Party narrowly won control.

The day after the election Livingstone challenged as the left's candidate for the leadership of the Labour group and won by 30 votes to 20. As GLC leader he immediately got headlines for measures such as refusing to use the official limousine and continuing to live in his bedsit flat.

But the first serious reform was the Fares Fair campaign. The GLC cut bus and tube fares by 25 percent. It was a brilliant success. After 30 years of steady decline, passenger traffic increased by 11 percent on the buses and 7 percent on London Underground. More buses were put on the roads, more trains on the track, and London Transport took on 600 extra staff.

But Fares Fair was not to last. Tory-controlled Bromley council took the GLC to court, on the grounds that its ratepayers' money was being used to support a policy that brought them no benefit. The Law Lords ruled that Fares Fare was illegal.

Propaganda by the right wing press was unremittingly hostile. A £3,500 donation to a refuge for prostitutes was branded as 'Pornography On The Rates' by the *Daily Mail*. When the GLC gave a £15,000 grant to a company to train black businessmen, the *Sun* accused it of 'reverse racism' and was soon to say that Livingstone was 'the most odious man in Britain'.

The Tories and the press did their best to undermine the GLC but they failed. So in 1986 they abolished it, putting Livingstone out of a job. A year later he was elected as MP for Brent East in north west London. For ten years he remained a well-known figure, but far removed from any real influence on Labour or on national events.

He tried to stand for the leadership in 1992 but could not get the required number of nominations, and the same happened in 1997 when he wanted to stand for the deputy leadership.

He returned to national prominence in September 1997 when he defeated the ultra-Blairite Peter Mandelson for a position on the party's national executive. Two years later he announced that he would stand to become Labour's candidate for the newly created post of London mayor, with opposition to the privatisation of the London Underground (tube) at the centre of his campaign. After losing a rigged selection procedure to the leadership's choice, Frank Dobson, Livingstone announced he would stand as an independent. He was expelled from the Labour Party, but won a clear victory at the election of May 2000. In September 2002 the party's ruling executive rejected his application to rejoin the party. But in January 2004 he was allowed back, becoming the Labour candidate for the 2004 mayoral election and then winning again.

The war on terror

The dreadful events of 7 July 2005, when bombs on tube trains and a bus in London killed 56 people and injured over 700 were a tragedy. They also were a challenge to every political force. The bombs killed innocent people including opponents of the war, and were no challenge to imperialism—as the whole anti-war movement made clear. But the key issue was whether they were linked to Iraq and Blair's policies. In the days immediately after the attack Livingstone did not make the link with Iraq. His initial statement simply denounced the bombers and said the bombs were 'just an indiscriminate attempt at mass murder and we know what the bombers' objective is. They seek to divide Londoners'.[7] Just crazed bombers it seemed, and no political implications.

Then on 20 July Livingstone was asked what he thought had motivated the bombers and he told Radio 4 listeners:

> You've just had 80 years of Western intervention into predominantly Arab lands because of the Western need for oil. We've propped up unsavoury governments. We've overthrown ones we didn't consider sympathetic. Under foreign occupation and denied the right to vote, denied the right to run your own affairs, often denied the right to work for three generations—I suspect that if it had happened here in England, we would have produced a lot of suicide bombers ourselves.[8]

This was a big shift. In August, Livingstone settled on what has become his final position:

> The London bombings demand clear thinking, not rhetoric. People's lives depend on the decisions made. These must be for every community to aid the police in preventing attacks; to treat Britain's Muslim community with respect, both because it is right and to shrink the pools terrorists operate in; and for Britain to withdraw from Iraq.

So he did make the link with Iraq and opposed a racist backlash against Muslims. But he went on:

> Nevertheless, I want to make the point to some opponents of the war. It is not a policy simply to explain to people: 'You are dying because Britain is in Iraq.' The bombers came to kill indiscriminately. Right now, only the police can stop bombers. Anyone who tries to avoid this is not dealing with what are literally life and death matters. Opponents of the war should continue to

oppose it. But they also have to say to London's communities: 'Cooperate with the police to catch terrorists'.[9]

Such an approach, which put cooperation with the police first, weakened the more general political points. It could also lead in some hands to demands on Muslims of whether they were 'doing enough' to 'root out terrorists' in their community. It opened the door to the line from home secretary John Reid and others that there is a problem with Muslims sheltering bombers in their midst and that they must demonstrate more forcefully their commitment to 'British values', preferably by backing the war in Iraq.

It was not the position that Livingstone had adopted in 1981 after the Irish Republican Army (IRA) had bombed London's Chelsea barracks. Then he said, 'Nobody supports what happened last Saturday in London. But what about stopping it happening? As long as we are in Ireland, people will be letting off bombs in London. I can see that we are a colonial power holding down a colony. For the rest of the time violence will recur again and again as long as we are in Ireland. People in Northern Ireland see themselves as subject peoples. If they were just criminals or psychopaths they could be crushed. But they have a motive force which they think is good'.[10]

The police and Blair praised Livingstone's August 2006 statement. Perhaps their support was based on the evidence Livingstone had already given them of his willingness to support the police to the hilt at a key moment.

On 22 July the police had shot and killed the innocent Brazilian Jean Charles de Menezes. There was outrage at the killing. But Livingstone said, 'The police acted to do what they believed necessary to protect the lives of the public. This tragedy has added another victim to the toll of deaths for which the terrorists bear responsibility'.[11] Note, not the government, not the police, but the 7/7 bombers alone were responsible for Jean Charles's death.

And Livingstone has not wavered an inch in his support for the police or Metropolitan Police chief Ian Blair since. Ian Blair, who said Muslims were in a 'state of denial' about terrorism, has come close to being driven from office as evidence emerged about the lies in the police account of the de Menezes killing. But Livingstone has repeatedly stressed that he has his full backing. This continued even after the Forest Gate raid in June 2006 when Mohammed Abdul Kahar was shot in a police raid which saw 250 officers following up 'good intelligence' of a chemical bomb—which was never found. 'I have great confidence in the Met police,' said Mr Livingstone. 'I was a deep critic 25 years ago but I realise that the force has been transformed'.[12]

Livingstone has both collapsed into support for the police and moved away from any linkage between terrorism and Iraq. As so often, he speaks well about events until it gets difficult, and then he collapses into support for the ruling order.[13]

The support has not just been in words. Livingstone has used nearly two thirds of the money which Londoners pay for the mayoralty on the police, with over 5,000 extra officers since he became mayor.

Livingstone and big business

Just before the London mayoral election in 2004 the bosses' *Economist* magazine dispensed advice which may have shocked some of its readers. It called for a vote for Livingstone. Its reasoning was simple: 'The former figurehead of Labour's "loony left" has shaved off his moustache, taken to television chat shows and decided that keeping businessmen happy so that they create more and better-paid jobs is a better way of improving the workers' lot than the class struggle.' It added, 'On planning, Mr Livingstone has delighted London's businessmen. He has used his powers to allow through schemes for a rash of new skyscrapers which outrage conservationists, but promise jobs, cash and the visual thrill that comes (at least from far away) when sharp new buildings slice the skyline'.[14]

Livingstone's views have been 'evolving' for a long time. In 1999 he said, 'Twenty years ago I would have said a central planned economy could be made to work better than the Western capitalist economy; I don't believe that any more. I think it is quite clear that as a system for the distribution and exchange of goods the market can't be bettered'.[15]

Once elected in 2000 Livingstone sought partnerships with business organisations such as the Confederation of British Industry and the London Chamber of Commerce. He called for 'a strong partnership with every section of London business, the City, large employers and small firms'.

The Mayor's London Plan was unveiled in June 2002, a strategic overview for the next two decades. There were many warm words about the environment, social planning, affordable housing and much else.

But at its heart was a vision to attract jobs for a city whose population was rising sharply. Of the 636,000 new jobs the mayor was projecting for London, 454,000 were expected to be in financial services. The immediate implication was the building of new office accommodation—the equivalent of an additional 75 Canary Wharfs. More seriously it meant attracting banks and financial institutions who had very little interest in notions of social planning and every interest in profits.

The bankers were wooed by accommodating planning decisions and no genuine moves against big business. The central elements of Livingstone's mayoralty—more police, the congestion charge and developments where 70 percent of housing is 'unaffordable'[16]—were perfectly acceptable to giant firms.

By 2006 the *Guardian* could report that:

> Post-Enron corporate regulations mean that Russian companies are choosing London instead of Wall Street to raise money via flotations. Livingstone says, 'Chinese firms are splitting 50-50 between us and New York. Clearly, the vast bulk of Indian investment is coming to London. All the emerging economies see London as the best place to do business. And if we can secure that position then we're set fair for another 100 years and not just getting me through to the next election.'

Such a strategy blunted any confrontation with Tony Blair. It would be very hard for Livingstone to criticise the Labour leader for making too many concessions to business when his core plan is based on such compromises.

It meant it was impossible, for example, to impose taxes on office building. If every office development paid a tax that was earmarked for public housing then it would have laid a basis for desperately needed low-cost rented accommodation. So would a tax on second homes in London and buy for let properties.[17]

But such polices might have alienated some of the bankers and finance houses that Livingstone had decided were crucial.

A privatised tube

Think of one solid achievement of the Livingstone mayoralty. Most people would say the congestion charge. He took the political risk of charging cars £5 to enter central London during weekdays. And it worked. A year after its introduction in February 2003 Livingstone could say:

> Congestion charging was a radical solution to a long-standing problem. London's roads were clogged with slow-moving traffic and congestion was costing business £2 million a week. This is the only thing that I have done or been associated with in 33 years of public life that has turned out better than I thought it would. Despite the dire predictions before the launch of the scheme, congestion charging has proved a success and that is why nearly 75 percent of Londoners now support the scheme—because it works.[18]

Leave aside the very New Labourish method of phrasing success in terms of what benefits business, and Livingstone could indeed point to improvements. Traffic delays inside the charging zone were 30 percent lower than before charging was introduced, traffic levels entering the zone during charging hours were down 18 percent and there was an increase of 29,000 bus passengers entering the zone during the morning peak period.

It should be noted that about a quarter of the displaced traffic simply moved to roads around the charging zone. But half of the displaced drivers moved to public transport and another quarter to walking or cycling.

In general it is only the 'Mr Toads' of this world that get really angry about the congestion charge. But there are genuine questions to be asked. The congestion charge, the same price for all, is regressive. A fiver is a lot for a postal worker or a secretary. It's the price of a Perrier water in a posh restaurant for a chief executive. The charge is rationing by price, and the poor are hit harder than the rich.

Livingstone argued that the poorest people don't use cars in London. He was right up to a point. In 2003 in London 37 percent of households, mainly the least well off, had no car and relied entirely on public transport. Among the poorest tenth of people in London 88 percent had no car.

Most of those who drive into central London each day are by definition better off, with parking at £4 an hour unless they have access to company car parks. But the effect of the scheme was to push off the roads those who felt the charge most—workers on average wages or less. The real answer to London's traffic nightmare is not rationing by wealth. The technology used to run the scheme could have been used to ration car use on the basis of need instead.

People who have a greater need to use cars—the disabled, some pensioners, parents of younger children, some workers doing essential jobs—could have been given free permits. Others could have been restricted to a maximum number of journeys a year into central London, limited by the overall need to keep traffic at a liveable level. That would have been a fair way to tackle the immediate congestion, while moving on to the crucial question of greatly improving public transport.

Livingstone has made some populist moves to rectify the regressive nature of the charge. The £8 a day rate (introduced in 2005) will rise to £25 for cars such as 4x4s—'Chelsea tractors'—that emit high levels of carbon dioxide. Livingstone says he wants this rate introduced by 2009 to combat climate change and that the charge would apply to vehicles in Band G, the top road tax rate—although this covers some family 'people carriers' as well as bankers' limousines.

There is another question—what happened to the congestion charge cash? Much of it of course went to Capita, the private firm brought in to run the system. But apart from that fat cat levy, the main destination for the money was not for improvements such as 'more buses', as Livingstone claimed. The real answer was, 'To Gordon Brown'.

Cuts in the London transport budget wiped out the money raised from the charge. Transport for London said ministers cut its budget for 2004-05 by £125 million and by £200 million in 2005-06. This almost exactly took away the £130 million a year raised from the charge.

But let's accept that Livingstone produced a very limited form of improvement through his congestion charge. It was class-biased and partial, but still an improvement.

That verdict can't be applied to the wider issue of public transport.

Opposition to the privatisation of the London Underground was the central element in Livingstone's 2000 manifesto, and as soon as he was elected the battle against Private Public Partnership (PPP) began. The argument was clear: from 1998 onwards the government had said that the new investment that was undoubtedly needed on the tube must come from involving the private sector, just as was proposed for the NHS and schools. Livingstone said that the public sector could do the job.

The fight was important enough in its own right, but it also focused attention on a central policy of the Labour government. The rail unions, which had supported Livingstone's election, were also prepared to fight. They had already struck in June and July of 1998 and February 1999 over the issue. The two main unions, Aslef and the RMT, were well organised. And a poll in the summer of 1999 had shown that two thirds of Londoners were against any form of tube privatisation. But the campaign failed.

One reason was that the unions, in order to keep within the anti-union laws, framed their dispute as being over the 'effects of privatisation' rather than privatisation itself. This meant they could strike legally, but it also meant the struggle was sidetracked into questions of the precise terms that would be acceptable for transfer. In the end this was disastrous. Despite the magnificent strike of February 2001, which saw RMT members refusing to cross Aslef picket lines, the unions first split over what was an acceptable deal, and were then all panicked into accepting agreements in case they were 'left behind' as privatisation rolled on.

But the biggest factor throughout was Livingstone himself. He never put himself at the head of a serious fight. He first proposed the issue of bonds as a revenue-raising device rather than privatisation. This deflected attention away from the basic confrontation over ownership, and he then allowed the battle to peter out.

Soon after his election victory, Livingstone's appointments showed where he was going. He found jobs for the Tory and the Lib Dem he had defeated. But a bigger surprise was in store. In the autumn of 2000 Livingstone encouraged Bob Kiley to come from the US to take a central role in London's transport system. The two described their relationship as 'a CIA activist working for an unreconstructed Trotskyite'.[19] Kiley had certainly worked for the CIA, rising to be executive assistant to the agency director. But if Livingstone had ever been a Trotskyist, he certainly wasn't now.

Kiley had a reputation for taking on organised workers. On the New York subway, supposed to be his greatest triumph, he had increased the pace of work, imposed lower pay for new starters, cut bonuses for night and weekend working, cut jobs, and brought in private companies to do maintenance work. He was a strange choice to fight a campaign alongside the unions against privatisation.

Kiley was appointed as commissioner of Transport for London, the public body which reports to Livingstone, and also chairman of London Regional Transport, the public body appointed by the government's transport secretary to run London Underground.

Kiley enjoyed a $4 million four-year contract, but his tenure of both positions did not last long. In 2001 he was sacked as chairman of London Regional Transport following a series of clashes with his boss, transport secretary Stephen Byers.

Remaining as commissioner of Transport for London, he and Livingstone took the government to court in trying to prevent PPP. But in August 2001 Livingstone gave up the legal fight and accepted he would work with the private firms involved. Since January 2003 London Underground's infrastructure has been maintained by private companies but the underground is owned and operated by Transport for London (TfL).

Having lost, the least that Livingstone should have done was to support workers when they fought back against the PPP structure and the firms involved within it. But, as the section below on trade unions shows, he signally failed to do so.

In 2004 Transport for London announced that Kiley had been awarded a new four-year contract worth a staggering £2.4 million—plus the continued use of a £2.1 million Belgravia townhouse. His salary rose to £318,000 a year plus an annual bonus of up to £285,000. In fact he left his post in January 2006. He received an unprecedented settlement package for a public sector worker in Britain, worth nearly £2 million. He remained a consultant to the mayor at £3,200 a day for up to 90 days in each year of 2006 and 2007, and 50 days in 2008. He was awarded £745,000 in severance pay plus £113,425 in benefits each year from 2006 to 2008. And he kept that house.

What new investment there has been on the tube has been very patchy and the work has been bedevilled by the inefficiencies of using a range of private firms.

There are some spruced-up stations and improvements. And, as part of the preparation for the Olympics, there will be more to come, but the private firms who honeycomb the system are incredibly inefficient, constantly causing overruns on work and delaying travellers. The verdict in general must be one of not nearly enough done, of a half-hearted approach constrained by the feeling that big business has to be kept sweet.

In truth there are now five classes of travellers in London. At the very top of the pyramid are taxi users, overwhelmingly the rich who are allowed to use the bus lanes and therefore travel more easily than at any time for decades in the capital.

Next come car drivers who are prepared to pay the congestion charge of £8 a day. Such a sum is enough to give any working person pause, but a mere trifle to the rich or to those who get their companies to pay.

The third category is tube users who have Oyster cards (the pre-payment cards). They can travel on the generally overcrowded and sweaty[20] tube system at less eye-watering prices than the next category. That is those who don't get an Oyster card because they are tourists or foreign workers or have come to London for a day from the rest of Britain, or simply don't know how to get one. Such people have the joy of paying £4—yes, £4—for a single journey in central London.

Finally there are bus users, who have seen some improvements in the last few years in both the quality and frequency of services. The number of bus journeys taken in London in 2005 was a third higher than in 2000.[21] But a large part of this is because the tube is so expensive that the bus becomes relatively more attractive even if it isn't a pleasant form of transport. In addition a rising population in the capital means bus use would have risen even if the service had remained the same. It remains true that only the bravest would ever gamble on a London bus reaching its destination on time during busy periods.

Beneath these five categories are motorcyclists, cyclists and pedestrians. Central London has seen a 30 percent increase in the number of cyclists since the introduction of the congestion charge. But the interests of such groups have been largely neglected and in many parts of London cycling and walking feel hazardous because of traffic.[22]

Simple matters could have been implemented by the mayor, such as 20 mph as the standard speed limit in all streets where Londoners live, work or shop, free cycle training for every London schoolchild including on-road training, safe routes to school for all London's children, sufficient secure cycle parking at all London schools, and a concerted action plan to reduce cyclists' deaths from HGVs and skip lorries.

This hasn't happened. Instead the scale of what has been achieved is small. In November 2006 Peter Hendy, commissioner of Transport for London, announced that 'since 2000 there has been a modal shift of just over 4 percent from car usage to public transport'. Four percent in six years! Welcome, no doubt, but hardly a transformation of the city or a body blow against climate change.[23]

Livingstone and organised workers

In June 2004, just two weeks after winning re-election as mayor, Livingstone faced a strike over pay by London Underground workers in the RMT union. Instead of seeking a deal, let alone standing in solidarity with the workers, Livingstone denounced their action. He said the pay offer of 6.5 percent over two years was 'extremely generous' and then added, 'Were I a member of the RMT, for the first time in my life I would cross a picket line next Tuesday.' Just to make sure there was no mistake, a spokesperson for the mayor said he did not 'retract the words'.[24]

Livingstone's words shocked even mainstream trade union leaders. Dave Prentis, the general secretary of Unison, Britain's biggest union, said, 'It's outrageous and shameful that someone in Livingstone's position, with his history and background, should be telling people to scab on their trade union.' Bob Crow, the general secretary of the RMT, resigned in protest from the board of the mayor's Transport for London body.

It was the worst example of Livingstone's attitude towards the unions, but not the first.

In 2003 tube driver Chris Barrett was spied on and then sacked while off sick. Livingstone's people told the media Barrett was a 'parasite' and Livingstone said, 'I don't know how he got away with it for so long,' when the driver's confidential attendance records were somehow leaked to the media. There was no apology when Barrett later won his case at an industrial tribunal.

Livingstone seems to believe the unions' strength is the crucial obstacle to creating an 'efficient' (more cheaply run) tube system. In fact the unions are the guarantors of workers' rights, safety, adequate staffing and a service that treats passengers as people rather than financial inputs.

In 2006 Livingstone returned to his union-bashing during a station staff strike. Speaking to the annual London Government Dinner at the Mansion House, he astonished the 300 well-fed guests—who included the capital's 33 borough leaders and key City figures—by his anti-union tone. They gave him an ovation when he said he 'had not the slightest intention' of giving in to the RMT union. One said afterwards, 'Red Ken has become Blue Ken.'

Livingstone has never put organised workers at the centre of his strategy. At the GLC in the 1980s he preferred vague 'people's campaigns' rather than militant action by trade unionists. When the Law Lords declared that the Fares Fair policy was illegal the Labour leaders of the GLC pinned their hopes on a propaganda campaign. Some councillors believed that consumer action was the way forward. They argued that on the crucial day when the fares were supposed to rise there should be a mass campaign of non-payment. It was a dismal failure, with just a few hundred people refusing to pay. Livingstone did not support the boycott, but had no alternative strategy. There was no real link with transport workers or any attempt to put strikes at the core of the fight. Yet just two weeks before the failed boycott day, a one-day strike by London Transport workers in defence of low fares was a magnificent success. Not a single bus or tube ran. Livingstone did not argue to deepen this struggle. The result was a tragic missed opportunity to turn the support for Fares Fair into aggressive anti-Tory defiance.

In October 1983 the Tory government published plans to abolish the GLC and the Metropolitan County Councils. In January 1984 a national demonstration in London saw almost 30,000 people march (on a weekday) to oppose the plan, with teachers, firefighters and council workers striking to take part. But the campaign was again pitched as a 'people's crusade', with a Tory GLC councillor allowed to speak as well.

The Tories then decided to put a limit on local councils' ability to increase the rates. This would force councils to make huge cuts. Some 25 councils banded together to say they would not set a rate. Ken Livingstone was at the head of the movement. In November 1984 up to 100,000 workers struck across London and over 20,000 marched in protest at the Tories' plans. Ken Livingstone was cheered when he said the £6,000 million owed by the councils to the banks would not be paid.

But as the Labour leaders urged compliance with the law, Ken Livingstone's GLC was the first to crack. In March the GLC set a rate and movement, just as t accepted huge cuts. This retreat led to the collapse of the anti-ratecapping he union and Labour leaders were betraying the great strike by the miners.

May Day and direct action

One of Livingstone's most famous statements came in April 2000, one month before the London Mayor election and four months after the anti-capitalist movement had burst on to the scene with the demonstrations against the World Trade Organisation in Seattle. In an interview with the *NME* music magazine he said:

> The IMF and the World Bank are still appalling and now the World Trade Organisation too. All over the world people die unnecessarily because of the international financial system. Susan George, the economist not the actress, estimates that in any year since 1981 between 15 and 20 million people have died unnecessarily from the debt burden. Every year the international financial system kills more people than World War Two. But at least Hitler was mad, you know?

His sharp and wholly correct criticism of the bankers' comments caused a storm of denunciation which Livingstone, to his credit, brushed aside. But he was soon faced with a concrete example of protest to deal with, and his tune was very different.

Just days before the mayoral polling day, anti-capitalist demonstrators gathered in London for a May Day protest. They were attacked by the police and a few protesters were drawn into attacking McDonald's and similar targets. Famously, a statue of Winston Churchill was made to look as though blood was dripping from its mouth. Graffiti was sprayed on the plinth and a green turf mohican was added to the statue's head.[25]

Rival London mayor candidates sought to link Livingstone's attacks on the banks and his support for direct action to the events. After all, in January 2000 Livingstone had told Sky news, 'Direct action is not violence', and a month later had told *The Face* magazine, 'I've always been in favour of direct action. One of my fondest memories was chasing the inspector of the Archway Road inquiry out onto the roof at Central Hall.'

Now Labour, Tory and Liberal Democrat tried to claim that Livingstone was 'soft' on protesters. He speedily condemned the violence and praised the very police who had caused the trouble. 'The police action concentrated on isolating the small minority of determined wreckers and thugs intent on violence and damage to property from any peaceful protesters,' he said. 'Throughout the four days of demonstrations the police thereby set the tone that London both upholds the right to peacefully demonstrate and that it will clamp down with the full force of the law on those who threaten mayhem in the capital. This is precisely the tone that should be set for policing in London.'

The next year, as May Day neared, Livingstone moved to destroy the protest before it began. He warned people 'not to be fooled by protesters' claims that their demonstrations are intended to draw attention to key issues, such as protection of the environment, the cancellation of Third World debt and the eradication of poverty'.

The other speaker at the press conference, which took place at New Scotland Yard, was Sir John Stevens, the Metropolitan Police commissioner. Livingstone said that he has been in regular contact with the commissioner about plans for May Day:

> This morning I received my second briefing from the commissioner on the expected activity on May Day. I welcome the close working relationship that my office has had with the commissioner. We will continue to liaise over the next few days to do what we can to keep London safe.

A newspaper advertising campaign was launched urging people not to take part in the protests. The press was wild with stories of 'foreign rioters' coming to London and papers ran pictures of individuals who had allegedly committed offences and must be 'rounded up'.

The police took their cue from Livingstone, mobilising 6,000 officers on the day to deal with a few thousand protesters, corralling them against their will for seven hours and then making dozens of arrests. It was an early glimpse of the way civil liberties could be swept away and the police given arbitrary powers. And having supported them in advance, Livingstone then backed the police fully afterwards.

Livingstone and the Labour Party

When he became mayor six years ago, Livingstone achieved the remarkable success of defeating Labour from the left in an important election. There are very few who have done so, and even fewer in such a big constituency or in such a high-profile election. Yet now he has returned to the party, with Tony Blair, the man he humiliated by winning the election, being the most insistent that he be readmitted to the party.

Amid all his contradictions, and even when he was expelled, Livingstone has always been dogmatically clear that the Labour Party is the only serious vehicle for progressive change. For over two decades his behaviour has been like that of the typical Labour Party elected official—occasionally criticising but basically loyal.

In 1986 he sealed his split with the party's hard left when he said, 'I take a much more pragmatic view than many people on the left about working with Neil Kinnock. Kinnock represents the best vehicle possible for achieving socialism now'.[26] This was the Kinnock who had failed to rally behind the Great Miners' Strike of 1984-85, was combing through Labour's every policy to remove anything which upset the people at the top of the society, and was witch-hunting the left.

Livingstone's readiness to embrace the 'new realism' was helpful in winning the nomination to be MP for Brent East against a left wing candidate, Diane Abbott.

In many ways it is remarkable that Tony Blair remained so blinkered to Livingstone's merits. Here was someone with the ability to excite electors and to make them believe that he was one of them. You might have thought Blair would have embraced him.

Livingstone certainly did his own wooing. While campaigning to win Labour's nomination for mayor, he declared he was '95 percent Blairite' and told Blair, 'I would work with your government, not against it. I am convinced that your administration has the potential to be a great reforming government on a par with those of 1906 and 1945'.[27] And this was after Blair's government had shown its ruthless determination to rule in the interests of British capital.

But Blair feared Livingstone would become a focus for the fightback against tube privatisation and might ferment wider revolt inside the party. So he insisted on the rigged system that delivered Frank Dobson as the candidate, despite every indication that Livingstone was far more popular than him, inside the party and out.

Livingstone then had to make a choice. A less astute (or less ambitious) figure might have lain low. But Livingstone could see the way in which politics was changing, and the space for a campaign that was critical of Blair.

In March 2000 he took a huge gamble and announced he would run as an independent. Livingstone said he had been forced to choose 'between the party I love and upholding the democratic rights of Londoners'. It was the biggest formal challenge to Blair since he became leader six years previously.

Livingstone apologised for breaking his word not to stand against an official Labour candidate, saying he offered 'no weasel words of equivocation'. But he claimed the Labour selection process had set a 'new standard in ballot-rigging'.

In words that would come to haunt him, Blair said, 'I believe passionately that Ken Livingstone would be a disaster—a financial disaster, a disaster in terms of crime and police and business.' The extent of the forces ranged against Livingstone was underlined when the Transport and General Workers Union said it would not support him, despite backing him to be Labour's candidate.

But Livingstone shrugged off such problems and when the votes were counted he had won fairly easily.[28]

However, when he was expelled Livingstone declared it was but a trial separation and that he would be 'back soon'. Although by standing as an independent he opened a big space for millions of workers to talk about an alternative to Labour, Livingstone himself did not encourage such moves. He advised a vote for Labour in the London Assembly's constituency seats, and a vote for the Greens in the top-up list.[29] He turned his back on the genuine left alternative, the London Socialist Alliance.

Even before the voting began he said, 'Clearly Tony Blair will want to wait and see for a couple of months how I'm performing as mayor. But then providing I haven't scared the chickens, they will most probably consider what to do around about conference time. It would be good at conference if I'm back in the fold and the whole party is reunited in the run-up to the general election'.[30]

And after the election he immediatly began to work for readmittance to the Labour Party. The executive had said he must wait at least five years before he came back, but many unions and left activists demanded he be let back sooner.

However, he suffered a setback in July 2002 when the party's national executive voted by 17 to 13 not to allow him back. The then Labour chairman, Charles Clarke, said there had been concern that Livingstone would not toe the party line on issues like the private public partnership for the tube.

'The single most important consideration in people's minds was whether the application to rejoin was effectively an application that the Labour Party should endorse his independent candidacy for mayor of London,' said Mr Clarke.

Both Tony Blair and John Prescott voted against the mayor's readmission. But in less than 18 months the executive had changed its mind and voted overwhelmingly to bring Livingstone back. One reason was the awareness that Livingstone was going to crush Labour's candidate (Nicky Gavron) at the next mayoral election. Another was that the mayor had shown no real diversion from New Labour policies. But the most powerful factor was that Labour was on the rocks nationally and needed every last help at the elections of 2004. Back in the party Livingstone would be shoring up Blair's war-damaged support. Outside he would be feeding the idea that a break with Labour could be credible and effective. Some in the party (Gordon Brown, John Prescott, Denis Skinner) did not accept this logic and wanted him kept out. But Blair was insistent.

In December 2003 the executive paved the way for his return and Livingstone could say, 'There are people who get married, then get divorced, have a few years apart and then decide they've missed each other terribly. I see it as very much like that—and they get remarried.'

He argued he had moved the government's agenda forward 'more spectacularly' than anywhere else in the country.[31]

And then in January 2004, by 22 votes to two, the executive let him back in.

Blair ruefully had to say that, despite his earlier fears, Livingstone had done 'a pretty good job' running the capital. 'My prediction that he would be a disaster has turned out to be wrong and I think when that happens in politics you should just be open about it,' he said. 'If the facts change you should be big enough in politics to say your mind changes'.[32]

The fact that weighed most heavily was impending electoral disaster—and Blair was right. In the 2004 local elections Labour did much better in London than the rest of the country. Blair had not helped Livingstone out; Livingstone had helped Blair out. Nationally the Labour Party got its lowest share of the vote since 1918. But in London it was not completely wiped out. Its assembly seats fell from nine to seven, but the Tories did not gain any seats, with UKIP being the main gainer.

Livingstone did worse as a Labour candidate than he had as an independent, winning 3 percent fewer votes in the first round than he had in 2000. The potential for the left was shown by Lindsey German, Respect's candidate for London mayor, who polled 61,731 votes. She came fifth in the contest, beating the British National Party and the Greens and three other candidates. The Respect coalition narrowly missed getting onto the London Assembly, pulling in 87,533 votes across the capital.

Red or blue?

Livingstone is a reformist politician who comes from the left but who wants to be part of the traditional structures of British politics. Through skilful management of his own media image, and with support from the left as rebellion rose against New Labour, Livingstone won the 2000 mayoral election despite the efforts of the official machine to destroy him.

As Alex Callinicos wrote:

> Being a reformist politician in an era where nation-states have capitulated before global capital means combining business-friendly policies with a bit of more radical rhetoric and a few crumbs for the poor. In Livingstone's case this mix comes out as a succession of zig zags. These include a neoliberal vision for London's future, the Olympic bid, denunciations of the RMT and opposition to the war in Iraq.

Having ruled out mass mobilisations to confront the system, Livingstone needs to keep the bankers and the financiers happy to maintain their investment. He also needs to keep the Treasury funds flowing. But to win elections he also needs a left wing base. Having that base gives him bargaining power against Tony Blair and Gordon Brown—and it could help him mount a challenge for the Labour leadership in the right circumstances.

To maintain this he offers reforms. These are weak, but they do exist. Those who deny the possibility of reform are either left denying the existence of what palpably does exist, or, on discovering that minor change is indeed possible, collapse into enthusiastic support for those who are tinkering with the system.

Livingstone's reforms are tiny—and they are also delivered from above and in a tokenistic way. Yet this has been enough to persuade former revolutionaries from the Socialist Action group to work for Livingstone as trusted advisors—and to use their influence (and GLA money) in order to get others to subordinate themselves to his approach. They seem to believe that they are somehow advancing the socialist cause by co-opting hand-picked 'representatives' to various bodies in such a way as to give a leftist veneer to the mayor's office while he happily courts business interests.

Livingstone is a puny example of the reformist process, of which other important examples include, say, President Luiz Inacio Lula da Silva (Lula) in Brazil. While strictly following neoliberal polices, and playing the game according to the rules of bourgeois politics, Lula also introduced the 'Bolsa Familia' (family grant). It guarantees £23 a month from the federal government to 11 million families or 44 million people—20 percent of the population of Brazil. Half those receiving the family grant live in the north east, Brazil's most impoverished region, and it's here that Lula did best in the elections.

This reform cannot be ignored, but neither does it change the essential nature of the Lula government, one which serves the interests of big business. Revolutionaries can accept that small changes are possible, but show how fragile and faltering they are compared to the great tide of neoliberalism which sweeps across the globe, wrecking people's lives.

That is true in Brazil; it is also true in London. Livingstone's example shows how important it is not to put our faith in reformist politicians who claim to be representing us. Instead we need to build a political movement independent of Labour, one that allows working people to fight for their own liberation.

NOTES

1: The issue was the employment by London Underground of Mohammed Kamel Mostafa, son of jailed Islamic cleric Abu Hamza. Livingstone initially said he was 'happy' for him to have the job. Livingstone later learnt that Mostafa had been jailed for three years in Yemen in 1999 for plotting a bombing campaign and therefore, he said, his employers 'are correct to dismiss him'.

2: *Socialist Campaign Group News*, no 143, April 1999. Such support for NATO came strangely from a man who in 1989 had criticised fellow Labour MP Gerald Kaufman by claiming he 'has crawled so far up the backside of NATO that only the soles of his feet are visible'.

3: Greater London Authority press release, 'Mayor Backs Consensus Against War on Iraq', 16 September 2002, www.london.gov.uk/view_press_release.jsp?releaseid=1368

4: Ross Lydall, 'Mayor's Amazing Attack on Bush', *Evening Standard*, 8 May 2003.

5: Nigel Morris, 'Livingstone Says Bush is "Greatest Threat to Life on Planet"', *Independent*, 18 November 2003. Livingstone did not, however, speak at the anti-Bush demonstration.

6: James Sturcke, 'Muslims Being Demonised, Says Livingstone', *Guardian*, 24 October 2006, http://www.guardian.co.uk/religion/Story/0,,1930352,00.html

7: Mayor's Statement, 7 July 2005 http://www.london.gov.uk/mayor/mayor_statement_070705.jsp

8: Fraser Nelson, 'Outrage as Livingstone Tries to "Explain" Suicide Bombers', *Scotsman*, 21 July 2006.

9: Ken Livingstone, 'Three Ways to Make us all Safer', *Guardian*, 4 August 2005, www.guardian.co.uk/attackonlondon/comment/story/0,,1542245,00.html

10: *Times*, 13 October 1981.

11: BBC News, 'Shot Man Not Connected to Bombing', 23 July 2005, http://news.bbc.co.uk/1/hi/uk/4711021.stm

12: *Guardian*, 'Police Leader and Mayor Back Police Chief', 13 June 2006 www.guardian.co.uk/menezes/story/0,,1796363,00.html

13: For a full treatment of this issue see Chris Harman, 'The Ruling Class, its Police and the Left', *Socialist Review*, July 2006, www.socialistreview.org.uk

14: *Economist*, 3 June 2004.

15: *Evening Standard*, 19 October 1999.

16: This is, of course, the other side of saying that 30 percent are 'affordable'. Livingstone has frequently championed a target of 50 percent affordable housing in all new developments. But the 2006 survey showed the mayor's delivery of affordable housing in London for 2004-05 was a mere 28 percent. See 'Delivering Increased Housing Output', April 2006 www.london.gov.uk/mayor/strategies/sds/lon_plan_changes/housing.jsp

17: Such policies were put forward by Respect's Lindsey German in her 2004 campaign for London mayor—and won widespread support. See www.socialist-worker.co.uk/article.php?article_id=392

18: http://news.bbc.co.uk/1/hi/england/london/3494015.stm

19: I give the BBC version. Other versions have Kiley calling Livingstone a 'Marxist socialist'.

20: In summer the temperature on some trains exceeds the limit for the transport of live animals.

21: The number of journeys in London by all methods of transport increased by 5 percent during this time period, so the bus increase is not quite as spectacular as it seems.

22: Class remains central to such statistics. Children in Britain whose parents are long-term unemployed or who have never worked are 13 times more likely than children at the top end of the socioeconomic scale to die from an injury or poisoning incident, according to a study published in the *British Medical Journal* in July 2006. See www.lshtm.ac.uk/news/2006/child-injury.html

23: *Tribune*, 10 November 2006, *City Limits* Climate Change supplement.

24: Kevin Maguire, 'Livingstone in "Scab" Row', *Guardian*, 26 June 2004, www.guardian.co.uk/guardianpolitics/story/0,,1247645,00.html

25: A former Royal Marine who had served in Bosnia was later convicted of the Churchill-altering offence.

26: *Ham and High*, 21 February, 1986.

27: *Guardian*, 29 January, 1999.

28: First round: Livingstone 39 percent, Norris (Conservative) 27 percent, Dobson (Labour) 13 percent, Kramer (Lib Dem) 12 percent. Second round: Livingstone 58 percent, Norris 42 percent.

29: Livingstone's support was crucial to them winning three assembly seats.

30: http://news.bbc.co.uk/1/hi/in_depth/uk_politics/2000/london_mayor/729269.stm

31 http://news.bbc.co.uk/1/hi/uk_politics/3327457.stm

32: http://news.bbc.co.uk/1/hi/uk_politics/3374509.stm

Muslim working class struggles[1]

Hassan Mahamdallie

One product of the demonisation of Britain's Muslims by those forces desperate to provide a scapegoat for the fallout from the 'war on terror' has been a concerted effort to separate them out from the rest of society, to make them seem 'alien' and culturally distant—especially in the eyes of the wider working class.[2] These attacks obscure the reality that the majority of Muslims (though not all, of course) belong to the working class.

Many people, including some who consider themselves on the left, seem to want to put Muslims in historical cul-de-sacs that deny, downplay or only nod briefly to their working class lives, background or heritage. Why should this be? Muslims have been living, working and struggling in Britain in increasing numbers for well over a hundred years, and early settlements go back much further, right back to the 1600s.[3] Other sections of the working class are assumed to have traditions and histories of struggle. Muslims seem to have no history, radical or otherwise. In an attempt to challenge this distortion I have sketched out three periods in which Muslim workers have fought exploitation and oppression—the struggles of Arab and Somali seamen in Britain's ports during the period of imperialism and colonialism, the first industrial struggles of Muslim workers during the period of post Second World War migration, and the radical Asian youth movements of the 1970s and 1980s.

I have had to pick the Muslim 'strands' out of the general narrative of 'Black History'. This is not easy because its principle works, meticulous, pioneering and inspirational as many are, were written in the 1980s when religious identity was regarded as subordinate to 'racial' identities, reflecting the unified struggles against racism which had taken place. This is not an indication of neglect or the passing over of religious identities. Rather it is because Muslim workers did not then see their religion as the defining part of their political identity. This did not change until the Rushdie affair (see below) at the end of the 1980s. In any case, the strength of their religiosity at any one period should not be automatically read as a sign of their willingness to engage or not in workplace or community struggles.

Part 1: 1850-1945—The portside struggles of the Muslim seamen and their communities

There had been a small Muslim presence in this country stretching back hundreds of years, itself an inconvenient fact for those who wish to cast Muslims as 'foreign' newcomers to our society.

However, the opening of the Suez Canal in 1869 marked the beginning of significant Muslim immigration. The port of Aden, seized by the British in 1837, became a major stop off and refuelling point and attracted migrants from Yemen and northern Somalia, doubling the port's population by the end of the 19th century.[4] Ship owners from Europe began to employ these migrants in increasing numbers predominantly as segregated unskilled labourers in shovelling coal in the engine rooms.

These Muslim sailors joined a floating multiracial and multinational proletariat that had up to that point been populated by Indian 'lascars', West Africans and West Indians, as well as British and Europeans. By the end of the 19th century small itinerant port communities were establishing themselves along the trade routes, including Europe's seaports, especially those of France and Britain. Arabs could be found boarding in the dockside areas of Cardiff, South Shields, and to a lesser extent Liverpool and Hull. In Cardiff they joined other migrant workers from Africa, the West Indies, India, China, Malta, Greece, Italy, Germany and other countries. Portside licensed boarding houses and cafes sprang up to service the Muslim sailors, becoming hubs for welfare and community needs.[5]

Richard Lawless, in his groundbreaking book about the Yemeni community in the north east of England, *From Ta'izz to Tyneside*, tells how, 'for Arab seamen arriving in a strange land with little knowledge of its language and customs, the Arab boarding-house was virtually essential for their survival', providing 'not only accommodation and food that was lawful according to their religion, but essential assistance in securing another ship, and credit if their resources ran out before they signed on for the next voyage'.[6]

Some seamen began to put down semi-permanent or permanent roots, often resulting from relationships that had grown up between them and local women. Women who married the seamen would often convert to Islam and take a Muslim surname, to be passed onto their children as the families became members of the dockside working class population. Prayer rooms and eventually mosques with koranic schools were established in both Cardiff and South Shields, where in the 1930s:

> Elaborate and colourful processions through the streets were organised to mark the major Muslim festivals, occasions when members of the Arab community were able to make a strong public declaration of their faith. Muslims from other parts of the north east sometimes took part in these processions and groups of Arabs from Cardiff also participated.[7]

In Cardiff the religious culture of the seamen could mark them out in some respects. An invaluable 1940s sociological study of the city's Butetown area observed of Muslims:

> The adherents of this creed not only carry out their ritual and religious obligations with vastly more fervour and enthusiasm than the rest of the community, but are correspondingly surer both of themselves and their own way of life. The principle injunctions of Islam are fulfilled assiduously, and the various prohibitions enjoined by the prophet are on the whole rigorously observed as are Ramadan and other fasts and festivals... This constant display of devotion is regarded by the rest of the community with a certain amount of respect and even a little admiration. There is a feeling that it gives 'tone' to the district.[8]

Nevertheless Muslim seamen, like the other black populations, met with fluctuating, sometimes extreme and sustained, levels of racism, hostility and prejudice. Modern racism had developed as a necessary ideological buttress for the transatlantic slave trade. During the era of empire it was 'refined' into a weapon to justify subjugation of the colonies. Former prejudices founded on notions of biological superiority of the 'white race' now mixed with assumptions of cultural superiority and a corresponding contempt for the histories, cultures and religions of the colonised.

The British colonisation of Muslim countries gave the racism of empire an anti-Islamic twist, an echo perhaps of older fears and prejudices produced at the time when Western Europe felt threatened by ascendant Islamic empires. Humayun Ansari in his recent history of Muslims has written how 'the early 19th century saw the emergence in Britain of 'a new sense of cultural superiority' with the decline of the Ottoman Empire that had once challenged Europe from the East. 'British elites saw their nation vibrant and expanding' and gained 'a sense of superiority' from 'the expansion and consolidation of European influence over Muslim territories' so that:

> popular prejudice again non-Europeans and Christian hostility towards 'heathens' in Britain...gained considerable currency; colour was an outward reflection of mental and moral inferiority... By the 1860s negative images of Islam and Muslims were embraced in the hardening religious and racial prejudices that were beginning to be articulated in the form of pseudo-scientific theories of race in Britain.[9]

The drive to unite British society, especially the working class, behind the imperial project inevitably had an effect on attitudes. A 1918 survey highlighted 'race prejudice' as especially strong towards the colonised peoples. 'Very little of this hostility was formed on the basis of personal contact; most of it was "derived" from the process of imperialism'.[10] However, it would be wrong to assume that British workers were a homogenous racist bloc. The British working class movement also had a significant tradition of anti-racism. The London Chartists in the 1840s chose a black tailor, the ultra-radical William Cuffey, as their leader. In the 1920s the working population of Battersea elected an Indian Communist, Shapurji Saklatvala, as their MP. He stood alongside the black mayor of Battersea, John Archer. As we will see later the British Communist Party would oppose racism and attempt to organise the black immigrant seamen.[11]

The general racism was sharpened by local antagonisms in the ports, especially when scarcity of employment could set British seamen against their black and Arab counterparts. The migrant seamen were herded into close-knit slum areas around the docks, with a colour bar in jobs and housing that tended to keep them from integrating with the local population. It was the official and open policy of Cardiff council and estate agents to refuse 'coloured' families housing outside of Butetown and as late as the 1940s they faced 'ostracism, oral or newspaper comment, refusal to serve, non-admission to dance halls, hotels etc'.[12] Officials could argue that 'coloured men who have come to dwell in our cities are being made to adopt a standard of civilisation they cannot be expected to understand. They are not imbued with moral codes similar to our own and they have not assimilated our conventions of life'.[13] The local press agitated for repatriation on the basis that the seamen did not 'belong to the social system we have evolved on these islands'.[14]

Black and Arab seafarers faced a further obstacle in the generally hostile attitude that the trade unions had towards them. The seamen's unions sought to bar foreigners from trade union membership, until union leader J Havelock Wilson[15] reversed it, seemingly just on the practical grounds that it was better to contain the foreign seamen inside the unions than give the ship-owners a free hand with them. By 1902 Wilson was taunting white seamen with claims that 40 percent of his union's membership was made up of foreign labour—which meant that in many areas they must have been the backbone of the union and a major contributor to its coffers.

The shipping bosses used pitifully paid and badly treated lascars to undermine the wages and conditions of white seamen, but instead of the unions making a common front against the owners to drive up wages and conditions of all workers, they fell into the trap of seeing the lascars as competitors and easily duped tools of the bosses. So when the National Sailors' and Firemen's Union (NSFU—later to become the NUS) emerged as a force out of a major strike in 1911 part of its attack on the shipping owners was the accusation that they were discharging British seamen and replacing them with lower paid foreign hands. The employers were happy to fuel this divisive stance by spreading it about that foreign crews were eager to do the work, and that Muslims seamen in particular were teetotal and compliant.

Articles and letters in the union journal show that the prejudice towards Arabs (and Chinese) went far beyond hostility arising from competition for jobs: 'It is no use trying to persuade us that the question of colour does not enter the national consideration; it does and very seriously. We had growing up in our midst a population, not of young Arabs, but of half-castes, which is undesirable in the extreme'.[16] Other headlines in the journal included 'Menace of Mixed Unions' and 'White Wives' Vain Regret'.[17] Sexual jealousy and a horror at the prospect of white women marrying Arab seamen and having children was a permanent racist motif throughout the first half of the 20th century.[18]

The seamen's representatives at the Trade Union Congress demanded that 'Asiatics should not be allowed to work west of Suez' and warned that 'in our seaport towns there were little half-bred Arabs and Greeks who were being brought into the world and who were going to be a serious menace to the country'.[19]

The South Wales popular press was ever eager to embellish this spectre, talking of 'an inferior race of Asiatics...men who can herd together like pigs, and are fed on cheap meals of grain or rice, have not got the pluck, endurance, grip or power of a man fed according to English ideas'.[20]

In Tyneside a correspondent to a local newspaper betrayed how racism encouraged by economic competition could fuse with the cultural racism of empire: 'No matter how bad conditions are aboard ship, Mohamed (who can live on the smell of an oily rag or a stick of incense for a week) will not complain, but a Britisher always does. This is why poor, puzzled, ostracised, uncomplaining Mohamed is given preference to Britishers'.[21]

The outbreak of the First World War resulted in a sudden increase in demand for seamen in the merchant navy, and the migrant seafaring population of Tyneside, made up mostly of Yemenis, increased fourfold.[22] But the situation dramatically altered again when the war drew to a close. The Arabs were hit by a double blow. They found themselves out of work, once more suffering pre-war racist hiring practices by the shipping lines. And they also faced hostile mobs of demobilised seamen accusing them of taking their jobs. A West African sailor, Earnest Marke, recalled:

> It now became scarcity of jobs, not men, with the demobbed men wanting their old jobs back and negroes being sacked to make room for them. Those who didn't get their jobs back immediately, began taking it out on the negroes—any negro... If the negro hadn't been there the confusion might have been worse. Perhaps even revolution. In a way, the negro saved the situation and the government by acting as a scapegoat.[23]

The antagonisms exploded into the 'race riots' in the first half of 1919. The attacks have, paradoxically, to be seen in the context of the huge outbreak in class struggle that rocked the British ruling class that year. The 1917 Boshevik Revolution in Russia had lit a flame across Europe and beyond. The First World War came to an end amid turmoil throughout British society as workers returning from the front found, not a 'land fit for heroes', but rising prices and the threat of being pushed into the ranks of the unemployed and poverty. They rebelled with a massive wave of strikes, with an average of 10,000 workers on strike for every day of the year.

The first confrontation between the working class and the state came early in January 1919 when 100,000 Clydeside engineering workers struck in a magnificent show of strength, demanding a 40-hour week. However, the leadership of the strike failed to provide the political leadership necessary to generalise the action. This left Glasgow isolated, and on Friday 31 January the police attacked a massive 35,000-strong demonstration in the city's George Square as the state sought to reassert its control: 'Glasgow was an armed camp, occupied by troops with bayonets, machine guns, tanks and aeroplanes'.[24]

One of the strike leaders was the future Labour cabinet minister Manny Shinwell, then the leader of the British Seafarers' Union, set up in Glasgow as a breakaway from Havelock Wilson's union. Evidently Shinwell reckoned that he could poach members from the rival union if he could be seen to be more hostile to foreign seamen (especially Chinese lascars). Shinwell urged in a public meeting four days before the Clydeside mass strike that 'action should be taken at once' against the Chinese. A racist gang attacked West African seamen in the Broomielaw docks area just a few hours later. As one historian has concluded:

> The clash on the Broomielaw can be taken as an example of how one element of the working class can be made the scapegoat, by those supposedly protecting the interests of all workers (in this case the two seamen's unions), in order to secure the best deal for their members, at the expense of the minority.[25]

The important point to add, of course, is that, although the black and Chinese seamen suffered most, the white trade unionists certainly didn't benefit either by being taken in by Shinwell's diversionary politics.

The threat to the British ruling class lessened as 1919 unfolded and there was a decline in class confidence, especially among the least organised sections of the workers. As this happened, there was a repeat on a nation-wide scale of the scenario Shinwell had more or less purposefully brought about in Glasgow, with some white workers attracted by the possibility of 'kicking down' those worse off than themselves.

Blacks and Arabs were set upon in all Britain's major ports and suffered savage beatings, fire bombings and murders. In February the violence erupted in South Shields, in April in the London docks; in May it hit Liverpool and Cardiff in June. The intensity of the violence seems to have increased at each stage. In Cardiff the rioting lasted several days, and resulted in three deaths. A Cardiff Somali, Ibrahim Ismaa'il, later remembered in his memoirs that;

> A Warsangeli [from a Northern Somali kabil or clan], Abdi Langara, had a boarding house right in the European part of town... As soon as the fight started all the Warsangeli went to defend Abdi's house... Seven or eight Warsangeli defended the house and most of them got badly wounded. Some of the white people also received wounds. In the end the whites took possession of the first floor, soaked it with paraffin oil and set it alight. The Somalis managed to keep up the fight until the police arrived—one of them was left for dead.[26]

A local newspaper report described how:

> A black man was spotted—he was first insulted and then attacked by three

> whites, one of whom blew a whistle. This seemed to be the expected signal, because hundreds of persons rushed up from the neighbouring street, including many women and girls—who had sticks and stones, and flung them at the unfortunate coloured man as they chased him along the street.[27]

Black and Arab seamen never took these attacks lying down, even when they were outnumbered. One account from the 1919 riots tells how a Somali imam, Hadji Mohammed, 'was prepared to face the mob, but his white wife pleaded with him, so he clambered up a drainpipe, hid on the roof and watched his residence being reduced to a skeleton'.[28] A white racist was killed on the first night of the race riot in Cardiff. One historian writes that 'the police protected the main black settlement around Loudoun Square (Because they feared the blacks would kill more whites if they didn't) but left unguarded a secondary area of largely Arab settlement nearer the city centre. This population moved into Butetown for self-protection'.[29] The subsequent police report, openly betraying its sympathies, concluded that 'if the crowd had overpowered the police and got through, the result would have been disastrous, as the black population would probably have fought with desperation and inflicted great loss of life'.[30]

In South Shields fighting broke out after an Arab seaman punched a racist trade union official outside the dockside union offices. A large crowd then attacked the Arabs who, outnumbered, 'armed themselves with knives, sticks and revolvers' and drove back their attackers',[31] while in Liverpool black seamen had defended their boarding houses against a police raid, one 'armed with a poker, others with revolvers, knives and razors. One policeman was shot in the mouth, another in the neck, a third was slashed on face and neck, and a fourth had his wrist broken'.[32] Soon afterwards a West Indian, Charles Wotten, escaping police clutches after one raid, was cornered by a crowd of 200 to 300 racists who threw him into the docks and pelted him with stones until he drowned.[33]

There were some reported spontaneous acts of solidarity from individual English people, and socialist newspapers such as Sylvia Pankhurst's *Workers' Dreadnought* would excoriate 'negro-hunting' and ask the rhetorical question, 'Do you wish to exclude all blacks from England? If so, do you not think blacks might justly ask that the British should at the same time keep out of black peoples' countries?'[34] But in the main the blacks and Arabs were left to put up resistance by themselves against the mobs and their organised collaborators in the forces of 'law and order'.[35]

Part 2: 1919-1950—The seamen and the inter-war years

The reaction of the authorities to the 1919 mob violence was to further crack down on the Muslim seamen. Arab and Somali sailors were reclassified from their previous status as British passport holding workers to unwelcome and problematic 'aliens', their rights as British subjects deliberately and callously stripped away.

In 1921 the Cardiff Town Clerk recommended that destitute seamen 'be repatriated forthwith, or accommodated in a concentration camp',[36] and in 1922 hundreds of Adenese were repatriated out of the city. Seamen, including numbers of Somalis and Yemenis in South Shields who had lived in Britain for a long time, many with white wives and British-born children, were told that they had to prove their citizenship rights from scratch, and many had their British status removed for lack of documentation or financial resources to register it.

The National Union of Seamen seized the opportunity to do a 'British First' deal with the shipping owner. The government and Home Office issued new restrictions in 1920 and then 1925 under the Aliens Act which had been targeted in the first place against poor Jewish immigrants:

> All coloured alien seamen were henceforth to be registered with the police and to carry an identity card marked 'SEAMAN' in red ink bearing a photograph and a thumb-print. It was argued that the last was necessary because it was more difficult to tell coloured men apart and some more positive means of identification was needed! The holder was not a person but an invisible man, a black; only the criminal associations of a thumb-print could give him an identity.[37]

The NUS was granted the sanction in 1930 that Arab and Somali sailors specifically should be picked last (if at all) and go on a forced rota that meant they had to take any job offered them if they were not to lose all rights not only to a job but the right to stay in Britain. The order specified that;

> A white card shall be issued...to any Somali or Arab who satisfies the Port Consultants that he is a bona fide seaman and lawful in this country. The white card shall only be issued after being stamped by the National Union of Seamen and the Shipping Federation... Officers engaging Somalis or Arab crews shall be informed that it is very undesirable to mix Somalis and Arabs of other races, and asked to specify which one they prefer.[38]

Soon Somalis, Arabs and their families were pushed into starvation and destitution.

Police harassment and a local authorities' ban on them moving out of the depressed port areas effectively segregated these 'aliens' and their families, treating them as a 'social menace'. Very top of the list of moral crusaders was Cardiff chief constable James A Wilson, who clearly had a pathological hatred of 'race mixing':

> The coloured seamen who live in our midst…are not imbued with our moral code, and have not assimilated our conventions. They come into contact with the female sex of the white race, and their progeny are half-caste, with the vicious hereditary taint of their parents.[39]

Wilson was delighted to hear of the South African Immorality Act of 1927 that forbade sexual relationships across racial boundaries.

The Arab and Somali seamen responded to the attack on their already precarious existence by launching a militant and vigorous campaign to smash the rota, picketing shipping offices and lobbying to get the union's position changed. The violent confrontations that took place in Cardiff and South Shields as a result ended with Arab and Somali sailors being prosecuted and receiving 'exemplary' sentences tagged with judicial recommendations of deportation.

The seamen looked to radical forces to help them. In Cardiff they were drawn via activists in the Seaman's Minority Movement and the International Transport Workers' Federation into a working alliance with the Communist Party and the Colonial Defence Association it influenced. One historian tells how 'the International Transport Workers Federation sprung to the defence of coloured men in one of the perennial conflicts over national insurance. The following year black men were involved in a movement to increase wages within the NUS.' As Neil Evans has written in his meticulous study of the period, 'Butetown was viewed by the Communist Party at the time as one of the most productive areas to hold corner street meetings and sell literature. In the late 1930s the Colonial Defence Association led protest marches and deputations about relief scales to the City Hall in Cardiff'.[40]

An article in the *Negro Worker* (edited by Trinidadian communist and Pan-Africanist George Padmore) in 1933 under the byline of Minority Movement port organiser Harry O'Connell was headlined 'Race Prejudice in England'. It reported a debate at a Cardiff City Council meeting over the issue of relief for blacks and concluded, 'Coloured and white workers in Cardiff must unite to fight for equal employment rates for all workers irrespective of colour and race. As long as the British Slavemasters are able to play out one section of the working class against another, they will be able to rob and exploit both alike'.[41] In 1934 the anti-socialist LCP leader Dr Harold Moody was forced to complain (with some exaggeration) that 'the coloured people of Cardiff are mainly Communists, simply because no one else has seen fit to give them a helping hand'.[42]

These Muslim communities organised among themselves for their political, social and religious needs as well as forging links with radical anti-racist organisations. In Cardiff the British Somali Society (BSS) and the Somali Youth League (connected to organisations in Somalia) were formed in the mid-1930s, and the BSS leadership collaborated with the Communist Party.[43] The United Committee of Coloured and Colonial Peoples Organisations, set up to unite the migrant seamen of Cardiff across national, ethnic and religion divides, sent an Arab delegate, Mohamed Hassan, to the landmark 1945 Pan-African Congress organised by George Padmore in Manchester, along with two delegates from a Somali Society.[44] There were also welfare organisations and a religious grouping, the Islamia Allawia Friendly Society, in Cardiff[45] and similar formations in South Shields. As Ansari has written, 'Muslims in Britain found themselves forming part of a broader multicultural identity, which coexisted with and sometimes transcended religion'.[46]

After the Second World War renewed migration from the colonies boosted the Yemeni populations. As Richard Lawless has written:

> In the 1950s and 1960s a new influx of Yemenis into Britain found employment not in shipping but in heavy industry, especially in the steel and metal-working plants in Sheffield and Birmingham... Some Arab seafarers moved to the Midlands where new employment opportunities were opening up in industry and in this way forged a link between the two phases of Yemeni migration to Britain.[47]

Meanwhile, harassment of Muslim sailors by the police and local authorities in Cardiff and South Shields continued. A sharp reminder came in 1952 when a Somali seaman, Hussein Mattan, was fitted up by the police for the murder of a local woman and hanged after a sham trial. It was not until 1998, 46 years later, that his widow Laura and sons Omar and Mervyn managed to get this gross miscarriage of justice recognised as such and Mattan's name cleared.[48]

Part 3: The Second World War—Shipboard militancy and early industrial roots

Labour shortages with the outbreak of the Second World War strengthened the position of lascars. They were in demand once again, but they were not prepared to put aside their maltreatment. Cynical demands for them to unite behind the war against fascism were evidently rejected, many probably recalling how in 1919 they had been 'rewarded' for their efforts at the end of the First World War.

As Rosina Visram has written:

> Three days into the war, by September 1939, as many as eight ships were on strike, Indian seamen demanding, in some cases, a 200 percent wage rise, including essential provisions like soap, warm clothing and bedding... The Board of Trade was forced into negotiations, enlisting the help of the India High Commissioner, Sir Firozkhan Noon, to act as mediator in order to minimize concessions.[49]

An attempt by ship-owners to impose a 25 percent across the board wage rise to head off militancy backfired, as did mass jailings of strikers. This bitter struggle continued throughout the war, led by a Bengal-born political activist named Surat Alley,[50] and eventually succeeding in achieving better pay and conditions for the seaman, although still way behind that enjoyed by their white counterparts.

Meanwhile employment was opening up in another sector—the war industries, drawing in ex-seamen and new migrants, especially from pre-partition India (Indians, Pakistanis and Bangladeshis). Visram describes how:

> Factories and war-related industries in London, Glasgow, but particularly in the Midlands, needed labour. Indeed, demand was so high that even their lack of English language was apparently no longer considered a handicap... Some gave up peddling [a trade traditionally occupied by Indian men] for more secure factory employment... The two most numerous ethnic groups engaged in industries in wartime Britain were Bengali Muslims, largely ex-seamen, and Punjabis, both Sikh and Muslim.[51]

By April 1943 there were up to 2,000 Indians labouring across Birmingham and Coventry.[52] Although they filled a crucial gap in the war industries, they were, as before, crowded into poor accommodation and faced discrimination at work. They responded by starting to organise themselves, socially, politically and through the trade unions.

The Indian Workers Associations (IWAs) had their origins in 1937, formed by Sikh activists living in Coventry with political connections to the Indian independence movement in Punjab, and by 1942 also existed in Birmingham, Bradford, London and other towns, with Sikhs, Hindus and Muslims joining together. The IWAs' early activity was heavily influenced by Indian socialist and communist organisations, and branches and individuals had close political and membership links to the Communist Party. The secret service described a founder member, Coventry-based Akbar Ali Khan, known as the 'driving force' behind the IWA, as holding 'advanced political views'.[53] Another founder member was Udham Singh, who became a martyr when he was hanged in Pentonville Prison in 1940 after shooting dead the colonial governor of Punjab responsible for the Amritsar Massacre, which Singh had witnessed as a boy. Singh called himself Ram Mohammed Singh Azad to embody Hindu (Ram), Muslim (Mohammed), Sikh (Singh) freedom (Azad) in unity against British colonial rule.

Part 4: Making their mark—post-war migration, new workers, racism and the industrial struggles

The long economic boom that followed the Second World War pulled significant numbers of migrant workers into Western Europe. As a commentator observed in the mid-1970s, 'migrant workers are used largely to fill jobs that native workers will not do, because of their low wages or low esteem. And yet they are jobs which are essential to the maintenance of public services that bolster our consumer economy.'[54]

Workers from the Indian subcontinent made up the majority of Muslim migration during this period, although there were other smaller groups—Turkish Cypriots fearing the prospect of ethnic conflict on their island, Moroccans to work in the hotel and catering industries, Yemenis in the steel industry in Sheffield. In all cases they followed in the footsteps of earlier settlers, but in larger numbers and into different industries.[55]

Muhammad Anwar describes the way in which this 'chain' migration took place in relation to Pakistani workers:

> The mass migration of Pakistanis started in the late 1950s and early 1960s when new migrants followed the routes established by the pioneer Pakistanis... The sponsorship and patronage by the early settlers helped to overcome the intervening obstacles for migrants. This led to a chain of migration on the kinship, friendship basis... It was estimated in 1951 that there were 5,000 Pakistanis (including Bangladeshis) in Britain... In 1961 the estimated number reached 24,900, and by 1966 it grew to 119,700.[56]

The IWAs as a movement had faltered in the period after the Second World War[57] but revived in the late 1950s as Indians, including Muslims, faced other challenges. The Southall IWA, for instance, went from a membership of 120 in 1957 to 12,500 by the late 1960s.[58] The branches gave a militant edge to community organisation, meeting welfare, social and cultural needs along with trade union and political leadership.

As Dilip Hiro has recorded:

> The leftist element continued to exhort IWA members to participate in trade union activities, and even to set up unions where they did not already exist. In this they were quite successful. Many local IWAs could justly claim that their members, in spite of victimisation and the threats of employers, managed to found unions. Also, without exception, IWA members supported whatever militant action was taken by established unions in factories and public transport, because they believed that the economic lot of Indian workers was intimately intertwined with that of British workers.

The IWAs also 'showed much vigour and initiative in combating racial discrimination and opposing racist immigration policies', taking the lead in organizing national demonstrations in 1961 and again in 1968.[59]

Immigrant workers, although doing long hours of shift work for poor pay, were not in peripheral sectors of the economy: 43 percent of black workers in the mid-1970s were in factories employing over 500 workers, compared to 29 percent of white workers. And 61 percent of male black workers were unionised compared to 45 percent of white male workers.[60]

They were soon to move into confrontation with the employers, and quite often obstructive and racist local union officials.

In May 1965 the first significant post-war 'immigrant strike' took place at Red Scar Mill in Preston, Lancashire, involving Indian, Pakistani and African-Caribbean workers. It was opposed by the local TGWU organisation who characterised it as 'tribal', 'racial' and 'unofficial'.[61] In May 1972 Pakistani workers struck at Crepe Sizes, Nottingham, and a month later African-Caribbean workers struck at Stanmore Engineering Works. In June 1973 another strike involving African-Caribbean workers hit Standard Telephone and Cables. Then Asians struck at Harwood Cash Lawn Mills in Mansfield and at EE Jaffe and Malmic Lace in Nottingham, and Indian and Pakistani workers at Perivale Gütermann in Southall, west London.

What then was the industrial and political background to this rash of strikes and the race and class dynamics within them?

In 1962 the Tory government passed the openly discriminatory

Commonwealth Immigrants Act. Harold Wilson's Labour government further turned the screws in 1965 and then in 1968 bowed before the racist hysteria unleashed by Enoch Powell to rush through parliament a law to block Asians with UK passports coming to Britain when they were driven out of East Africa. Further waves of racist hysteria accompanied the plight of Ugandan Asians in 1972 and Malawi Asians in 1976.

Those who did get through the barriers settled predominantly in areas of London, especially west London and Middlesex, Birmingham and the East Midlands. Although many had arrived in Britain penniless, that did not mean they were prepared to be passive in the face of hostility or unequal treatment. About half were from Hindu backgrounds, the rest being Muslims and Sikhs.[62] One contemporary report recorded, 'The newcomers include traders, doctors, teachers, bank clerks, civil servants, motor mechanics and labourers. Most of the young people have received an English education'.[63]

East African Asians, whatever their previous status or profession, found only badly paid textile factory work open to them in Leicester and other nearby towns.[64] Their entry into the manual workforce coincided with the first weakening of the long post-war boom and disillusion with the record of the 1964-70 the Wilson government. There was a rising tide in workers' militancy:

> There were more than 200 occupations of shipyards, factories, offices and workshops between 1972 and 1974. Workers also won important battles on the wages front... The total of strike days reached 10,980,000 in 1970 and 13,551,000 in 1971, climbing to 23,909,000 in 1972—the highest figure since the 1920s.[65]

The 1972 miners' strike had been won after mass picketing at Saltley Gate stopped a strategically important Midlands coke depot. In 1974 the Tory government was to fall after it lost another confrontation with the miners. Against this background, why should Asian workers hold back?

But alongside the rising level of struggle there was also an underbelly of racist scapegoating, exacerbated by the ability of the far right to exploit disillusion with Labour's failure to fulfil the expectations of its supporters. The response of important groups of Asian workers marked a fundamental shift in the landscape of British trade union politics and its approach to black and immigrant workers. It was in June 1972 that the first of the series of major industrial confrontations involving East African Asians took place at Mansfield Hosiery Mill in Loughborough:

> The lowest paid workers, bar loaders, all of whom were Asian, asked for a

> pay rise and in October struck—against union advice. All the other workers came out with the bar loaders, although the whites returned to work within a week. What underlay the bar loaders' anger was the refusal of management to train them as knitters (all the knitters were white). Eventually the bosses agreed to train two Asians as knitters and the white workers struck in protest. The outcome was a new deal which the bar loaders then rejected and struck against. Their strike was eventually made official in December after they occupied the union offices. A return to work eventually took place when the Asian workers accepted that 30 of the 80 knitters' jobs be reserved for them.[66]

The politicised strike committee afterwards called a 'trade unions and racialism conference' that was attended by 350 delegates from the left, black organisations and the trade unions, and offered solidarity to other workers in their position.

Mansfield Hosiery was followed by a larger confrontation at Imperial Typewriters in Leicester in 1974. This strike involved 400 mostly East Asians, lasted for four months and quickly became political, with the focus moving from the issue of wages to that of racism and democracy in the trade unions. The strikers, many among them young women, fought against open and ugly racism on the part of white union members and their leaders. They organised mass pickets, resisted intimidation by National Front thugs, held three mass rallies, won widespread support inside and outside the local Indian community, and appealed successfully to the TGWU national leadership for an inquiry into the lack of Asian representation on the factory shop stewards committee. The casually bigoted attitude of the local union leadership was shown by the TGWU's district official who in an interview not only sympathised with the company, but attacked the women strikers: 'They have got to learn to fit in our ways, you know. We haven't got to fit into theirs'.[67] He clearly couldn't comprehend that the Asian women 'fitted in' more with 'the ways' of British trade unionists than he did.

The Imperial Typewriters strike committee refused to mirror this hostility. It put out a statement saying, 'Our struggle has taught us also that black workers must never for a moment entertain the thought of separate black unions. They must join the existing unions and fight through them'.[68]

Those white workers inside Imperial Typewriters who opposed the strike were soon proved to be ultimately acting against their own interests. As one contemporary account described:

> When Littons [the US multinational that owned the factory] decided to close its two UK factories in 1974, the Leicester plant put up no resistance, while

the Hull workers occupied their factory in an attempt to save their jobs. The Leicester workforce, weakened and demoralised by racist divisions, was in no position to fight back over the closure, and black and white workers alike lost their jobs.[69]

The challenge to the trade union movement reached its height at Grunwick's two years later. The workforce at this film-processing factory in north east London was 80 percent East African Asian. In August 1976 nearly half of them walked out demanding union recognition. The ensuing strike was to last two years, with the trade union movement, black community and radical organisations and the left on one side and George Ward, the Anglo-Indian boss, the courts, the police and organised right forces on the other. It also drew in the TUC and the Labour cabinet, albeit kicking and screaming. The inspirational leader of the strike was Jayaben Desai, a Kenyan East Indian whose bitter experience of the lack of TUC backbone led to her trenchant comment, 'Official action from the TUC is like honey on your elbow: you can smell it, you can see it, but you can never taste it'.[70]

The secretary of the strike committee was Mahmood Ahmad. He told a mass meeting of 2,000 trade unionists at a British Leyland convenors' conference that TUC promises of real support were so much hot air: 'If the British trade union movement wants to recruit Asian workers then it has to do better than this.' It was reported that 'Mahmood was the only speaker that day to receive a standing ovation'.[71]

But if the top of the trade union movement was failing the Grunwick strikers, that accusation could not seriously be levelled at the rank and file. The mass picket deployed at Saltley Gate manifested itself at Grunwick's. As the 'official' account of the dispute pointed out:

> It was the mass picket that transformed the strike... It was the arrival in Willesden of thousands of trade unionists from all over Britain which was to reassure the strikers that they were not, after all, alone and that besides the right wing section of the labour movement there was also a left wing, a radical and a militant section which responded with class feeling to the call of all workers in struggle, whether male or female, manual or clerical, black or white.[72]

The police, including the paramilitary Special Patrol Group, attacked the mass pickets but they did not stop building the mass actions, building to a peak on 11 July 1977 when 20,000 turned out, including Yorkshire miners led by Arthur Scargill. But national trade union leaderships would not defy a court ban on postal workers refusing to move Grunwick's mail, and the struggle eventually ended in a defeat for the strikers. It was an important episode in the development of the downturn of workers' struggle that would culminate in the 'Winter of Discontent' as the Labour government turned on its own supporters, ushering in the Thatcher years. However, the wider lesson of Grunwick's was not lost:

> Grunwick's was the most important dispute in the history of the British labour movement concerning the immigrant community. It laid the ghost of black and brown workers not being prepared to join unions and undercutting the wages of white workers. Gone forever is the image of the passive and unorganisable traditional Asian women. There are still problems with race within the trade union movement, but Grunwick did much to erase the painful memory of disputes in which black and brown workers were not supported by their white colleagues.[73]

Grunwick's set down a marker for the British working class and trade union movement. National union leaders had used the annual Trades Union Congress since the 1950s to argue against racism and for immigrant workers to be recruited into the unions. This reflected a massive step forward from the 1930s when the congress had conducted rancid racist debates and could happily unite around seamen's unions calls to bar lascars. However, the TUC had rarely been under pressure to deliver on this stance. Grunwick's changed that and paved the way for a new black presence inside the union structures. The TGWU union, which had been the union of choice for Asian workers despite the position of many local union leaders, would go on to elect Bill Morris as the first black trade union general secretary in 1991.

It had been a hard struggle since the Red Scar Mill strike in Preston. Muslim workers, including women workers, were among those actively involved in the strikes of these years.[74] The strikers were class conscious and prepared to use the most radical and advanced tools in the class struggle to achieve their collective aims. It is not what set Muslim workers apart that stands out from an analysis of this period: rather it is what they had in common with other workers.

Part 5: The Asian youth movements—radicalisation and the fight against racism and fascism

The radical period detonated by the events of 1968 had its effect on Muslim and other black and Asian workers in Britain. The rising class struggle internationally, the anti-imperialism of the fight against the Vietnam War and the black movement that emerged from the United States civil rights period all made their mark, especially on the younger generation of Asians confronted by the rising threat of the National Front and ever more barbaric immigration controls from Tory and Labour administrations.

The Imperial Typewriters strikers had had to confront counter-pickets by the National Front (carrying banners saying 'White Workers of Imperial Typewriters'). Two years later in 1976 the National Front polled 15,000 votes in Leicester, against the backdrop of a powerful racist campaign against the entry of Malawi Asians to Britain. A series of racist murders followed. In Southall, west London, in an area of major Punjabi settlement, a young man, Gurdip Singh Chaggar, was struck down by a gang of drunken racist white youths. The Metropolitan Police commissioner rushed to say that it was not necessarily racially motivated. A leading fascist and Blackburn councillor, John Kingsley Read, celebrated the murder of Chaggar with the notorious phrase 'One down, one million to go'. As a historian writes, 'This senseless murder made most of the members of the local Asian community realise that they were being overly optimistic in thinking racism would subside... Out of this traumatic experience arose the Southall Youth Movement'.[75]

The Southall Youth Movement considered itself more radical than the 'old guard' who were connected with the IWAs and the Communist Party. Many members of the youth movements had moved in and out of Trotskyist organisations, and although some later ended up hostile to the far left, there is no doubt that they were influenced by its politics and methods. The success of a mass mobilisation initiated by the International Socialists in stopping the National Front from marching through a black area of Lewisham had been followed by the rise of the Anti Nazi League and Rock Against Racism, and the strategy of building mass organisation and direct action dominated the political culture.[76]

A flavour of the times and the rapid development of the Southall Youth Movement is reflected in this contemporary report:

> The emergence of a militant anti-racist Indian youth movement in Southall in the last few weeks took the entire local left by surprise. In fact, youth organisation was the inevitable conclusion to the spontaneous youth movement that sprung to life in the hours and days following the brutal murder of Gurdip Singh Chaggar in the heart of Southall... The Southall Youth Movement...has brought out hundreds on a number of demonstrations... Further the Southall youth astonished...by organising a mass sitdown in Piccadilly Circus on the 11 July [1976] demonstration when two of their number were arrested for chasing racists.[77]

A Sivanandan, commenting on the period, pointed out that:

> Various youth movements sprang up from this initiative—whenever and wherever there was a need and in response to specific circumstances. But since these circumstances were invariably connected with fascist attacks and murders, and/or police inability either to protect or apprehend...the youth movements tended to centre largely around the defence of these communities, and their organisations to reflect that purpose.[78]

Youth movements were established in Luton, Nottingham, Leicester, Manchester, Bradford, Sheffield and Birmingham and elsewhere.[79] There were several set up in London, for example among the Bangladeshi and Pakistani populations. The Bangladeshi Youth Movement was organised in response to the racist murder of Altab Ali in Whitechapel.

In Newham a youth movement was organised after the murder of 29 year old Akhtar Ali Baig. He was 'savagely attacked on East Ham High Street by a skinhead gang—two boys, two girls, aged 15 to 17—who stopped him, abused him and spat in his face before one of them, 17 year old Paul Mullery, pulled out a sheath knife and stabbed him in the heart. 'I've just gutted a Paki', Mullery was said to have boasted'.[80]

The youth movements had different ethnic and religious membership reflecting the geographical area which they operated from, but, as Anandi Ramamurthy has pointed out, they all 'worked with white anti-racists'.[81]

It was members of the Bradford Youth Movement who came to national prominence. In the summer of 1981 there were rumours that the Asian community was to be the target of an organised fascist attack (not for the first or last time). The youth put in preparations for self-defence, much in the manner of the Cardiff seamen over 60 years before. Petrol bombs were discovered by the police on some waste ground. Twelve members of the Bradford Youth Movement were arrested and charged with conspiracy to cause an explosion and endanger lives—a charge of 'terrorism' up to then more commonly used against Irish Catholics.[82]

'The Bradford 12' were put on trial a year later, prompting and inspiring a huge political campaign in their defence. Over half of the defendants came from Muslim families.[83] Their lawyers ran what was seen as an audacious defence—rather than lodge a guilty plea they would argue that the 12 had been acting in legitimate self-defence and in defence of their communities. The jury agreed with them and the Bradford 12 were acquitted.[84]

Although the youth movements could incorporate and unify activists across different faith backgrounds, it would be a simplification to describe them as purely secular movements. Members of the youth movements could hold strong religious convictions or be influenced by the religious cultures of their families.[85] Tariq Mehmood looking back explains that:

> Most of the people in the youth movements were religious, but religion was not an issue for the members, it was their own affair. Many Sikhs, Hindus and Christians helped to protect mosques, as Muslims did of temples when they were attacked. We had very close relationships with gurdwaras and mosques. There were many among the Muslim [members] who kept all fasts... The unity was in anti-racism and anti-imperialism... Ishaq Mohammed Kazi came to me about the question of God. Two weeks later he was in jail as part of the Bradford 12... Any divisions were political, either Labour Party or left party. Or else caste or national.[86]

The youth movements went into decline through the 1980s, partly as a result of the general downturn in workers' struggles that removed a unifying outward-looking focus for Asian youth. Another weighty factor in their decline was the 'carrot' dangled by substantial state funding of 'community' resources and the consequent co-option of activists. This state funding was also increasingly organised on ethnic and religious lines.

It is argued that the Rushdie affair in 1988-89 had a decisive and destructive polarising effect. On the one hand Conservative forces in the Muslim communities campaigned against his novel *The Satanic Verses* as 'sacrilegious' and supported an Iranian fatwa against him, while on the other the media launched a wave of Islamaphobia which led to Muslims of all sorts being taunted with the chant, 'Rushdie'. Many youth movement members or ex-members were divided on where they stood, (or, as one activist put it, 'there was no middle ground left'.[87]) However, the common interpretation that the response to *The Satanic Verses* desecularised the youth movements and set in motion a wholly reactionary religious identity ignores political and organisational splits and stresses that were already in existence. It would be more accurate to say that Rushdie exposed a decline that had been in motion for some time. This was a downward trend mirrored in the other social movements that had sprung up in the 1970s, for example among women.

It is also increasingly clear that the assertion of a religious identity in the face of Islamophobia or anti-Muslim racism contains a strong positive element and the potential to engage in militant mass action with others, religious or otherwise. It would be wholly wrong to counterpose the politics of the youth movements against those of today's anti-war movement. They should not be placed in opposition to one another—if anything they should be regarded as varied manifestations of a militant and proud tradition.

The youth movements should be viewed in the broader sweep of the history of struggles of working class Muslims in Britain. As such they became part of an historical and political continuum set in motion many decades previously. From the courageous and radical struggles by the pioneering seamen and their families, through the tenacious and uncompromising struggles of the factory workers to the radical formations against fascism and racism, this is a history that anyone can be proud of. The future chapter in this narrative is already in the making.

In all the periods I describe groups of black workers were defending themselves, moving into struggle and asserting their rights. They all demanded solidarity from the wider working class—sometimes they gained it; sometimes they didn't. The role of the left, of anti-imperialists and anti-racists, was crucial to how much solidarity was delivered, to the degree to which racist attitudes were challenged, and whether or not the struggles of black workers began to interact with the class struggles in general. The same remains true today.

NOTES

1: I would like to dedicate this article out of respect to Peter Fryer who died on 31 October 2006. His book *Staying Power* remains unsurpassed in the study of British black history.

2: For more on my analysis of Muslims and the war on terror see 'Racism: Myths and Realities', *International Socialism* 95 (Summer 2002); 'Racism', in Farah Reza (ed), *Anti Imperialism: A Guide for the Movement* (Bookmarks, 2003); and 'Racism: A Boost for the Bigots', *Socialist Review*, November 2005, http://www.socialistreview.org.uk/article.php?articlenumber=9579

3: For good accounts of this early history see Humayun Ansari, *The Infidel Within: Muslims in Britain since 1800* (Hurst & Company, 2004), and Nabil Matar, *Turks, Moors & Englishmen in the Age of Discovery* (Columbia University Press, 1999).

4: Richard I Lawless, *From Ta'izz to Tyneside: An Arab Community in the North East of England During the Early 20th Century* (University of Exeter Press, 1995), p31.

5: In the east London docks in the early 1940s there were still Somali and Bangladeshi cafes open along Cable Street, giving rise to speculation that Muslim seamen may have taken part in the 1936 Battle of Cable Street against Mosley's fascists.

6: Lawless, as above, p48.

7: As above, p220.

8: Kenneth Little, *Negroes in Britain* (Routledge and Kegan Paul, 1972), pp171-172.

9: Humayun Ansari, as above, pp60, 61.

10: Colin Holmes, *John Bull's Island: Immigration & British Society, 1871—1971* (Macmillan, 1988), p106.

11: See Rozina Visram, *Asians in Britain 400 Years of History* (Pluto Press, 2002), pp304-319.

12: Little, as above, p127.

13: As above, p104.

14: As above.

15: Havelock Wilson started off as a militant fighter, a working activist like Tom Mann, but moved to the right and by the end of the First World War was getting secret payments from an anti-Labour pro-empire organisation.

16: Kenneth Lunn, 'Race Relations or Industrial Relations?: Race and Labour in Britain, 1880-1950', in Kenneth Lunn (ed), *Race and Labour in 20th Century Britain* (Frank Cass, 1985), p12.

17: As above, p16.

18: See Kenneth Little for details of racism directed against relationships between Arab sailors and white women. The white women were denigrated as either prostitutes or 'loose women'. Little in his surveys finds there was a cross-section of women married to Arab men: 'It would be a mistake to assume that the origins of all the Loudoun Square womenfolk are of such "poor class". There are examples of girls coming straight from middle class families whose marriage to a coloured man has proved socially inauspicious from the point of view of parents or friends, and who as a consequence, partly for convenience, partly through social pressure, were obliged to move to the coloured quarter of the town. With the arrival of children their position in the district became consolidated more or less for good. Other whites have arrived here in a variety of ways. A few have left home from a spirit of adventure, or because they have found the ideas and customs of their original social group too restrictive and have "taken up" with a coloured man'—Little, pp136-137. Lawless in his book on the South Shields Muslims quotes articulate and well argued letters from white wives in response to racist attacks in the local press. One, who signed herself 'White Woman', replied to an attack on 'half caste' children, 'No matter what colour we are all flesh and blood... As for our kiddies being outcastes I think those who say that do not know the meaning of the word; one thing we can send our children to school clean and tidy, and they can come home to a good dinner... If the white men were out of the coloured man's country, we would be quite willing to go back with our men to their country.' Quoted in Lawless, pp186-187. Lawless also reproduces posed family photos from the 1930s that visually demonstrate that the Arabs and their families considered themselves wholly 'respectable' members of the working class.

19: Trades Union Congress Minutes 1925, pp100-101, www.unionhistory.info/reports

20: Kenneth Lunn, as above, p12.

21: Lawless, as above, p92.

22: Peter Fryer, *Staying Power: The History of Black People in Britain* (Pluto Press, 1984), p299.

23: Earnest Marke, *In Troubled Waters: Memoirs of my Seventy Years in England!* (Karia Press, 1986).

24: Chanie Rosenberg, *1919: Britain on the Brink of Revolution* (Bookmarks 1987), p38.

25: Jacqueline Jenkinson, 'The Glasgow Race Disturbances of 1919', in Kenneth Lunn (ed), as above, p65.

26: Quoted in Fryer, as above, p306.

27: As above, p306.

28: As above, p307.

29: Neil Evans, 'Regulating the Reserve Army: Arabs, Blacks and the Local State in Cardiff, 1919-45', in Kenneth Lunn (ed), as above, p73.

30: Fryer, as above, p304.

31: Lawless, as above, p81. At the 1925 Trades Union Congress a seamen's union leader in his speech dramatically 'produced some clubs and other weapons that [he said] the Arabs and Somalis took down to the shipping office'. See TUC website above.

32: Fryer, as above, p300.

33: As above.

34: *Workers' Dreadnought*, Issue 7, June 1919. During this time Pankhurst employed black radical poet Claude McKay as a journalist, as well as a black sailor, Reuben Samuels.

35: See Marke, as above, pp30, 31, for an account of how he was helped by a local woman to escape mob attack and on one occasion was rescued from a beating by a group of women factory workers.

36: Visram, as above, p204.

37: Evans, as above, p80.

38: Lawless, as above, pp251-2.

39: Evans, as above, p88.

40: As above, p102.

41: *Negro Worker*, April-May 1933 (nos 4-5, vol 3). Four years earlier Harry O'Connell had been sentenced for eight months in jail after taking part in an Arab and Somali picket in South Shields that led to a violent confrontation with local NUS officials and the police (see Lawless, p138). An Arab boarding house owner Ali Said, who had emerged as a forceful leader allied to O'Connell, was sentenced to 16 months hard labour with a recommendation for deportation at the end of his sentence (Lawless, p147). A photograph from the time shows maybe 40 Arab and white members of the Seamen's Minority Movement posing outside the Minority Movement's offices in South Shields (Lawless, plate 5).

42: Evans, as above, p98. During the 1920s a Gujarati communist, Upadhyaya (Paddy), had attempted to organise 'lascars' in Britain into the Indian Seamen's Union. His leaflets were translated into several Indian languages by the imam of the Ahmadiya Mosque in Southfields, south west London. See Visram, p231.

43: Ansari, as above, p113.

44: See Hakim Adi and Marika Sherwood, *The 1945 Manchester Pan-African Congress Revisited* (New Beacon Books, 1995), p119.

45: See Evans, as above, p114. During this period Cardiff Muslims successfully lobbied for a special section in Ely Cemetery to be set aside for them (see Evans, p101).

46: Ansari, as above, p116.

47: See Lawless, as above, p246 (the Sheffield Yemeni's most famous son is the boxer Prince Naseem—full name Naseem Salom Ali Hameed).

48: Duncan Campbell, 'Seaman Wrongly Hanged in 1952', *Guardian*, 25 February 1998. See also the case of the late 1980s miscarriage of justice concerning 'The Cardiff Three', three black men, one of them named Yusef Abdullahi, who were framed for murder. In both cases the real murderers were eventually identified.

49: Visram, as above, p236.

50: As above, p239.

51: As above, pp267-8.

52: As above, p269.

53: As above, p271.

54: Robert Moore, *Racism and Black Resistance in Britain* (Pluto Press, 1975), p7.

55: Ansari, as above, p151.

56: Muhammad Anwar, *British Pakistanis: Demographic and Economic Position* (Centre for Research in Ethnic Relations, 1996), pp7,8. (In the 2001 census the number of Pakistanis in Britain was estimated at 658,000).

57: As above, p273.

58: Dilip Hiro, *Black British, White British: A History of Race Relations in Britain* (Grafton, 1991), p140.

59: As above, pp139—140.

60: As above, p20.

61: As above, pp269-270.

62: Douglas Tilbe, *The Ugandan Asian Crisis* (Community and Race Relations Unit of the British Council of Churches, 1972), p9.

63: As above, p4.

64: From 1968 to 1978, Leicester received more than 20,000 displaced East African Asians, more than anywhere else in the country (Leicester City Council figures).

65: Tony Cliff and Donny Gluckstein, *The Labour Party—A Marxist History* (Bookmarks, 1988), pp308-309.

66: Kim Gordon, *Black Nationalism and Socialism* (SWP, 1979), p69.

67: Amrit Wilson, *Finding A Voice: Asian Women in Britain* (Virago, 1978), p58.

68: Crisis Special Report, 'Rascism: Who Profits?', Counter Information Services *CIS Anti Report*, no 16 (Autumn 1976), p22.

69: As above.

70: Jack Dromey and Graham Taylor, *Grunwick: The Workers' Story* (Lawrence and Wishart, 1978), p102.

71: As above, p102.

72: As above, p103.

73: As above, p198.

74: Significant soldidarity was subsequently delivered in 1980 to Asian women workers on strike at the Chix bubble gum factory in Slough.

75: Dilip Hiro, as above, p169.

76: As Ramamurthy records, 'Among the founding members of the Bradford Asian Youth Movement were young Asians who had left the International Socialists (IS, forerunner of the Socialist Workers Party, Militant and the Revolutionary Communist Group). Anandi Ramamurthy, 'The Politics of Britain's Asian Youth Movements', *Race & Class* (Institute of Race Relations), vol 48, 2006, p43.

77: John Rose, 'The Southall Youth Movement', in *International Socialism* 91 (first series), September 1976, pp5-6. An important role in leading the sitdown was played by an Indian female International Socialists activist.

78: A Sivanandan, *A Different Hunger: Writings on Black Resistance* (Pluto Press, 1987), p40.

79: Ramamurthy, as above, p44 (see also the Tandana-Glowworm digitalised archive of Asian Youth Movement political ephemera at www.tandana.org).

80: *From Newham: the forging of a black community* (Newham Monitoring Project, 1991), p40.

81: Ramamurthy, as above, p44.

82: As above, p53.

83: See 'Reflecting on the Trial of the Decade: The Bradford Twelve', in *Race Today* (vol 14, no 4, August/September 1982), pp124-132. The two leading members of the group on trial were Gata Aura, who had previously been prominent in the successful fight of Rochdale Pakistani Anwar Ditta to overcome the immigration laws that were preventing her children joining her in Britain, and Tariq Mehmood Ali. Both had been members of the International Socialists. Tariq Mehmood is today a novelist and co-director of the award-winning film *Injustice*—a documentary exposing black deaths in custody. Another defendant was Marsha Singh, who is now a local Labour MP. Lawyers involved in the defence included Helena Kennedy (now a Labour peer) and Ruth Bundy (involved in the Stephen Lawrence inquiry).

84: The contrast between the successful Bradford 12 campaign and its outcome and the trials and 'exemplary' sentences handed down following the similar circumstances in Bradford in2001 is painfully obvious.

85: Ramamurthy, as above, p46.

86: Tariq Mehmood, email conversation with the author, 13 November 2006.

87: Ramamurthy, as above, p57.

Snapshots of capitalism today and tomorrow

Chris Harman

What is really happening to world capitalism today? In this article I use diagrams and graphs to provide some snapshots of the present shape of the system, deliberately minimising wider theoretical issues, which I have dealt with elsewhere.[1]

The first significant thing about the world economy is the way in which global economic growth, averaging out booms and recessions, has not only declined from the 'golden age of capitalism' in the 1950s and 1960s, but also from the levels known in the late 1970s and 1980s. This is shown in Figure 1.[2]

The decline in growth rates has been accompanied by a continual rise in the amount of investment per employed worker—what Marx called the 'organic composition of capital' (see Figure 2).

This ratio rises because competition between firms causes each to invest ever larger amounts in means of production per worker employed in order to raise labour productivity and keep ahead of its rivals. The amount of value that goes into investment rises much more quickly than the amount of new value created by the workforce.

Total material output may rise (assuming there is not a recession), but there is a fall in the value—and ultimately the price the producing firm gets—for each unit of output. Hence the plummeting in recent years of the prices of things produced in high investment industries like personal computers, televisions and DVD players.

Figure 1: World GDP per capita growth 1961-2003 (annual change in percent)

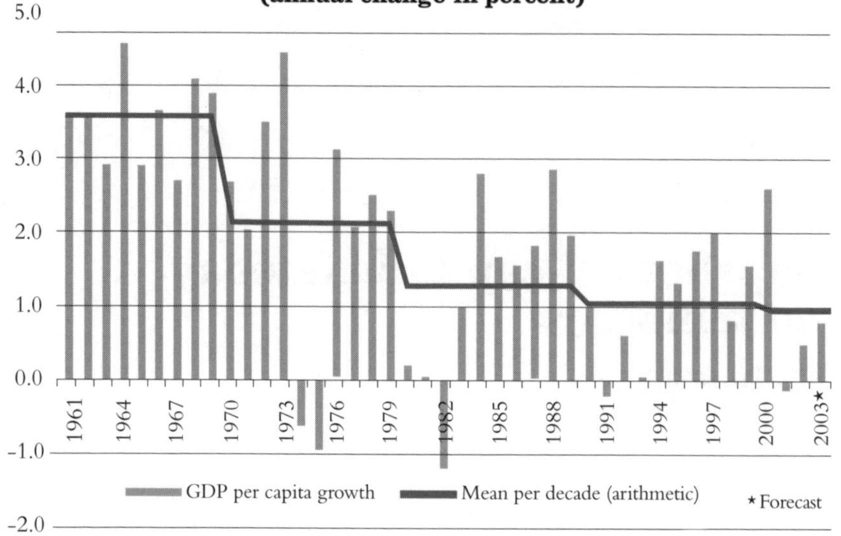

Sources: World Bank, ***World Development Indicators 2003*** *(online version) and World Bank,* ***Global Economic Prospects 2004.***

Figure 2: Capital-labour ratio (thousands of 1990 dollars per hour): Europe (Germany, France and the UK) and the United States, all firms

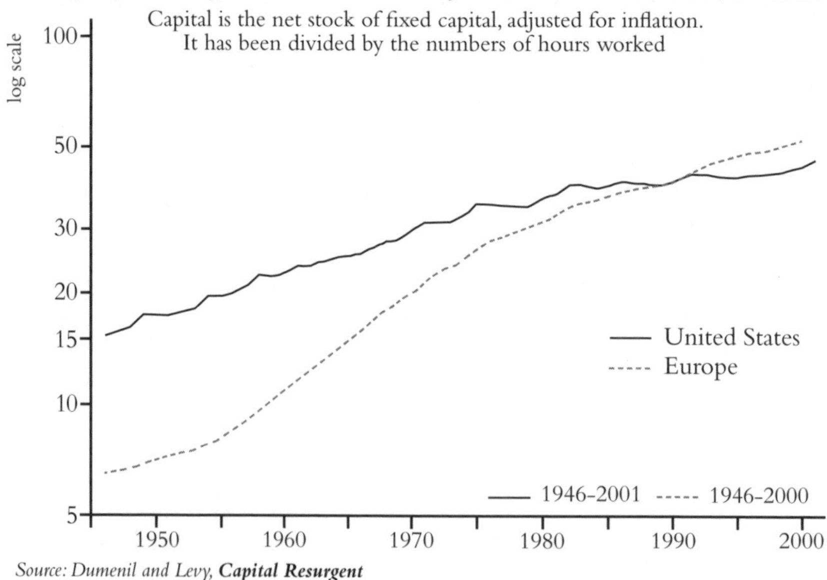

Source: Dumenil and Levy, ***Capital Resurgent***

So through the system as a whole total investment rises more rapidly than value produced. But profits come from this value. There will be a tendency of the ratio of profits to investment to decline unless capitalists can increase the share of the value going to themselves rather than to workers. This is Marx's well known 'tendency of the rate of profit to fall'.[3] The figures for the last three decades show the tendency at work for manufacturing industry (Figure 3).

Figure 3: US, Japanese and German manufacturing net profit rates 1949-2001

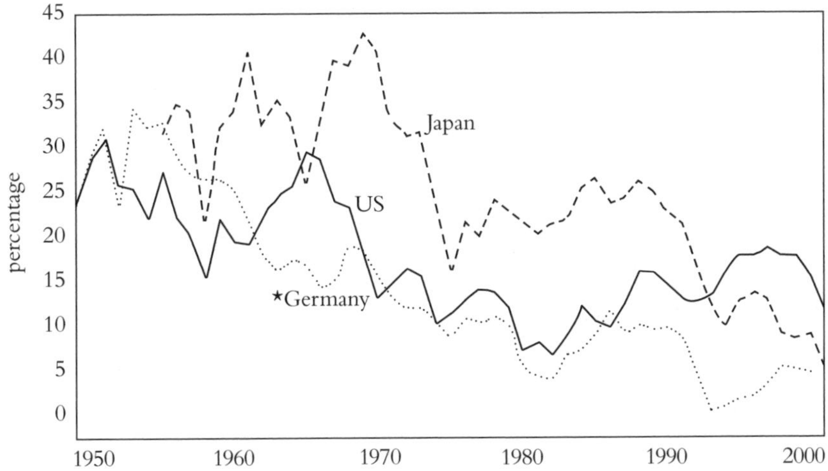

*Profit rate for Germany covers West Germany 1950-90 and Germany 1991-2000

Source: Robert Brenner, The Economics of Global Turbulence, 2006 edition, p7

Such falls in the rate of profits necessary have three consequences:

- Increased competition between capitalists
- Increased efforts by capitalists to put pressure on workers and other exploited groups
- Increased instability of the system as a whole

Global competition

One of the most significant developments in the last four decades has been the rise of the multinationals. The top 500 multinationals dominate international business, accounting for over 90 percent of the world's FDI and nearly half its trade.

UNCTAD reported in 1999 that 'the world's 60,000 multinational companies and their 500,000 local partners now control a quarter of the world's total output, amounting to $11 trillion. More than half of that output is produced by the top 100 multinationals…'[4] UNCTAD added in 2002 that '29 of the world's 100 largest economic entities are transnational corporations' if the output of corporations and countries is compared.[5]

Such developments have led many commentators to conclude that the multinationals are big enough not to care about the state. But this is wrong on three counts.

• The most important states are still much bigger than the biggest multinationals. There are 44 states (including Turkey, Egypt, Thailand and Argentina) with bigger economies than the biggest multinational, Exxon, which has only 0.75 percent of the output of the US and 3 percent of that of Germany.

• All the multinationals depend upon states as bases from which to operate globally.

Figure 4 shows the average 'transnationality' of corporations, a composite measurement of the degree to which their markets, workforces and investments are outside their home country.

Figure 4: Average Transnationality of the world's largest transnational corporations (TNCs), 2003

Top 100 TNCs	55.8
Top 50 TNCs	47.8
Those based in:	
United States	45.8
United Kingdom	69.2
Japan	42.8
France	59.5
Germany	49.0
Small European countries	72.2

Source: UNCTAD/Erasmus University database, (Ratio of overseas to domestic assets, sales and employment) see UNCTAD, ***World Investment Report 2001***

These figures are sometimes said to show how little multinationals depend on a national base. But in fact they show that the top 50 multinationals still rely on their home base for over half their business. And this dependence increases every time the world economy slows down or goes into recession—see Figure 5.

Figure 5: Average transnationality index for the world's 100 largest TNCs 1990-1999

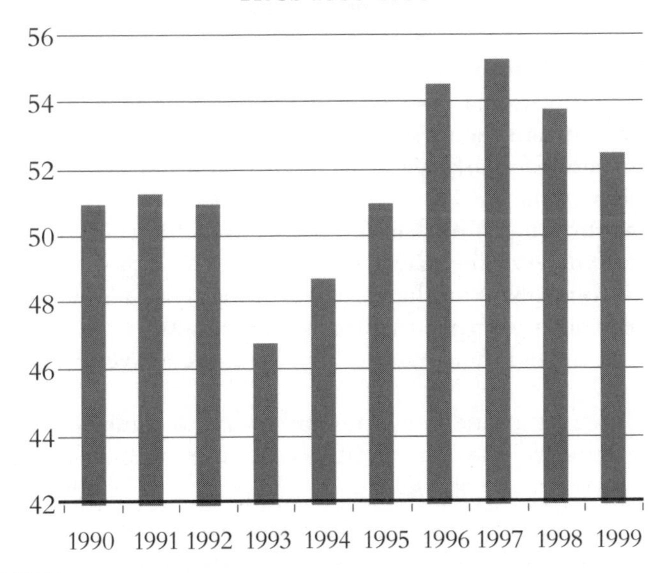

Source: UNCTAD

In other words, the national state remains very important to multinationals, particularly at times of economic crisis.

Multinationals are dependent on national states to protect their global interests. There is no world state to do so. And so each looks to a state (or sometimes a group of states like the European Union) to push for its interests when it comes to trade negotiations (for instance through the WTO), exchange rates between currencies, the allocation of government contracts, protection against expropriation, the defence of intellectual property rights and the enforcement of debt repayments.

The hierarchy of national capitalisms

The playing field on which states seek to advance the interests of domestically based multinationals is not even.

At the top of the hierarchy are those who are most powerful in negotiations with particular trade partners, and at the bottom those who find themselves in the weakest position. The multinationals based in the states towards the top find they have a political edge over firms based towards the bottom when it comes not only to getting the best trade deals but also to important other associated issues—opening up countries to their investment, accepting their interpretations of intellectual copyright, maintaining low levels of taxation on remitted profits, getting advantageous exchange rates.[6]

Uneven development

The hierarchy of national capitalisms is not a static one. Economies grow at different speeds and their firms have different degrees of success in penetrating international markets and accumulating investments beyond their national bases.

The multinationals react in three ways to the shifts in the world economic pecking order of the states.

- They try to compensate for their state's growing weakness by putting pressure on their workers to make them more competitive.
- They seek to spread their bets by increasing their investments in other states.
- They pressurise their state to use political means to compensate for weakening economic weight—the political use of economic aid, pressures through the world financial system and displays of military power.

Figure 6: Share of world exports (percent)

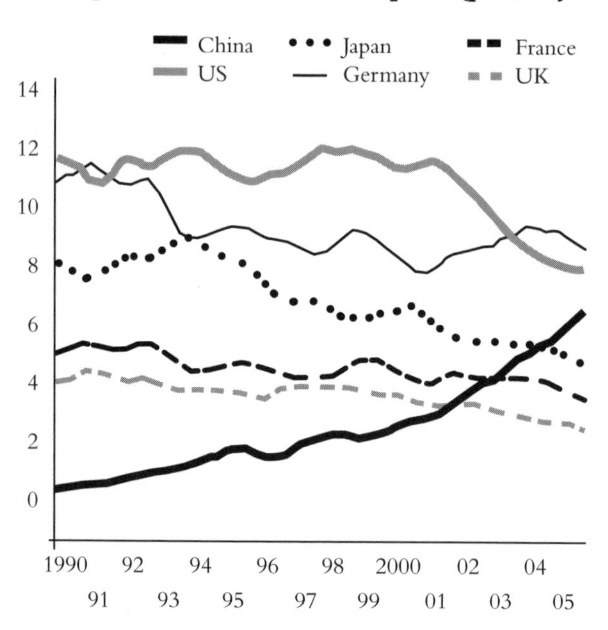

Source: IMF, UNCTAD, McKinsey

The terrain of competitive struggle

Capitalism is a system in which investment chases profit. So figures for foreign investment provide an indication of where capitalists see the most likely sources of stable, long term profitability. Figures 7 and 8 for Foreign Direct Investment provide a glimpse of where that profitability has been sought in recent years.

Figure 7 shows that on average more than two thirds of the great bulk of overseas investment has been to already industrially advanced countries—the so-called 'triad' of North America, Japan and Europe—with a huge upsurge towards them in the boom of the late 1990s and a falling back to a figure still twice that of the rest of the world since. These countries are not only where the wealth of the world is concentrated, but also where capitalists expect to be able to gain most profit from further exploitation. Intercapitalist competition is, above all, competition to control marketing and investment opportunities in these countries.

The old 'third worldist' notion that capitalism lives mainly off the exploitation of the poorer countries of the 'Global South' does not fit with the realities of the system today. Of course, capitalists take what they can from the poorer countries ('every little helps') and this has a terrible effect on the people of those countries. But it is not the most important sort of exploitation.

A third of investment is to the 'Global South'. But here too a handful of countries are important to capital, while many are marginal to it.

Nearly half of the foreign investment to these countries (or about one sixth of worldwide investments) is concentrated in three places—China (including Hong Kong), Brazil and Mexico. By contrast the 176 poorest countries are targets for less than 8 percent of total world foreign investment. The pattern of 'Global South' manufacturing exports (Figure 8) shows the impact of this uneven distribution of investment.

This picture does not fully tell the story as regards capital's interests. There is also the question of the raw materials and, in particular, oil. This is behind the strategic importance of the Middle East and, to a lesser extent at a time of high oil and gas prices, Venezuela and parts of West Africa and, often forgotten, Russia.

But the sources of the major raw materials tend to be concentrated in the same handful of states that dominate the investment statistics. People often conceive of the poorest countries as suppliers of raw materials to the richest. But the reality is very different.

The US exported more than 80 million tons of cereals in 2000-2001, Asian countries only 15 million tonnes, South American countries only 17.5 million, and African countries only 3 million. Brazil is now the

Figure 7: Foreign Direct Investment inflows, global and by groups of economies 1980-2004 (billions of dollars)

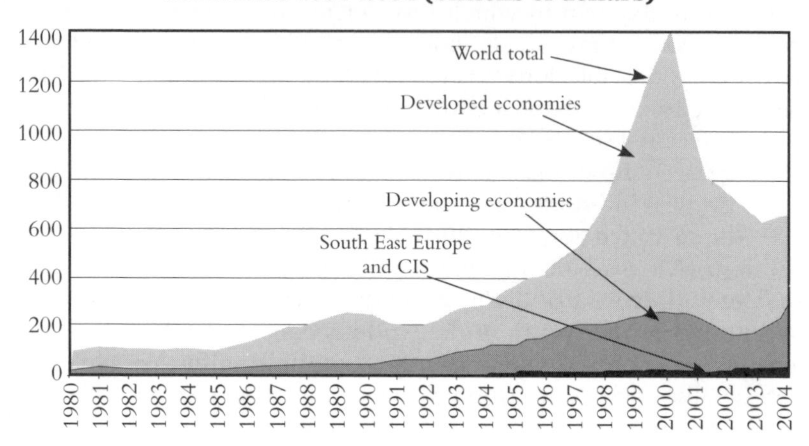

Source: UNCTAD, FDUTNC database (www.unctad.org/fdistatistics)

Figure 8: Distribution of developing countries' manufacturing exports total for 1990s (percent)

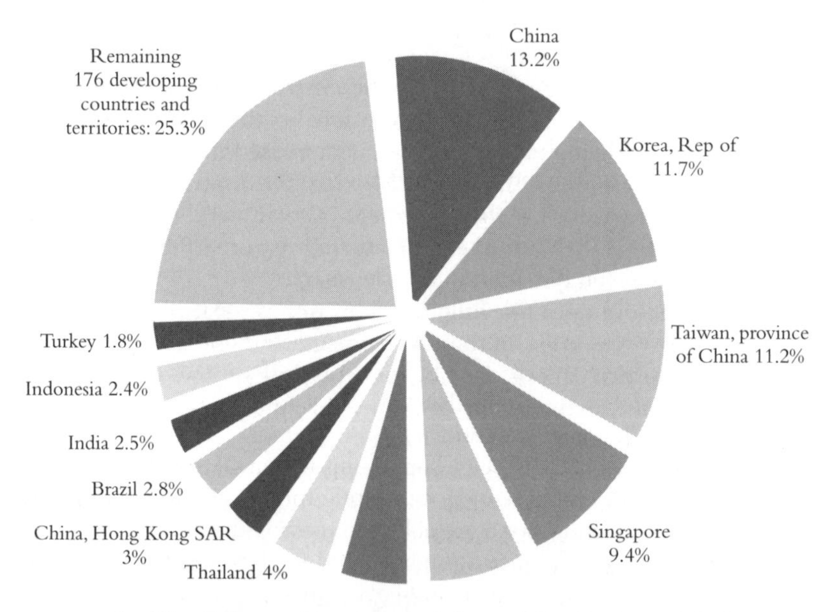

Combined share of top 12 countries and territories: 74.67%

Source: Based on UNCTAD, ***Handbook of Statistics 2002***

world's biggest sugar producer. The picture is not all that different with minerals. 'Among the top 10 non-fuel mineral exporters, only two, Chile and Brazil, are less developed countries, and they ranked ninth and tenth respectively'.[7] Most countries of the Global South are dependent on their exports of raw materials and foodstuffs—but that is not the same as the global system being dependent on them for more than a fraction of its profit-making and essential imports.

So a map of the world in terms of importance for capitalist exploitation would be dominated by Europe, North America, Japan, China, Brazil, Mexico and the three or four largest oil and gas producers

Centuries of pillage by the ruling classes of the advanced countries mean that not a lot of wealth remains in vast areas of the world. It is nonsense to claim, as New Labour does, that most Third World countries can trade their way out of poverty, since they have not been left with the resources necessary to trade successfully within the system as it exists today.

The US fights to retain its hegemony

In the 1980s the West European countries and Japan grew faster than the US. In the last decade it has been the other way round. The US ruling class has been able to achieve this turnaround through the use of three interrelated methods.

1: There has been a massive increase in the rate of exploitation of US workers .This is shown by the figures for real wages (Figure 9) and working hours (Figure 10). These are the figures give by the US Department of Labour. International Labour Organisation figures, calculated in a slightly different way, show a rise in the average working year in the US over the last quarter of a century from 1,883 hours in 1980 to 1,966 in 1997.[8]

2: The US has been relying on its dominance of the world financial system—entrenched by the dollar's role as the 'reserve currency' for other countries to borrow from the rest of the world—to bolster the US domestic economy. For more than a decade US consumption and investment have been rising much faster than domestic incomes or savings. The US has become the world's largest debtor nation (Figure 11).

Essentially what has been happening is that national banks in Japan, China, Korea and so on have been depositing money coming in from exports to the US in US treasury bonds, which then provide the basis for banks to lend to American capitalists and consumers —and for US based multinationals to undertake overseas investment, including in the countries lending to the US.

So the US economy has been able to keep expanding, despite a trade deficit now equal to around $800 billion (about £420 billion) a year.

Figure 9: Weekly Pay of US production workers (1996 dollars)

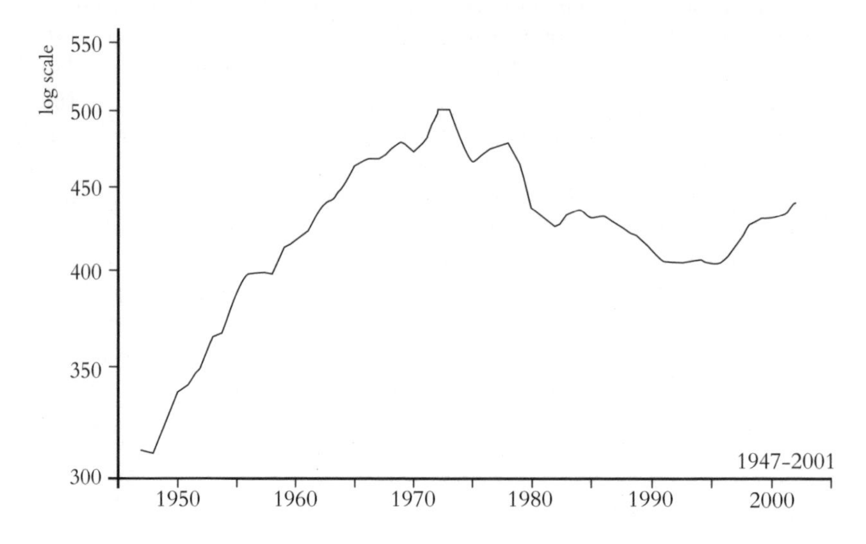

Source: Dumenil and Levy, ***Capital Resurgent***

Figure 10: Annual hours worked per worker, 2004

Koreans:	2,380
Mexicans:	1,848
Americans:	1,824
French:	1,441
Dutch:	1,357
Britain:	1,689

Source: US Department of Labour

US investments in the rest of the world are only worth 80 percent of foreign investment in the US—but nevertheless rake in a higher total in interest and profits. In effect capitalists and governments elsewhere in the world are paying a subsidy to the US economy in return for being able keep their funds there.

Figure 11: Net US Foreign Debt as percentage of GDP

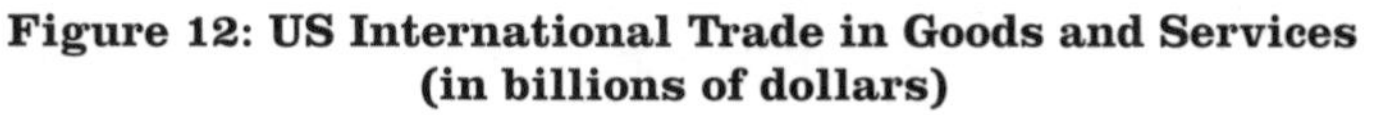

Figure 12: US International Trade in Goods and Services (in billions of dollars)

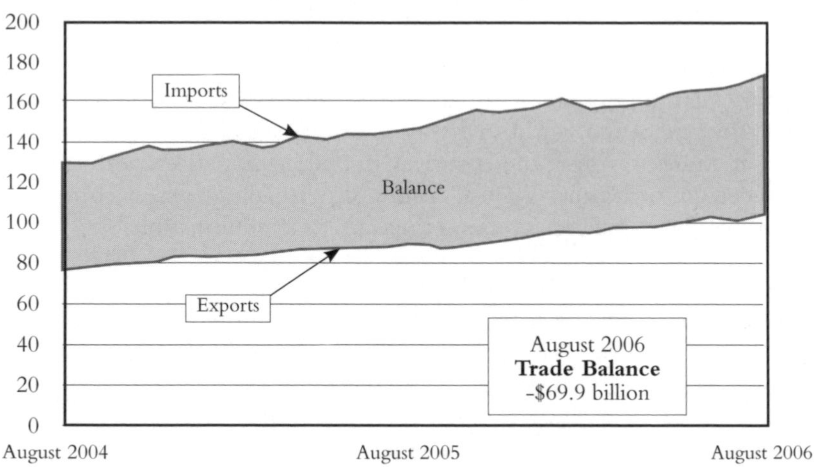

Source: US Census Bureau, foreign trade statistics, 12 October 2006

Capitalists and governments are not philanthropists. They only follow such a course because of the power of the US state.

3: Such use of this state power has been the third weapon used by the US ruling class in its struggle for hegemony. Its ideology may be neoliberal, but its practice at home has been rather different. It has been using the state to intervene in financial and economic matters to push through measures that protect the domestically based multinationals and banks, even while it demands other economies turn to neoliberal measures that reduce the role of their states.

• One function of an expansion in arms spending has been to provide a helping hand to the corporations: the Pentagon played a significant role in the reorganisation of the US computer industry to face up to the challenge from Japanese firms in the early 1990s, and the Clinton administration played an active part in encouraging the 1996 merger of Boeing and McDonnell Douglas to create an aerospace giant bigger than any European competitor.

• The Federal Reserve and successive governments have worked to try to achieve an exchange rate for the dollar (most notably through the Plaza Accord with Japan and Germany in the mid-1980s) favourable to US industry; the US treasury has used supposed bail outs for debt-burdened countries as the opportunity to strengthen the global influence of US financial corporations.

• Republican and Democrat administrations alike intervened to prevent the collapse of big companies: Chrysler in 1980, the Saving and Loans (the US equivalent of building societies) in the mid-1980s and Long Term Capital Management in 1998.

• Above all, the US state, with its military might, is seen as a tool that can shape the rest of the world in a way that suits US business interests, both when it comes to trying to get its way in trade negotiations with the other advanced countries and when it comes to persuading weaker countries to adopt neoliberal policies, opening them up to its multinationals.

Europe caught in the middle

European capitalism finds itself under pressure on two fronts. On the one side there is increasing competition from the Far East. Not only has China emerged as a major competitor across a wide range of industries—importing components from Japan and the 'tiger' economies, putting them together and then competing with European products elsewhere in the world. But Japanese capitalism has continued investing over the last 15 years, despite the stagnation of the Japanese economy.

On the other side is the pressure that comes from US-based capitalism, with its three decades of a rising rate of exploitation of its workforce. So although some of the mainland European countries have succeeded in raising their output per hour worked until it is higher than that in the US, the longer hours worked in the US mean that its output per worker is still considerably higher than Europe's.

This has been happening while European capitalists face the same pressure on the rate of profit as elsewhere. And their problems are aggravated by the means they used to maintain political stability in the aftermath of the Second World War—the institutionalisation of 'social partnership' through collaboration with the union bureaucracy, cemented by concessions to workers in terms of working hours, rights at work, welfare provision, pensions and so on. As Figure 13 shows, they are paying much more for welfare provision to maintain social peace than their American rivals.

All this creates political difficulties for them when they go on the offensive to increase their own rate of exploitation. But they feel they have no choice but to do so if they are going to protect their position in global

Figure 13: Welfare contributions as a percentage of labour costs 2005

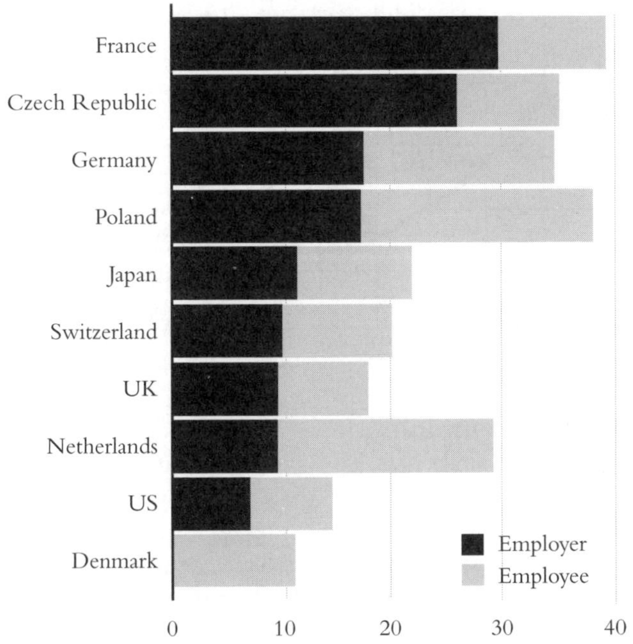

Source: Financial Times

markets. Hence they pressurise governments to implement neoliberal policies at home while they try to soften up their workforces by threatening to move production to Eastern Europe and elsewhere.

Germany is the biggest European economy—and still the world's biggest exporter. But German capitalism has had to turn on its workers in order to try to preserve its position. The BBC could report last year, 'Real wages have fallen dramatically and working hours are nearly back to 40 a week—to the point where some employers say they don't see much difference between the cost of hiring a German or British worker'.[9] What has been happening to German workers is shown clearly in Figure 14.

The same logic is at work for capitalists based in France, Britain, Italy, etc. They are faced with competition from capitalists based in the US, Japan, the East Asian tigers and China, all of which benefit from working hours at least 300 hours more than those in France and Germany. They will respond with one offensive after another against what they conceded to workers in the past to maintain 'social peace'—and the result could well be outbreaks of class struggle on a scale not known for decades.

Figure 14: German labour costs

Source: European Commission

Financial instability

The scale of US debt has provided an additional boost to financial speculation. Investors always look for quick profits elsewhere when there is downward pressure on profit rates in productive sectors of the economy.

The last decade has seen worldwide a growing dependence on new forms of speculative borrowing and lending—derivatives (see Figure 15). These began as ways for corporations and banks to protect themselves against unexpected changes in currency exchange rates and have since developed into a form of gambling on all sorts of possible economic and financial shifts. The 'hedge funds' that engage in such gambling are now multibillion concerns.

By mid-2004 the total value of the derivatives traded had already grown until it was more than six times the total GDP of the whole world. The derivatives market, because it is a global market, escapes regulation by any national government. There are recurrent fears in business circles of the damage to the financial system that would occur if there were a major mishap in the derivatives market, such as forced the bail-out of Long Term Capital Management eight years ago.

Figure 15: Derivatives at banks (national value, billions of dollars)

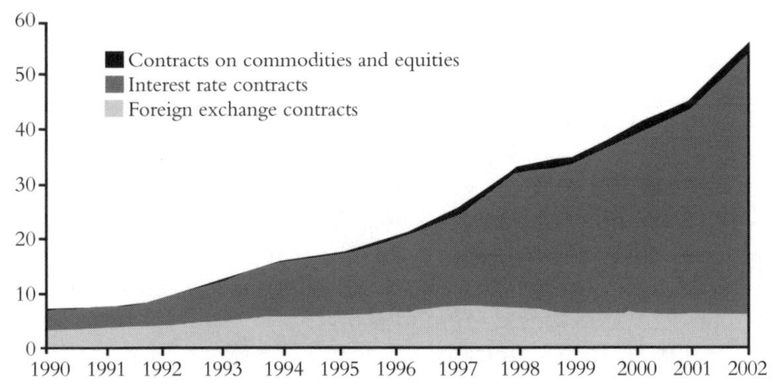

Source: ***Report of Condition and Income****, Federal Financial Institutions Examination Council*

The China question

A real and massive expansion of the Chinese economy has been taking place. But there are fears that it is being accompanied by some of the symptoms of a classic capitalist bubble.

The very high levels of investment are not matched by anything like the same rate of growth of the employed labour force: 'Between 1978 and 1993 employment expanded by 2.5 percent per annum, but between 1993 and 2004, when the investment share of GDP was much higher than in the 1980s, employment growth slowed to only slightly over 1 percent'.[10]

There is strong evidence that the rising ratio of capital investment to workers is exerting a downward pressure on profits, which is exacerbated by the competition between different firms (each linked to different multinationals) to get rid of excess supplies of goods. But these pressures on profitability are concealed by the willingness of the banking system to take on an ever greater number of bad debts. The official figures for 'non-performing loans' in the Chinese banking system vary between the official figure of 20 percent of the total loans, and some unofficial estimates suggesting they amount to 45 percent of GDP.[11] The potential for a massively destabilising crisis in the medium term is enormous—and the crisis would have an enormous impact on the whole world economy.

For the moment, though, Chinese growth is having more immediate effects on capitalism elsewhere. The massive growth has led to a sucking in of raw materials from elsewhere, pushing up the prices that firms everywhere in the world have to pay for them. At the same time the flood of consumer goods from China is exerting a downward pressure on the prices of consumer goods that these firms want to sell. This pressure exacerbates the problems world wide arising from the long term tendency of profit rates to decline.

A glimpse of the future

It is impossible to foresee how the contradictions shown in these snapshots work themselves out. But the key thing is not to pontificate over whether there will be another slump in the near future (even if it is worth noting that the old cycle with recessions roughly every ten years seems to have re-emerged since the early 1980s). Much more significant is the political impact such contradictions are bound to have.

• European-based capitals increasingly fear being caught in a nutcracker. Hence the increasing desperation of their political friends to impose neoliberal 'reforms' in welfare provision, pensions, working hours and education, even if this disrupts all the mediating structures (social democratic parties, trade union bureaucracies) that have bound workers to the system for decades

• The enormous expansion of the networks of credit, with less and less connection with the real world of production and trade, can only continue so long as there are no sudden panics—over exchange rates, over the threatened bankruptcy of some great multinational, over the capacity of a major country to cover its foreign debts, or over a sudden movement in raw material prices. Such panics could suddenly cause firms and banks to withdraw loans from each other, threatening a cumulative collapse of the whole credit system. Faced with fears for the financial system as a whole and of the impact on the multinationals based in their states, governments would be compelled to intervene, to use their political power for national capitalist ends, regardless of neoliberal ideology. But the rise of the multinationals and the massive expansion of cross-border economic actively make government intervention much more difficult than in the past.

• Domestically there will be more splits down the middle of national ruling classes as their members turn on each other, with each section trying to get the state to protect it, even if this means damaging other sections.

• Internationally states will increasingly see their political power—and an important component of that political power, their military might—as a way to protect 'their' firms' as opposed to those based in other states. An indication of the direction in which things are going is the attempt of the US state to guarantee a 'New American Century' by grabbing the country with the world's second biggest reserves of oil. So too is the increasing tension between Japan and China, and Russia's assertiveness over the bargaining power it gets from its gas reserves.

• So globalisation and neoliberal ideology do not mean the end of state intervention and of clashes between states—even if the clashes of interest between those towards the front of the global pecking order tend to be acted in bloody 'proxy' wars in countries much further back in that order.

Figures for arms expenditure show the political-military tendencies that are built into the system today more than anything else (Figure 16).

But it is not only US military spending that is rising, even though it dwarfs that of other powers.

There are currently two great belts of political instability. There is that stretching across sub-Saharan Africa. And, more important for the system as a whole (though not for the millions who have suffered from Africa's wars), there is the one stretching eastwards from the Mediterranean to the Indus and northwards into central Asia. We can expect the dynamics of intercapitalist competition to produce more military conflicts and political earthquakes as nationally based multinationals battle for survival in an unstable global economic system.

There will be the sudden explosion of political crises—and with them sudden splits within and between ruling classes. Lenin defined a 'pre-revolutionary situation' as one where the mass of people could not tolerate the old conditions any more, but neither could the ruling class. Bitter divisions within its ranks could suddenly snap the repressive and ideological ties holding the mass of people in check, allowing long concealed bitterness to come to the surface.

We are nowhere near that state of affairs today in any of the developed capitalist countries—nor for that matter in overwhelming majority of the less developed ones. But we have seen a few notable examples of Lenin's model in recent years, producing, if not full blown revolution, enormous popular mobilisations and political crises—Indonesia, Ecuador, Bolivia, Venezuela, Nepal, and most recently the southern Mexican city of Oaxaca. The 'snapshots' suggest that we will see many more in the decades ahead—and not only in places that are peripheral from the point of view of those who run the world system.

Figure 16: US military spending 1945-2008

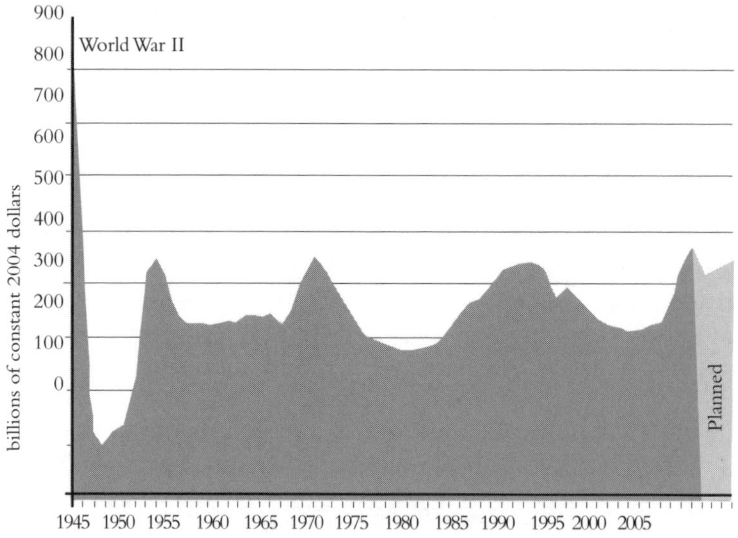

Based on SIPRI figures

NOTES

1: See my book, *Explaining the Crisis* (Bookmarks, 1984 [reissued 1997]), based upon four pieces from this journal in the early 1980s, and my articles, 'Poland and the Crisis of State Capitalism', *International Socialism* 1:94 and 1:95 (1977); 'Better a Good Insight than a Bad Theory', *International Socialism* 1:100 (1979); 'Where is Capitalism Going?, *International Socialism* 58 and 59 (Spring & Summer 1993); 'The State and Capitalism Today', *International Socialism* 51 (Summer 1991), available at www.isj.org.uk; 'Globalisation', *International Socialism* 73 (Winter 1996); 'Analysing Imperialism', *International Socialism* 99 (Summer 2003); and 'China's Economy and Europe's Crisis', *International Socialism* 109 (Winter 2006).

2: The diagram has been used before in this journal—see Alex Callinicos, 'Making Sense of Imperialism: A Reply to Leo Panitch and Sam Gindin', *International Socialism* 110 (Spring 2006).

3: I remind readers with more than a basic knowledge of Marxist economics that I am putting things as simply as I can here. For a much fuller discussion of the tendency of the rate of profit to fall and the countertendencies, see my *Explaining the Crisis*, as above, chapter one.

4: BBC report, 28 September 1999.

5: UNCTAD press release, on www.unctad.org/Templates/webflyer.asp?docid=2426&intItemID=2079&lang=1

6: For an attempted depiction of this hierarchy, see Valentino Piana, 'Hierarchical Structures in World Trade', Economics Web Institute (2004), http://www.economicswebinstitute.org/main.htm

7: John T Thoburn, *Tin in the World Economy* (Edinburgh, 1995).

8: www.ilo.org/public/english/bureau/inf/pr/1999/29.htm International Labour Organisation figures. The figures given by various sources vary considerably, depending on how they count part time working and whether they take into account unpaid overtime. So the OECD figures do not show the rise in the US working years, while other measures, based on reports from firms, show it as rising much more than do the ILO figures.

9: BBC report, 5 September 2005.

10: Kuijs and Wang, quoted in Nicholas R Lardy, 'China: Towards a Consumption-Driven Growth Path', *Policy Briefs in International Economics* (October 2006).

11: For a fuller discussion of the contradictory pressures in the Chinese economy, see my 'China's Economy and Europe's Crisis', *International Socialism* 109 (Winter 2006).

The return of strategy

Daniel Bensaid

Daniel Bensaid is a leading member of the Ligue Communiste Révolutionnaire (LCR) in France. This article takes up issues arising in a discussion on revolutionary strategy to be found in the LCRs theoretical journal Critique Communiste in March 2006[1] *and continued at a seminar in Paris in June. Other participants included the editor of Critique Communiste Antoine Artous, LCR members Cedric Durand and Francis Sitel, and Alex Callinicos of the British SWP. The issues involved ranged from the nature of socialist revolution today to the attitude taken to non-revolutionary but anti-neoliberal forces in France.*

There has been an 'eclipse' in the debate about strategy since the beginning of the 1980s, in contrast with the discussions prompted by the experiences in the 1970s of Chile and Portugal (and then Nicaragua and Central America). The neoliberal offensive made the 1980s at best a decade of social resistance, characterised by a defensiveness in the class struggle, even in those cases when popular democratic pressure forced dictatorships to give way—notably in Latin America.

The withdrawal from politics found expression in what could be called a 'social illusion', by analogy with the 'political illusion' of those criticised by the young Marx for thinking 'political' emancipation through the achievement of civil rights was the last word in 'human emancipation'. There was an illusion about the self-sufficiency of social movements reflected in the experiences after Seattle (1999) and the first World Social Forum in Porto Alegre (2001).

Simplifying somewhat, I call this the 'utopian moment' of social movements, which took different forms: utopias based on the regulation of free markets; Keynesian utopias; and above all neo-libertarian utopias, in which the world can be changed without taking power or by making do with counter-powers (John Holloway, Toni Negri, Richard Day).

The upturn in social struggles turned into political or electoral victories in Latin America—Venezuela and Bolivia. But in Europe the struggles ended in defeat, except with the movement against the CPE attacks on the rights of young workers. The push towards privatisation, reforms in social protection and the dismantling of social rights could not be prevented. This lack of social victories has caused expectations to turn once more towards political (mostly electoral) solutions, as the Italian elections showed.[2]

This 'return of politics' has led to a revival in debates about strategy. Witness the polemics round the books of Holloway, Negri and Michael Albert, and the differing appraisals of the Venezuelan process and of Lula's administration in Brazil. There has been the shift in the Zapatistas' orientation with the sixth declaration of the Selva Lacandona and the 'other campaign' in Mexico. The discussions around the project for a new LCR manifesto or Alex Callinicos's *Anticapitalist Manifesto*[3] belong in the same context. We are coming to the end of the phase of the big refusal and of stoical resistance—Holloway's 'scream' in the face of 'the mutilation of human lives by capitalism', slogans like 'The world is not a commodity' or 'Our world is not for sale'. We need to be specific about what the 'possible' world is and, above all, to explore how to get there.

There is strategy and strategy

Notions of strategy and tactics are military terms that were imported into the workers' movement—above all from the writings of Clausewitz or of Delbrück. However, their meaning has varied greatly. At one time strategy was the art of winning a battle, with tactics being no more than troop manoeuvres. Since then there has been no halt to the expansion of the field of strategy over time and space, from dynastic wars to national wars, from total war to global war. So we can make a distinction today between global strategy operating on a world scale and 'limited strategy' concerned with the struggle for the conquest of power within a particular area. In some ways, the theory of permanent revolution sketched out a global strategy. The revolution starts from the national arena (in one country) to expand to the continental and world level; it takes a decisive step with the conquest of political power but is prolonged and deepened by 'a cultural revolution'. It thus combines act and process, event and history.

This dimension of global strategy is even more important today than it was in the first half of the 20th century, faced as we are with powerful states whose economic and military strategies are worldwide. The emergence of new strategic areas at the continental or world level shows this. The dialectic of the permanent revolution (as against the theory of socialism in one country), in other words the intertwining of national, continental and world levels, is tighter than ever. One can seize the levers of power in one country (like Venezuela or Bolivia), but the question of continental strategy (etc) immediately becomes a matter of domestic policy—as in the Latin American discussions over Alba versus Alca,[a] the relationship to Mercosur, to the Andes Pact. More prosaically, in Europe resistance to neoliberal counter-reforms can be reinforced by the balance of forces at the national level and by legislative gains. But a transitional approach to public services, taxation, social protection, ecology has to be pitched at the European level from the outset.[4]

Strategic hypotheses

I confine myself here to the question of what I have called 'the limited strategy'—the struggle for the conquest of political power at the national level. The framework of globalisation can weaken national states and some transfers of sovereignty take place. But the national rung, which structures class relationships and attaches a territory to a state, remains the decisive rung in the sliding scale of strategic spaces.

Let us straightaway put aside the criticisms from those like John Holloway and Cédric Durand[5] that ascribe to us a 'stagist' vision of the revolutionary process, according to which we would make the seizure of power the 'absolute precondition' for any social transformation. The argument is either a caricature or it stems from ignorance. Vaulting from a standing start is not something we have ever been keen on.

The concepts of the united front, of transitional demands and of the workers' government—defended not just by Trotsky but by Thalheimer, Radek and Clara Zetkin[6]—have a precise aim. This is to link the event to its preparatory conditions, revolution to reforms, the goal to the movement. The Gramscian notions of hegemony and 'war of position' operate along the same lines.[7] The opposition between the East (where power would be easier to conquer but more difficult to maintain) and the West arises from the same concern.[8] We have never been admirers of the theory of the mere collapse of the system.[9]

---

a: Alba—the Bolivarian Alternative for Latin America and the Caribbean, proposed by Chavez. Alca—the Free Trade Area of the Americas, proposed by the US.

We have insisted on the role of the 'subjective factor' as against both the spontaneist view of the revolutionary process and the structuralist immobilism of the 1960s. Our insistence is not on a 'model' but on what we have called 'strategic hypotheses'.[10] Models are something to be copied; they are instructions for use. A hypothesis is a guide to action that starts from past experience but is open and can be modified in the light of new experience or unexpected circumstances. Our concern therefore is not to speculate but to see what we can take from past experience, the only material at our disposal. But we always have to recognise that it is necessarily poorer than the present and the future if revolutionaries are to avoid the risk of doing what the generals are said to do—always fight the last war.

Our starting point lies in the great revolutionary experiences of the 20th century—the Russian Revolution, the Chinese Revolution, the German Revolution, the popular fronts, the Spanish Civil War, the Vietnamese war of liberation, May 1968, Portugal, Chile. We have used them to distinguish between two major hypotheses, or scenarios: that of the insurrectional general strike and that of the extended popular war. They encapsulate two types of crisis, two forms of dual power, two ways of resolving the crisis.

As far as the insurrectional general strike is concerned, dual power takes a mainly urban form, of the Commune variety—not just the Paris Commune, but the Petrograd Soviet, the insurrections in Hamburg in 1923, Canton in 1927, Barcelona in 1936. Dual power cannot last long in a concentrated area. Confrontation therefore leads to a rapid resolution, although this may in turn lead to a prolonged confrontation: civil war in Russia, the liberation war in Vietnam after the 1945 insurrection. In this scenario the task of demoralising the army and organising the soldiers plays an important part. Among the more recent and meaningful experiences in this respect were the soldiers' committees in France, the SUV 'Soldiers united will win' movement in Portugal in 1995, and the conspiratorial work of the MIR[b] in the Chilean army in 1972-73.

In the case of the extended popular war strategy, the issue is one of territorial dual power through liberated and self-administered zones, which can last much longer. Mao understood the conditions for this as early as his 1927 pamphlet *Why is it that Red Political Power can Exist in China?* and the experience of the Yenan Republic[c] shows how it operates.

According to the insurrectionary general strike scenario, the organs of alternative power are socially determined by urban conditions; according

---

b: MIR—Chilean Movement of the Revolutionary Left.

c: The remote region of China run by the Chinese Communists from the mid-1930s to their taking of Beijing in 1949.

to the extended popular war scenario, they are centralised in the (predominantly peasant) 'people's army'.

There are a whole range of variants and intermediary combinations between these two hypotheses in their ideal form. So the Cuban Revolution made the guerrilla foco ('focus') the link between the kernel of the rebel army and attempts to organise and call urban general strikes in Havana and Santiago.[11] The relationship between the two was problematic, as shown in the correspondence of Frank Païs,[d] Daniel Ramos Latour and Che himself about the tensions between 'the sierra' and 'the plain'. Retrospectively, the official narrative privileged the heroic epic of the *Granma*[e] and its survivors. This contributed to bolstering the legitimacy of that element in the 26 July Movement and of the ruling Castro group, but was detrimental to a more complex understanding of the process.

This simplified version of history was set up as a model for rural guerrilla war and inspired the experiences of the 1960s in Peru, Venezuela, Nicaragua, Colombia, Bolivia. The deaths of De La Puente and Lobatòn in Peru (1965), Camillo Torres in Colombia (1966), Yon Sosa and Lucio Cabañas in Mexico, Carlos Marighela and Lamarca in Brazil, the tragic expedition of Che to Bolivia, the near annihilation of the Sandinistas in 1963 and 1969, the disaster of Teoponte in Bolivia in 1970, mark the end of that cycle.

The strategic hypothesis of the Argentinian PRT[f] and the MIR in Chile made greater use, at the beginning of the 1970s, of the Vietnamese example of extended popular war (and, in the PRT's case, of a mythic version of the Algerian war of liberation). The history of the Sandinista front up to its victory over the Somoza dictatorship in 1979 shows a mixture of different outlooks. The Prolonged People's War tendency of Tomàs Borge stressed the development of a guerrilla presence in the mountains and the need for a long period of gradually accumulating forces. The Proletariat Tendency of Jaime Wheelock insisted on the social effects of capitalist development in Nicaragua and on the strengthening of the working class while retaining the perspective of a prolonged accumulation of forces with a view to an 'insurrectional moment'. The 'Tercerist' Tendency of the Ortega brothers was a synthesis of the other two tendencies which allowed for coordination between the southern front and the uprising in Managua.

Looking back, Humberto Ortega summed up the differences thus:

---

d: The leader of the urban resistance in Cuba, killed in 1958 shortly before the victory of the revolution.

e: The boat from which the group of guerrillas led by Castro landed in Cuba at the end of 1956.

f: PRT—Revolutionary Workers Party, an Argentinian section of the Fourth International with a guerrilla group, the ERP.

> The politics which consists of not intervening in events, of accumulating forces from cold, is what I call the politics of passive accumulation of forces. This passivity was evident at the level of alliances. There was also passivity in the fact that we thought we could accumulate arms, organise ourselves, bring human resources together without fighting the enemy, without having the masses participate.[12]

He recognised that circumstances shook their various plans up:

> We called for the insurrection. The pace of events quickened, objective conditions did not allow us greater preparation. In reality, we could not say no to the insurrection—such was the breadth of the mass movement that the vanguard was incapable of directing it. We could not oppose this torrent. All we could do was to put ourselves at its head in the hope of more or less leading it and giving it a sense of direction.

He concluded, 'Our insurrectional strategy always gravitated around the masses and not around some military plan. This must be clear.' In reality, having a strategic option implies a sequencing of political priorities, of when to intervene, of what slogans to raise. It also determines the politics of alliances.

Mario Payeras's narrative of the Guatemala process[13] illustrates a return from the forest to the town and a change in relationships between the military and the political, the countryside and the town, and Régis Debray's 1974 *A Critique of Arms* (or self-criticism) also provides an account of the start of this evolution in the 1960s. There were the disastrous adventures of the Red Army Fraction in Germany, of the Weathermen[g] in the US (to say nothing of the ephemeral tragi-comedy of the Gauche prolétarienne[h] in France and the theses of July/Geismar[i] in their unforgettable *Vers la Guerre Civile* ('Towards Civil War') of 1969. All these and other attempts to translate the experience of rural guerrilla war into 'urban guerrilla' war came to a close in the 1970s. The only instances of armed movements to have lasted successfully were those whose organisations had their social base in struggles against national oppression (Ireland, the Basque Country).[14]

These strategic hypotheses and experiences were not simply reducible to militarism. They set political tasks in order. Thus the PRT's conception of

---

g: A guerrilla group formed from a split in Students for a Democratic Society, led by Bernadine Dohn and Mark Rudd.

h: A French Maoist organisation formed in 1969.

i: Serge July was editor of the daily *Liberation* from 1974 to 2006, steering it from Maoism to the neoliberal 'centre-left'; Alain Geismar, secretary of the lecturers' SNE-Sup union during the events of May 1968, then a Maoist, now Inspector General of Education.

the Argentinian Revolution as a national war of liberation meant privileging the construction of an army (the ERP) at the cost of self-organisation in workplaces and neighbourhoods. Similarly, the MIR's orientation of putting the stress, under Popular Unity, on accumulating forces (and rural bases) led to its downplaying the threat of a coup d'état and above all underestimating its long term consequences. Yet as MIR's general secretary Miguel Enriquez clearly perceived, following the failure of the first, abortive, coup of 29 June there was a brief moment favourable to the creation of a combat government which could have prepared for a trial of strength.

The Sandinista victory in 1979 no doubt marked a new turn. That at least is the view of Mario Payeras who stressed that in Guatemala (as in El Salvador) revolutionary movements were not confronted by clapped out puppet dictatorships but by Israeli, Taiwanese and US 'advisers' in 'low intensity' and 'counter-revolutionary' wars. This increasing asymmetry has since gone global with the new strategic doctrines of the Pentagon and the declaration of 'unlimited' war against 'terrorism'.

This is one reason (in addition to the tragic hyperviolence of the Cambodian experience, the bureaucratic counter-revolution in the USSR, and the Cultural Revolution in China) why the question of revolutionary violence has become a thorny, even taboo, subject, whereas in the past the epic sagas of the *Granma* and of Che, or the writings of Fanon, Giap or Cabral made violence appear innocent or liberatory. What we see is a groping towards some asymmetrical strategy of the weak and the strong, an attempt to synthesise Lenin and Gandhi[15] or orient towards non-violence.[16] Yet the world has not become less violent since the fall of the Berlin Wall. It would be rash and otherworldly to bet on there being a 'peaceful way'. Nothing from the century of extremes ratifies this scenario.

The hypothesis of the insurrectional general strike

The guideline for our strategic hypothesis in the 1970s was the insurrectional general strike, which, for the most part, bore no resemblance to the variants of acclimatised Maoism and its imaginary interpretations of the Cultural Revolution. It is this hypothesis of which we are now the 'orphans', according to Antoine Artous.[j] What might have had a certain 'functionality' yesterday is lost today. He does not deny, however, the continuing relevance of notions of revolutionary crisis and dual power. The hypothesis needs, he insists, serious

j: Antoine Artous—editor of the LCR's theoretical journal *Critique Communiste*. Bensaid is referring to Artous's article in that journal, translated as 'The LCR and the Left: Some Strategic Questions' in the International Socialist Tendency's *International Discussion Bulletin* 7 (January 2006), www.istendency.net

reformulation—one that avoids wallowing in the term 'rupture' and in verbal trickery. Two points crystallise his concern.

On the one hand, Antoine insists that dual power cannot be totally situated outside existing institutions and be made suddenly to spring from nothing in the form of a pyramid of soviets or councils. We may once upon a time have surrendered to this oversimplified vision of real revolutionary processes that we used to pore over in political study groups. But I doubt it. Be that as it may, other texts[17] swiftly corrected whatever vision we may have had. We may even, at the time, have been disturbed or shocked by Ernest Mandel coming round to the idea of 'mixed democracy'[k] after he had re-assessed the relationship between the soviets and the Constituent Assembly in Russia. Yet clearly one cannot imagine a revolutionary process other than as a transfer of legitimacy which gives preponderance to 'socialism from below' but which interacts with forms of representation, particularly in countries with parliamentary traditions going back over more than a century, and where the principle of universal suffrage is firmly established.

In practice, our ideas have evolved—as they did, for example, during the Nicaraguan Revolution. In the context of a civil war and a state of siege, organising 'free' elections in 1989 was open to question but we did not challenge the principle. Rather we criticised the Sandinistas for suppressing the 'council of state',[l] which might have constituted a sort of second social chamber and have been a pole of alternative legitimacy to the elected parliament. Similarly, though on a more modest scale, the example of the dialectic in Porto Alegre between the municipal institution (elected by universal suffrage) and participatory committees over the budget is worth consideration.

The problem we face is not in reality that of the relationship between territorial democracy and workplace democracy (the Paris Commune, the soviets and the Setubal popular assembly of Portugal in 1975 were territorial structures), nor even that of the relationship between direct and representative democracy (all democracy is partially representative). The real problem is how the general will is formed.

Most criticism of soviet-style democracy by the Eurocommunists[m] or by Norberto Bobbio[n] is targeted at its tendency to corporatism: a sum (or pyramid) of particular interests (parochial, workplace, office), linked by

---

k: ie of a combination of parliament and workers' councils.

l: A body of around 50 people nominated from the political parties, the Sandinista defence committees, the unions, professional associations and private enterprise organisations.

m: Communists who broke with Stalinism in the late '60s and '70s to embrace left wing parliamentarianism.

n: Norberto Bobbio—a left of centre Italian political philosopher.

a system of mandation, could not allow for the creation of the general will. Democratic subsidiarity has its drawbacks too. If the inhabitants of a valley are opposed to a road passing through it or if a town is against having a waste collection centre (in order to palm both off on their neighbours), then there really has to be some form of centralised arbitration.[18] In our debates with the Eurocommunists we insisted on the necessary mediation (and plurality) of parties so that a synthesis of propositions could emerge and a general will arise out of particular viewpoints. Our programmatic documents have increasingly incorporated the general hypothesis of a dual chamber. But we have not ventured into speculation about institutional nuts and bolts—the practical details remain open to experience.

Antoine Artous's second concern, notably in his criticism of Alex Callinicos, bears on the assertion that Alex's transitional approach halts at the threshold of the question of power. This would be left to be resolved by some unconvincing *deus ex machina*,[o] supposedly by a spontaneous tidal wave of the masses and a generalised outburst of soviet democracy. Though defence of civil liberties figures prominently in Alex's programme, he would appear to make no demands of an institutional nature (for example, the demand for proportional representation, a constituent assembly or single chamber, or radical democratisation). Cédric Durand, on the other hand, would seem to conceive of institutions as mere intermediaries for autonomous protest strategies. This, in practice, might boil down to a compromise between 'below' and 'above'—in other words, crude lobbying by the former of the latter, which is left intact.

In reality all sides in the controversy agree on the fundamental points inspired by *The Coming Catastrophe* (Lenin's pamphlet of the summer of 1917) and the *Transitional Programme of the Fourth International* (inspired by Trotsky in 1937): the need for transitional demands, the politics of alliances (the united front[19]), the logic of hegemony and on the dialectic (not antinomy) between reform and revolution. We are therefore against the idea of separating an ('anti-neoliberal') minimum programme and an (anti-capitalist) 'maximum' programme. We remain convinced that a consistent anti-neoliberalism leads to anti-capitalism and that the two are interlinked by the dynamic of struggle.

We can argue about exactly how the balance of forces and existing levels of consciousness should structure transitional demands. Agreement is easy, however, on targeting the privatisation of the means of production, communication and exchange—whether in relation to public sector education, humanity's

---

o: Latin phrase—'A god from a machine', ie sudden emergence of a solution from nowhere.

common goods or the increasingly important question of the socialisation of knowledge (as opposed to intellectual private property). Similarly, we can easily agree on exploring ways to socialise wages through systems of social protection as a step towards the withering away of the wages system altogether. Finally, in opposition to the generalisation of the market we open up the possibilities of extending the free provision of, not merely services, but basic items of consumption (thus of 'de-marketisation').

The tricky question about the issue of transition is that of the 'workers' government'. The difficulty is not new. The debates at the time of the fifth congress of the Communist International (1924) on the record of the German Revolution and the Social Democrat-Communist governments of Saxony and Thuringia in the late summer of 1923 before show this. They reveal the unresolved ambiguity of the formulae that came out of the early congresses of the Communist International and the range of interpretations which they could give rise to in practice. Treint[p] underlined in his report that 'the dictatorship of the proletariat does not fall from the sky; it must have a beginning and the workers' government is synonymous with the start of the dictatorship of the proletariat.' Nevertheless he denounced the 'saxonisation' of the united front: 'The entry of the communists into a coalition government with bourgeois pacifists to prevent an intervention against the revolution was not wrong in theory' but governments of the Labour Party or Left Bloc type cause 'bourgeois democracy to find an echo within our own parties'.

The Czechoslovak Smeral declared in the debate on the activity of the International: 'As far as the theses of our congress in February 1923 on the workers' government are concerned, we were all convinced when we drew them up that they were in line with the decisions of the fourth congress. They were adopted unanimously.' But 'what are the masses thinking about when they speak of a workers' government?' 'In England, they think of the Labour Party, in Germany and in other countries where capitalism is decomposing, the united front means that the communists and social democrats, instead of fighting one another when the strike breaks out, are marching shoulder to shoulder. For the masses the workers' government has the same meaning and when we use this formula they imagine a united government of all the workers' parties.' And Smeral continued: 'What deep lesson does the Saxon experiment teach us? Above all, this: that one cannot vault from a standing start—a run-up is needed.'

Ruth Fischer's[q] answer was that as a coalition of workers' parties the

p: Albert Treint—leader of the pro-Zinoviev wing of the French Communist Party in the mid-1920s.

q: Ruth Fischer—leader of the ultra-left in the German Communist Party in the early and mid-1920s. She later became a fervent cold warrior.

workers' government would mean 'the liquidation of our party'. In her report on the failure of the German Revolution Clara Zetkin argued:

> As far as the workers' and peasants' government is concerned I cannot accept Zinoviev's declaration that it is simply a pseudonym, a synonym or god knows what homonym, for the dictatorship of the proletariat. That may be correct for Russia but it is not the same for countries where capitalism is flourishing. There the workers' and peasants' government is the political expression of a situation in which the bourgeoisie can no longer maintain itself in power but where the proletariat is not yet in a position to impose its dictatorship.

In fact, what Zinoviev defined as the 'elementary objective of the workers' government' was the arming of the proletariat, workers' control over production, a tax revolution...

One could go on and quote other contributions. The resulting impression would be of enormous confusion. This expresses a real contradiction and an inability to solve the problem, even though it was raised in a revolutionary or pre-revolutionary situation.

It would be irresponsible to provide a solution that is universally valid; nevertheless, three criteria can be variously combined for assessing participation in a government coalition with a transition perspective:

a) The question of participation arises in a situation of crisis or at least of a significant upsurge in social mobilisation, and not from a vacuum;

b) The government in question is committed to initiating a dynamic of rupture with the established order. For example—and more modestly than the arming of the workers demanded by Zinoviev—radical agrarian reform, 'despotic incursions' into the domain of private property, the abolition of tax privileges, a break with institutions like those of the Fifth Republic in France, European treaties, military pacts, etc;

c) Finally, the balance of forces allows revolutionaries to ensure that even if they cannot guarantee that the non-revolutionaries in the government keep to their commitments, they have to pay a high price for failure to do so.

In this light participation in the Lula government in Brazil[r] appears to have been mistaken:

a) For ten years or so, with the exception of the landless movement, the mass movement has been on the retreat.

b) the colour of Lula's social-neoliberal politics was clearly shown in

r: By members of the DS current which is part of the Fourth International.

his electoral campaign and in his *Letter to the Brazilians* (promising to keep to the previous government's financial commitments). The financing of his agrarian reform and 'zero-hunger' programme was mortgaged in advance

c) Finally, the social balance of forces within both the party and the government was such that to be a half-minister in agriculture[s] was not to support the government 'like a rope supports a hanged man' but rather like a hair that could not. That said, and taking into account the history of the country, its social structure and the formation of the PT, we chose not to make this a matter of principle (though we expressed our reservations orally to the comrades about participation and alerted them to the dangers). We preferred to go along with the experiment so as to draw up the balance sheet alongside the comrades, rather than give lessons 'from a distance'.[20]

About the dictatorship of the proletariat

The question of the workers' government has inevitably brought us back to the question of the dictatorship of the proletariat. An LCR conference decided by a majority of more than two thirds to remove mention of it from its statutes. That was fair enough. Today the term dictatorship more readily invokes the military or bureaucratic dictatorships of the 20th century than the venerable Roman institution of temporary emergency powers duly mandated by the Senate. Since Marx saw the Paris Commune as 'the political form at last discovered' of this dictatorship of the proletariat, we would be better off understood as invoking the Commune, the soviets, councils or self-management, rather than hanging on to a verbal fetish which history has rendered a source of confusion.

For all that we haven't done with the question raised by Marx's formula and the importance he gave it in his celebrated letter to Kugelman. Generally speaking, the 'dictatorship of the proletariat' tends to carry the image of an authoritarian regime and to be seen as a synonym for bureaucratic dictatorships. But for Marx it was the democratic solution to an old problem—the exercise for the first time by the (proletarian) majority of emergency power, which till then had been the preserve of a virtuous elite as with the Committee of Public Safety of the French Revolution, even if the committee in question emanated from the Convention and could be recalled by it. The term 'dictatorship' in Marx's time was often counterposed to 'tyranny', which was used to express despotism.

The notion of the dictatorship of the proletariat also had a strategic significance, one often raised in the debates of the 1970s upon its abandonment

s: The position taken by a leading member of DS.

by the majority of (Euro)communist parties. Marx clearly grasped that the new legal power, as an expression of a new social relationship, could not be born if the old one remained: between two social legitimacies, 'between two equal rights, it is force that decides'. Revolution implies therefore a transition enforced by a state of emergency. Carl Schmitt,[t] who was an attentive reader of the polemic between Lenin and Kautsky, understood perfectly what was at issue when he distinguished between the 'chief constable dictatorship', whose function in a state of crisis is to preserve the established order, and the 'sovereign dictatorship', which inaugurates a new order by virtue of a constitutive power.[21] If this strategic perspective, whatever name we give it, remains valid then there necessarily follows a series of consequences about how power is organised, about legitimacy, about how parties function, etc.

The actuality or otherwise of a strategic approach

The notion of 'the actuality of revolution'[u] has a double meaning: a broad sense ('the epoch of wars and revolution') and an immediate or conjectural sense. In the defensive situation the social movement finds itself in, having been thrown back for more than 20 years in Europe, no one will claim that revolution has an actuality in an immediate sense. On the other hand, it would be a risky and not a minor matter to eliminate it from the horizon of our epoch. Perhaps Francis Sitel intended to use this distinction in his contribution to the debate. If he wants to avoid 'a wild-eyed vision of the actual balance of forces' as 'a current perspective' 'and prefers instead a 'perspective for action which informs present struggles about the necessary outcomes of these same struggles', then there is not much to quarrel about. But more debatable is the idea according to which we could maintain the objective of conquering power 'as a sign of radicalism but admit that its realisation is currently beyond our horizon'.

For him the question of government is not linked to the question of power, but to 'a more modest demand', that of 'protection' against the neoliberal offensive. The debate about the conditions for participation in government does not go 'through the monumental gate of strategic reflection', but 'through the narrow gate of broad parties'. Our fear here is that it may no longer be the need for a programme (or strategy) which dictates the construction of the party but the size of an algebraically broad party which determines what is seen as the best party policy. The issue of government would then be scaled down as a strategic question and recast as a

---

t: Right wing German legal theorist of the inter-war years, joined Nazi Party.

u: Term used by the Hungarian Marxist philosopher Georg Lukács in 1922.

mere 'question of orientation' (which, to some extent, is what we did with Brazil). But a 'question of orientation' is not disconnected from the strategic perspective unless we fall into the classic dissociation between minimum and maximum programme. And, if 'broad' is necessarily more generous and open than narrow and closed, there are different degrees of broadness: the Brazilian PT, the Linkspartei in Germany, the ODP in Turkey, the Left Bloc in Portugal, Rifondazione Comunista, are not of the same nature.

'The most erudite developments in matters of revolutionary strategy appear quite airy fairy,' Francis Sitel concludes, 'compared with the question of how to act in the here and now.' Certainly, this worthy pragmatic maxim could have been uttered in 1905, in February 1917, in May 1936, in February 1968, thus reducing the sense of the possible to one of prosaic realism.

Francis Sitel's diagnosis, and his programmatic adjustment to this side of the horizon, is not without practical implications. Once our perspective is no longer limited to seizing power but is inscribed in a longer process of 'subverting power', we would have to recognise that 'the traditional[22] party which concentrates on the conquest of power is led to adapt to the state itself' and consequently 'to transmit within itself mechanisms of domination which undermine the very dynamic of emancipation'. A new dialectic has therefore to be invented between the political and the social. Certainly; this is the practical and theoretical task we set ourselves, when we reject 'the political illusion' as much as 'the social illusion', or draw principled conclusions from past negative experiences (about the independence of social organisations towards the state and parties, about political pluralism, about democracy within parties).

But the problem does not lie in the way a party 'adapted to the state' transmits the state's mechanisms of domination so much as in the deeper and commoner phenomenon of bureaucratisation, rooted in the division of labour. Bureaucratisation is inherent in modern societies: it affects trade union and associative organisations as a whole. In fact, party democracy (as opposed to the media-driven, plebiscitary democracy of so called 'public opinion') would be, if not an absolute remedy, at least one of the antidotes to the professionalisation of power and the 'democracy of the market'. This is too easily forgotten by those who see in democratic centralism only a mask for bureaucratic centralism. Yet some degree of centralisation is the very condition for democracy, not its negation.

The stress on the adaptation of the party to the state finds an echo in the isomorphism (picked up by Boltanski and Chiapello in *The New Spirit of Capitalism*) between the structure of capital itself and the structures of the workers' movement, which are subordinate to it. This question is a crucial one and cannot be evaded or resolved easily: the wage struggle and the right to a job (sometimes called the 'right to work') is indeed a struggle that is subordinate to (isomorphic with) the capital/labour relationship. Behind that is the whole problem of alienation, fetishism and reification. But to believe that 'fluid' forms—organising in networks and the logic of affinity groups (as opposed to the logic of hegemony)—escape this subordination is a grotesque illusion. Such forms are perfectly isomorphic with the modern organisation of computerised capital, flexible working, the 'liquid society', etc. That does not mean that the old forms of subordination were better or preferable to the emergent forms—only that there is no royal road of networking to lead us out of the vicious circle of exploitation and domination.

On the 'broad party'

Francis Sitel is fearful that talking of 'the eclipse' or 'the return of strategic reason' means simply bracketing things off, returning to the same old themes or taking up the question in the terms posed by the Third International. He insists on the need for 'fundamental revisions', for reinvention, for 'constructing something new', as fitting the requirements of the workers' movement. Of course. But we are not speaking of a blank screen. The rhetoric of novelty is no guarantee against falling back into the oldest, and most hackneyed, ways of thinking. Some new ways of thinking (about ecology, feminism, war and rights) are genuine. But many of the 'novelties' our epoch indulges in are no more than fashionable effects (feeding like any fashion on quotations from the past), which recycle old utopian themes from the 19th century and the workers' movement in its infancy.

Having rightly recalled that reforms and revolution form a dialectical couple in our tradition and not an opposition of mutually exclusive terms, Francis Sitel hazards the prediction that a 'broad party will be defined as a party of reforms'. That's as maybe. But it's an idea that is speculative and sets up a norm in advance. And that certainly is not our problem.

We don't have to put the cart before the horse and invent among ourselves a minimum programme (of reforms) for a hypothetical 'broad party'. We have to define our project and our programme. It is from that starting point that, in concrete situations and with tangible allies, we shall weigh up what compromises are possible, even if it means accepting some loss in clarity, in exchange for greater social spread, experience and dynamism. This is not new. We participated in the creation of the PT. Our comrades are active as a current in Rifondazione. They play a decisive part in the Left Bloc in Portugal. But these are all specific configurations and should not be brought together under some all-inclusive category of 'broad party'.

The structural situation in which we find ourselves certainly opens up a space to the left of the major traditional formations of the workers' movement (social democrats, Stalinists, populists). There are many reasons for this. The neoliberal counter-reform, the privatisation of the public arena, the dismantling of the welfare state, the market society, have sawn off the branch on which sat social democracy—and populist adminstrations in certain Latin American countries. The communist parties in Europe have suffered the after-effect of the implosion of the USSR at the same time as the erosion of the social bases they acquired in the pre-war years and the period of liberation from the Nazis, without gaining new roots. There really does exist what we often call a radical 'space', which has found diverse expression in the emergence of new social movements and electoral formations. This is the present day basis for reconstruction and regroupment.

But this 'space' is not homogenous and empty so that all we have to do is fill it. It is a highly unstable force field, as shown spectacularly by the conversion in less than three years of Rifondazione from lyrical movementism, at the time of Genoa and Florence,[23] to government coalition with Romano Prodi. This instability stems from the fact that the social mobilisations have suffered more defeats than they have won victories and that their link to the transformation of the political landscape remains overstretched. In the absence of meaningful social victories, the hope of the 'lesser evil' ('anything but Berlusconi—or Sarkozy, or Le Pen!') moves, for lack of real change, to the electoral terrain where the weight of institutional logic remains decisive (in France, that of plebiscitary presidentialism and a particularly anti-democratic electoral system). That's why the symmetry of the happy medium, between an opportunist and a conservative danger is a false perspective: they don't carry the same weight. We must know how to dare to take risky decisions (the most extreme example being that of the October insurrection)—but we must also know how to weigh up the risk and calculate the chances if we are to avoid pure adventurism. As the great dialectician Pascal said, we are already committed—we must wager. Yet racegoers know that a bet of two to one is small time, and that a bet of a thousand to one, though it may hit the jackpot, is a desperate throw. The margin is between the two. Daring too has its reasons.

The evolution from right to left of currents like Rifondazione or the Linkspartei remains fragile (even reversible) for the very reason that the effects of social struggle on the field of political representation remain limited. It depends in part on the presence and weight within them of revolutionary organisations or tendencies.

There are very general common factors. But over and beyond these, conditions vary enormously, depending on the specific history of the workers' movement (for instance, whether social democracy is totally hegemonic or whether there subsist important communist parties). It also depends on the balance of forces within the left. Apparatuses are determined not only by ideology, but by social logics. They cannot be shifted by whispering in the ears of their leaders, but only by modifying the real balance of forces.

The perspective of a 'new force' remains an algebraic formula for now (this was true for us before 1989-91 and is even truer since). Translating it into practice cannot be mechanically deduced from formulae as vague and general as 'the broad party' or 'regroupment'. We are only at the start of a process of reconstruction. What counts in the approach to this is our programmatic compass and strategic aim. This is one condition that will allow us to discover the organisational mediations we need and to take calculated risks. That way we avoid throwing ourselves headlong into some impatient adventure and dissolving ourselves into the first ephemeral combination that comes along. Organisational formulae are in reality very variable, depending on whether at issue is a new mass party (like the PT in Brazil in the 1980s, though this is an unlikely pattern in Europe), minority splits from a hegemonic social democracy, or yet again parties that we might previously have termed centrist (Rifondazione five years ago), or a coalition of revolutionary currents (as in Portugal). This last hypothesis remains, however, the most likely for countries such as France, where there is a long tradition of organisations like the CP or the far left and where, without a really powerful social movement, for them simply to merge in the short or medium term is difficult to imagine.

But, in every case, reference to a common programmatic background, far from being something that obstructs future reconstruction, is on the contrary its precondition. Strategic and tactical questions can then be prioritised so that we are not torn apart because of this or that electoral outcome. We can distinguish the political base on which organising open theoretical debate makes sense. We can assess which compromises allow us to forge ahead and which pull us back. We can adjust to forms of organisational existence (whether to be a tendency in a shared party, part of a front, etc.), depending on our allies and how their dynamic fluctuates (from right to left or left to right).

NOTES

1: They are available on the website of the ESSF (Europe solidaire sans frontières). Texts by Artous and Alex Callinicos are translated in the *International Discussion Bulletin* of the International Socialist Tendency at www.istendency.net

2: This was Stathis Kouvelakis's emphasis in 'The Triumph of the Political', *International Socialism* 108 (Autumn 2005).

3: Alex Callinicos, *An Anti-Capitalist Manifesto* (Cambridge, 2003).

4: I shall go no further on this aspect of the question. It is simply a reminder (see in this respect the theses proposed in the debate organised by *Das Argument*).

5: Durand appears to attribute to us a 'stagist view of social change' and 'a temporality of political action centred exclusively on the preparation of the revolution as a decisive moment' (to which he opposes 'an altermondialist and Zapatista historical time' ??!!), see *Critique Communiste* 179. For a detailed critique of John Holloway's approach, see the detailed critique in Daniel Bensaïd, *Un monde à changer* (Paris, Textuel 2006); *Planète altermondialiste* (Textuel, 2006), and in articles in *Contretemps*.

6: In the debate about the programme in the Communist International up till its sixth congress.

7: See Perry Anderson, 'The Antinomies of Gramsci', *New Left Review* 100, 1977.

8: See the debates around the report on the German Revolution at the fifth congress of the Communist International.

9: See Giacomo Marramao, *Il Politico e le trasformazioni*, and the pamphlet *Stratégies et partis*.

10: As Antoine Artous reminds us in his article in *Critique communiste*.

11: Despite the simplified myth of the foco, notably in Regis Debray, *Revolution in the Revolution* (London, 1967).

12: 'The strategy for victory', interview by Marta Harnecker. Asked about the date on which the insurrection was called, Ortega replied: 'Because a whole series of more and more favourable objective conditions arose: the economic crisis, the currency devaluation, the political crisis. And because after the September events we realised that it was necessary to combine simultaneously and within the same strategic space the rising of the masses at a national level, the offensive of the military forces at the front and the national strike in which the employers were involved or in practice acquiesced. If we had not combined these three strategic factors simultaneously and in the same strategic space, victory would not have been possible. On several occasions there had been a call for a national strike, but it had not been combined with the mass offensive. The masses had already risen, but the rising had not been combined with strike action and took place at a time when the military capacity of the vanguard was too weak. And the vanguard had already delivered several blows to the enemy but without the presence of the other two factors.'

13: Mario Payeras, *Los días de la selva* ('Days of the Jungle', Monthly Review Press, 1983) and *El trueno en la cuidad* ('The Thunder in the city', 1987).

14: See *Dissidence, Révolution, Lutte armée et Terrorisme*, vol 1 (L'Harmattan, 2006).

15: This is notably the theme of recent texts by Balibar.

16: The debate about non-violence in Rifondazione comunista's theoretical review (*Alternative*) is certainly not without a bearing on its present course.

17: Notably Mandel's, in his polemics against the eurocommunists' theses. See his book in the Maspero little collection and above all his interview in *Critique communiste*.

18: The experience of the participatory budget at the Rio Grande do Sol state level offers many concrete examples in this respect: credit allocation, ranking of priorities, territorial sharing of collective supplies, etc.

19: It may be worth coming back to a discussion of this notion of a united front, or a fortiori the anti-imperialist united front which some revolutionaries in Latin America have made flavour of the month, in the light of the evolution of social formations, of the role and composition of political parties, etc.

20: At stake here, as far as the orientation in Brazil is concerned, was a conception of the Fourth International and its relationship to the national sections. But this question goes beyond the context of this text.

21: See Carl Schmitt, *La Dictature* (Paris, 1990).

22: By 'traditional' does Sitel mean communist parties or, more broadly, social democratic parties whose aim is the conquest of governmental power through parliamentary means?

23: See the book by Fausto Bertinotti, *Ces idées qui ne meurent jamais* (Paris, Le temps des Cerises, 2001), and critical approach to it (which appeared at the time of the ESF in Florence) in Daniel Bensaïd, *Un monde à changer* (Paris, Textuel, 2003).

The French Revolution is not over

Neil Davidson

A review of Henry Heller, ***The Bourgeois Revolution in France, 1789-1815*** *(Berghahn Books, 2006), £36.50*

Marx and Engels were born into a world shaped by the French Revolution—literally so in the case of Marx, who grew up in the Rhineland where the French occupation between 1807 and 1813 greatly accelerated the dismantling of feudalism in that region. It is unsurprising then that this cataclysmic event should have influenced the formation of their theories. By the mid-1840s the revolution had acquired a three-fold significance in their thought.

First, in terms of the past, France provided the clearest example of how capitalism had first emerged within feudalism as a subordinate mode of production and then become dominant across a particular national territory. But this outcome was not simply the inevitable evolutionary triumph of a more dynamic economic system; it also required a successful struggle for political power by the capitalist class against the existing feudal-absolutist order.

Second, in terms of the present, it provided an inspiration for those national bourgeoisies—at this stage the vast majority—who were still excluded from political power. Marx was particularly concerned that the German bourgeoisie should learn the lessons of the French Revolution, although he rightly remained pessimistic about its capacity to do so. He was not so naive as to think, however, that bourgeois leadership involved industrialists and financiers personally mounting the barricades. He was quite aware that the actual fighting had been carried out by classes below the bourgeoisie in the class structure, and on some occasions suggested that without these plebeians the revolution would not have succeeded or even survived.

Third, in terms of the future, it also provided the emergent proletariat with lessons in the need for revolutionary intransigence on its own behalf, rather than on behalf of a new class of exploiters. But more generally, the mobilisations which characterised the crucial 'days' of the revolution involved far greater levels of mass involvement and higher levels of popular initiative than the preceding bourgeois revolutions in the United Netherlands, England, Scotland or America. Its mass character was therefore paradoxical, making possible the period of bourgeois ascendancy *and* prefiguring the form of the coming proletarian revolutions. As Georg Lukács later noted, 'From the Great French Revolution on, all revolutions exhibit the same pattern with increasing intensity'.[1] Indeed the actual pattern of events—the initial unity of the revolutionary forces, their increasing polarisation into left and right under pressure from the counter-revolution, the ultimate stabilisation on the basis of a conservative reaction within the revolution—seemed to offer a general pattern of development.

For Marx, therefore, the French Revolution involved three key elements: bourgeois leadership that gave the revolution its class character; mass mobilisations of peasants, urban masses and revolutionary armies that were necessary to take power and defend the new state; and the removal of obstacles to capitalist development that constituted the outcome. In France itself this interpretation gave rise to an extraordinarily rich socialist historiography, from Jaurès to Mathiez, and from Lefebvre to Soboul, much of which can still be read with profit today. But because Marx wrote specifically about the French Revolution and, to a lesser extent, its immediate predecessors, he did not leave behind a general theory of bourgeois revolution. The outline of one did emerge in Engels's later writings and was further developed by Lenin, Trotsky, Lukács, Gramsci and many other thinkers, although by no means in a systematic way. The underlying theme was that bourgeois revolutions were not the sum total of a checklist of 'tasks' which had to be accomplished before they could be declared complete. The only *necessary* component of a bourgeois revolution was not the nature of the process or the identity of the class actors, but the outcome: the establishment of a state committed to ensuring the accumulation of capital.

Unfortunately, this approach, like so much else of value in Marxist theory, was suppressed for decades by Stalinism. In its place the orthodoxy became a model of bourgeois revolution based on the French Revolution—or, to be more exact, a particular reading of the first five years of the French Revolution—a model accepted even by people who were not Stalinists, people who were in most other respects opposed to Stalinism. The problem was that the 'French model' was a positive obstacle to understanding how the bourgeoisie had come to power on a global scale. By using France as an example against which all other bourgeois revolutions were judged, it was inevitable that even those countries, like England, in which the revolutions were structurally quite similar to the French, would be found wanting, while some countries, like Germany, would be found not to have undergone bourgeois revolutions at all, because they had failed to reproduce the French experience. But what would become of this conception of bourgeois revolution if even the French Revolution was found not to live up to its image? This was exactly what began to be argued, first in the 1950s, then with greater confidence and frequency, from the 1970s.

The French Revolution did not take place

'Revisionism' is the catch-all term for a range of arguments which deny that the French Revolution was a 'bourgeois revolution'. Some versions go so far as to deny that it can be explained in social terms at all. The arguments have developed in three main phases.

The first, relatively isolated, expressions of the case were made over 50 years ago in Britain and Israel. In his inaugural lecture as chair in French History at the University of London, first published in 1955 as 'The Myth of the French Revolution', the British historian Alfred Cobban made four points. First, France was no longer a feudal society by 1789. Some dues and services still survived, but these were functionless survivals whose significance may have been deliberately over-emphasised by the Constituent Assembly so that their abolition, under pressure from the peasantry, would not set a precedent which could be extended to bourgeois property rights. Second, the main representatives of the Third Estate were not capitalists, but lawyers or, more precisely, venal office holders, functionaries and professional men who used the revolution to ascend the state structure at the expense of the nobility. Third, both the formal abolition of feudal dues and the ascendancy of the bourgeois office holders had been achieved by 1791—the subsequent events were violent, but essentially irrelevant, since by 1799 the situation had simply reverted to that at the beginning of the decade. Fourth, the impact of the revolution on capitalist development was limited and may even have retarded it until much later in the 19th century.[2] What then had led to the Jacobin dictatorship, the September Massacres, the Terror and all those other supposedly pointless events which Cobban regarded with such fastidious British distaste? The answer had been independently provided, not by a historian, but by the political scientist J L Talmon, then based at the Hebrew University in Jerusalem. His focus was on the Enlightenment beliefs which he claimed had taken on a life of their own and led to the Dictatorship of Virtue, an abstract set of truths which empowered the Jacobins and their supporters to kill in the name of ideological purity.[3] Both Cobban and Talmon were committed Cold Warriors. Cobban helped ensure that one of his own students, George Rudé, was blacklisted from lecturing in Britain. Talmon contributed towards the 'end of ideology' thesis during the 1950s and drew parallels between the 'totalitarian democracy' of the Jacobins and that of the supposedly equivalent modern totalitarianisms of Fascism and Communism.[4]

What was significant about the second phase moment of revisionism was where it arose and who was responsible. From the mid-1970s onwards these arguments began to be expressed in France itself by people on the left, or at least people who had been on the left. The most important of these was François Furet, a member of the Communist Party of France. In a history of the revolution written in 1965 with Denis Richet, Furet introduced the idea of 'the skidding off course of the revolution' after 1791.[5] If his first contribution echoed Cobban's claim that the real goals of the revolution had been achieved by 1791, his second, a decade later, recalled Talmon's emphasis on ideology. In this essay, 'The French Revolution is Over', Furet specifically attacks the connections which the French left in particular drew between the French and Russian Revolutions. Furet was, however, concerned less with the historical accuracy of this claim than with highlighting what he thought the real connections were, namely the comparable totalitarian systems embodied in the Terror and the Gulag.[6]

How have Marxists responded to the revisionist critique of the concept of bourgeois revolution? On the one hand, some have attempted to construct a more defensible version of the Cl assical Marxist position, drawing the scattered insights of the Second and early Third Internationals into a new synthesis. (The first attempts to do so actually predate the emergence of revisionism and were undertaken, in the context of a discussion of the nature of the USSR, by Cliff, Deutscher and Shachtman—a trio of very different Trotskyists—in books and articles written in 1948-49.) This version of the theory shifts focus from the *role of* the bourgeoisie in the bourgeois revolutions—although they did of course play a major role, above all in the Dutch, English and French revolutions—to the *consequences for* the bourgeoisie of the bourgeois revolutions; it therefore accepts at least some of empirical criticisms of the revisionists, but regards them as irrelevant.[7] On the other hand, the 'political Marxism'[a] of

a: 'Political Marxism' essentially argues that fundamental change occurs as a result of class struggles leading to changes in the relations of production. It is opposed, in other words, to the classical Marxist position in which these struggles emerge out of the prior development of the forces of production.

Robert Brenner, Ellen Meiksins Wood and their followers not only accepts the empirical criticisms of the revisionists, but agrees that they invalidate the entire concept. Here the focus is on the transition from feudal to capitalist social relations, rather than the revolutions which had hitherto been regarded as essential to the process, which this position sees as quite separate.[8] In effect, this is not so much a response to revisionism as a third and, one hopes, final phase of the thing itself.

Here, as with the influence of Cobban on Furet, there are connections with the preceding phase. George Comninel, for example, makes the apparently curious claim that the 'only' bourgeois aspect of the revolution was the fact that the bourgeoisie led it against their aristocratic opponents. Bourgeois leadership and aristocratic opponents may sound like reasonably decisive criteria, but it is important to understand that Comninel does not regard the 'bourgeoisie' as having any necessary connection with capitalism or the 'aristocracy' as having any necessary connection with feudalism. In the absence of 'a system entirely structured about commodity production as the self-expansion of capital through the reduction of labour to labour power', capitalism did not exist in France prior to 1789. Rather the bourgeoisie essentially belonged to the same social class as the aristocracy because both ultimately drew their income through the same method of surplus extraction. The revolution should therefore be seen as 'an intra-class conflict' or 'civil war' over distribution of the surplus. Unsurprisingly, Comninel does not think that the revolution did anything to promote capitalism either: 'The revolution was not fought by capitalists, and it did not produce capitalist society.' If anything, it restricted it further by preserving small-scale peasant production.[9] Virtually the only difference between Comninel and the earlier generations of revisionists is his belief that capitalism, rather than having already surpassed feudalism in France by 1789, did not exist at all.

A new synthesis

From the preceding discussion it should be obvious why a book called *The Bourgeois Revolution in France* should be of interest to readers of *International Socialism*, particularly when the author begins with this assessment:

> It seems evident that a connection exists between the predominance of revisionism, the decline of revolutionary movements of the 1960s and 1970s, and the conservative or neoliberal ideological offensive of the last decades. Whether or not the modern world came into being by revolution is more than an academic question. It bears on the present and future as well as on the interpretation of the past.[10]

So writes Henry Heller, a Canadian Marxist scholar who, over the last 20 years, has increased our understanding of 16th century France with a series of books reassessing the French experience of Calvinism, the Wars of Religion and the relationship between economic development and technological change.[11] It is only now, in his latest book, that Heller broaches the moment in French history during which classical Marxism has traditionally seen the breakthrough to capitalist economy and bourgeois society as finally taking place. And he has a specific purpose in doing so: 'This work seeks to reclaim the idea that the French Revolution was a bourgeois revolution'.[12] Indeed, it is the first book in English explicitly to defend a Marxist interpretation of the French Revolution since revisionism became entrenched.

Heller seeks 'confirmation of the Marxist view' in what he modestly calls 'a review of existing scholarly literature'.[13] In a relatively short but densely packed book, Heller has synthesised recent work by other historians which is either difficult for non-specialists to obtain or as yet untranslated into English. In the first category are mainly Anglo-American historians who have challenged specific revisionist claims on empirical grounds, without seeking to reject the entire approach. In the second are mainly French Marxists like Michel Vovelle and Guy Lemarchand (but also the Russian, Anatoli Ado), who are concerned not only with grounding their work in primary research, but also with engaging the revisionists in theoretical terms.[14] Heller assumes that his readers are aware of both the course of events and the main conflicting interpretations. Although the book proceeds through chronological periods, it does not really provide a narrative account, despite claims to this effect by Heller in the Preface. Consequently, readers seeking an introduction to the history of the French Revolution should turn instead to the short book written by Albert Soboul during the 1960s (which is also a fine example of the 'classic' position) or to the article by Paul McGarr published in this journal on the bicentenary of 1789.[15] That said, Heller writes simply and accessibly, and conveys a vast amount of information about who was doing what to who and why. Not that Heller is dismissive of theory, but his own theoretical approach differs from that of most previous historians in three main ways.

First, he does not focus his attention on the popular movements of either the peasants or *sans-culottes*: 'Rather, the focus will be on the step-by-step development of the bourgeoisie as a new ruling class'.[16] He clearly regards much of the writing about the movements from below as a way of sidestepping discussion of the revolutionary role of the bourgeoisie. But Heller goes further. From Daniel Guérin onwards, many historians have stressed the anti-capitalist possibilities of working class power emerging from the activity of the *sans-culottes*.[17] As far as France is concerned, most of the debate among socialists has not been about the accuracy of this assessment, but about how far an anti-capitalist programme could have succeeded. In a splendidly iconoclastic move Heller rejects the entire premise, writing that, 'far from being an impediment to capitalism, the popular democratic phase of the revolution was an essential element to the further development of French capitalism'.[18] Following the work of Richard Mowbery Andrews, Heller argues that many of the classic histories of the revolution 'took the egalitarian ideology of the *sans-culottes* too much at face value', losing sight of 'the fact that those who dominated the movement were solid bourgeois, notably the master artisans'.[19]

Second, he deals with the revolutionary period as a whole: 'This history will make a point of investigating not merely the 18th century background and the most tumultuous years of the revolution, but also the period of its consolidation under the Directory and Napoleon'.[20] Just as any serious discussion of the English Revolution has to span the period from the Scottish Covenanting rebellion of 1637 through to the Restoration of 1660, so too must one of the French Revolution extend from the Assembly of the Notables in 1787 to the Restoration of 1815. This may seem obvious, but many of the greatest works on the subject—such as the major books by Lefevbre and Soboul—conclude in 1799 with Napoleon's seizure of power, and many finish earlier with Thermidor in 1794.[21] By dealing with the period as a whole Heller affirms that the unheroic later stages are just as central as the years of mass mobilisation to the issue of capitalist dominance.

Third, although he foregrounds economic developments in a way that will undoubtedly scandalise the revisionists, Heller does not advocate a crude economic determinism. Rather 'the view advanced here will be one that insists that the economic, political and cultural factors cannot be seen as separate from one another...such factors will be treated dialectically as coexistent features of a great civilisational transformation'.[22] And, although he does not use the term, Heller is here invoking the notion of totality:

> From a Marxist point of view it is not the primacy of the economic that is the distinguishing feature. Rather it is an insistence on a knowledge of the historical process in its entirety or as a whole.[23]

Indeed, his main criticism of the revisionists is their blindness to the inner connections between changes to different aspects of French society. Heller accepts that they may have brought some gains in the study of areas like gender and political culture: 'But in the final analysis, the maintenance of a perspective that rejects the idea of the French Revolution as a capitalist revolution, is only possible by refusing to comprehend these events as part of a unified process or by rejecting the idea that such comprehension is possible'.[24]

How then does Heller's approach deal with some key themes thrown up by the revisionist debates?

Capitalism and crisis before 1789

If capitalism were already totally dominant in a society, there would be no *need* for a bourgeois revolution, because there would be no forces capable of opposing it. But if capitalism did not exist at all in a society, then there would be no *possibility* of a bourgeois revolution, because there would be no forces capable of supporting it. To what extent had capitalism developed in France by 1789? As Heller writes:

> The initial success of the bourgeoisie did not mean that France was a fully developed capitalist economy led by a fully conscious and self-confident capitalist class. It meant only that the bourgeoisie had developed enough economic as well as political strength to get rid of the *ancien régime*. It would take an extended process over the next 25 years for it to mature as a class while further developing its economic underpinnings.[25]

Heller argues that capitalist production existed to varying degrees across the different sectors of the economy in 18th century France. The uneven spatial development of agriculture effectively divided the country into three regions, but only in the north did capitalist agriculture emerge, bringing with it social differentiation between proprietors and large farmers on the one hand, and day labourers and teamsters on the other. Although the point is not original, it is extremely important as a demonstration that the type of productive relations typical of English capitalist agriculture were also present on a geographically more restricted basis in France.[26]

In relation to trade, once the demand for commodities expanded beyond a certain point, it had implications for how production—not simply the division of labour, or the labour process more generally—was organised. Heller shows that there was certainly a massive increase in French trade across the 18th century.[27] It is true that much of the production of commodities took place in small workshops and on a seasonal basis, but large factories also began to appear. The greatest of all, the Le Creusot iron and steel factory built during the 1780s, 'had a workforce of over 1,300, used the advanced coke reduction process in the manufacture of steel, and operated with the help of at least five steam engines and between 12 and 15 miles of railway tracking'.[28]

And what of the labourers who worked in these enterprises? In many respects they were not fully-formed proletarians, completely separated from both the means of production and the means of subsistence. But as Heller points out, people may be driven to work for wages, not because they have no access to subsistence production, but because it is insufficient to support them. Equally, capitalists are quite content for workers to partially provide for themselves, since this allows the level of wages to be held down.[29] To imagine otherwise is to abandon the possibility of a transitional economy at all: an economy must either be feudal or capitalist (or something else altogether), but nothing in between. This is highly unrealistic, to say the least:

> The full emergence of abstract labour and value are not capitalist preconditions but the end product of a prolonged historical process in which struggle over the means of production and their further development are primary factors... At a certain stage in the evolution of the economy of the *ancien régime*, the creation of value began to occur within the structures of the guilds and corporations, institutions that likely facilitated the process.[30]

But capitalist developments were opposed, and from more than one source. Heller cites the example of Jacques Vaucanson, a mechanic who entered the *Académie des Sciences* at the insistence of Louis XV because of his inventions, including 'a mechanical silk loom, a draw loom for brocade and figured silk, a silk throwing mill, and a mangle to achieve the effect of moiré or "clouded silk".' His entry to the *Académie* was opposed by the aristocratic members who opposed the practical application of scientific theory for the vulgar purposes of commerce. But he was also opposed by the corporate guilds of the artisans, themselves already under attack from the merchant capitalists, and who rioted to prevent the introduction of the mechanical loom.[31] The kind of support the absolutist state could give to innovators like Vaucanson against noble opposition was limited, since the nobility was the ultimate basis of its support.[32]

The absolutist state concentrated power, drawing it away from the local lordships to the centralised state as guarantor of surplus extraction and defence against peasant revolt.[33] Yet, centralisation did not necessarily mean that the state was all-powerful, despite its propaganda to that effect.[34] As Heller writes, 'The absolutist state had deprived the French nobility of much of its ability to control the rural population or to withstand revolt.' But it could not always replace that ability with its own power, which mattered in a situation where peasant resistance to the payment of tithes and enforcement of seigneurial rights had been increasing since 1775.[35]

Heller agrees with most commentators that the fiscal crisis of the state was a major precipitant of the revolution, in particular the increased share of taxation falling on the commoners. Not only were the nobles largely exempt from these, but they increased their own income levels by squeezing greater rents from their tenants. As we have seen, however, Heller also insists that there was an economic as well as a financial crisis: 'Economic crisis galvanised the mass of the population to throw its weight behind the political struggle of the bourgeoisie, allowing it to take power'.[36] Heller follows the Marxist Guy Lemarchand in arguing that there was a shortage of investment capital in both industry and agriculture, 'because too much of the economic surplus was drained off in the form of agricultural rents'. 'In the final analysis the paralysis of the leading sectors of an emergent capitalism reflected the ongoing stranglehold of the seigneurial class over the economy.' The crisis was also agricultural: 'The growth in population rendered the holdings of many of the peasants progressively smaller and increasingly fragile.' The two were connected by the limitations to French development:

> The domestic market was clearly inhibited by growing rural poverty. But the market was also blocked by the persistence of tolls and tariffs, local systems of weights and measures, a lack of adequate means of transport, and the burden of indirect taxes. Such a situation encouraged the persistence of too large a degree of domestic or local subsistence inhibiting urbanisation and the commercialisation of agriculture.

In short, the revolution had three underlying economic causes. The crisis of industrial underinvestment in the capitalist manufacturing sector and 'a classic Malthusian' crisis of subsistence in feudal agriculture set the context for 'the financial insolvency of the state', which in turn 'led to an ultimate political crisis'. The alignment of the joint crises of capitalism, feudalism and the absolutist state suggests the transitional, combined nature of French economy, but also that the transition had reached the point where it would be increasing difficult for the process to continue without radical political change.[37]

Both bourgeois and capitalist

Who then were the bourgeoisie who took the leadership of the revolution once the crisis had broken? Heller points out that, in terms of social weight, there were simply many more members of that class by the end of the 18th century than at the beginning: 'It is estimated that the size of the bourgeoisie grew from 700,000 to 800,000 at the beginning of the 18th century to perhaps 2.3 million in 1789, vastly outnumbering the 120,000 or so nobles.' Partly because of this, from 1720 onwards the nobility began to force through measures which excluded the bourgeoisie from joining them, including the ending of ennoblement through office in 1728. The bourgeoisie were opposed to the tax exemptions of the nobility, particularly as taxation increased, although membership of the nobility based on merit was still their goal. As this suggests, the development of their class consciousness was subject to contradictory pressures. On the one hand, their capacity for collective self-organisation was limited, for fairly obvious reasons: 'Before the onset of the revolution, the sphere of autonomous political activity was quite circumscribed by the authorities of the *ancien régime* as a matter of policy.' On the other hand, a bourgeois way of life involving distinct forms of dress, manners, speech and so on began to develop. So too did organisations where new ideas could be discussed and other activities besides. The Freemasons were one such organisation: 'The meeting of the lodges became sites not only for philosophical discussions, but for the creating and financing of new business partnerships.' It was clear to many young bourgeois that careers were not open to their talents: 'As a result, late 18th century France produced a large stratum of alienated intelligentsia who played an important role in the Revolution'.[38]

But what was the relationship of these bourgeois intellectuals to capitalism? As we have seen from the work of George Comninel, some 'political Marxists' claim that capitalists and the bourgeoisie are quite distinct classes, a position which has implications for how we assess revolutions, notably the English and French, which otherwise appear decidedly similar. Benno Teschke, for example, claims that 'while the English Revolution was not bourgeois, it was capitalist, and while the French Revolution was bourgeois, it was not capitalist'.[39] This distinction is completely untenable and relies on a fixation on the etymological origin of the word 'bourgeois'—as if the fact that it originally meant 'town dweller' in the middle ages continued to determine how it was used in the 18th century! Capitalists are *part* of the bourgeoisie. The latter is a far broader category, but one which could not exist as a class without the centripetal economic core of people committed to capital accumulation. Heller makes two points in this context.

First, there are perfectly good reasons why leadership should be exerted by individuals at the economic periphery. In one of his few direct references to the classical Marxist tradition, Heller notes Gramsci's insistence on the formation of 'organic intellectuals' to a revolutionary class: 'As a new class develops within the world of economic production, it tends to create from out of itself a stratum of intellectuals that helps to give it a sense of homogeneity and a sense of its economic as well as its social and political functions.' In France these included 'physicians, journalists, writers and, above all, lawyers'. 'In this light', Heller justly remarks, 'to demand why business people and not lawyers were to be found sitting in the Estates General for the third estate in 1789 is to invoke an argument based on a crude reductionism—a position of which Marxists have often been accused'.[40]

Second, it is in any case untrue that capitalists in the narrow sense were uninvolved in the revolution. Their direct intervention in government tended to be exercised outside the capital, something which has often been ignored because of the decisive impact of events in Paris. But as Heller says, 'the weight of the economic bourgeoisie made itself felt directly at the level of local rather than national government'.[41] Their most obvious impact, however, can be seen in the laws passed by the Convention. Take three components of the legislative programme of 1791, which clearly embody capitalist interests. Under the Law of Allaire of 2 March feudal guilds were abolished and restrictions on businesses removed. The Le Chapelier Law of 14-17 June banned combinations and industrial action. Finally, the decree on agrarian property rights of 5 June, the most important of a series of enactments concerning agriculture, established freedom of ownership, including the right to enclose common land.[42]

Because of their date, these examples may not convince revisionists who believe that the bourgeois content of the revolution ended after 1791. But the majority of the Jacobins saw political dictatorship, economic centralisation, the Law of the Maximum and all the rest as temporary measures made necessary by civil war and invasion. Only at the outer edges of Jacobinism did members see them as being anti-capitalist in themselves, and this was the anti-capitalism of small producers, not workers: 'The creation of the Jacobin state was not simply based on countering the threat of counter-revolution, but on the determination to oppose the threat from economic competition from its English rival by using political means'.[43]

The arms industry provides a good example of how military necessity contributed to capitalist expansion. In what can retrospectively be seen as early measures of state capitalism, the Committee of Public Safety effectively nationalised the existing armouries and organised the building of new ones in Paris and elsewhere. The majority of forges (about 1,000) were confiscated from their noble and ecclesiastical owners and transformed into state property, leased out to the *maîtres de forges* who had previously run them. Under the Directory and Napoleon they were ultimately sold off to the same individuals who, over the entire revolutionary period, began through a process of internal competition to centralise ownership and control: 'The stage was set for a future transformation of this industry—key to the development of 19 century industrial capitalism—under the auspices of these *maîtres de forges* who now operated these means of production as their private property.' Steel production nearly doubled between 1789 and 1801. And the new owners prospered too: by 1811 more than a dozen of the *maîtres de forges* had assets of between one and three million francs.[44]

In his discussion of the ideology of the revolutionary bourgeoisie Heller focuses on unjustly neglected figures like Pierre Louis Roederer and Etienne Clavière. The latter was a Genevan financial speculator and banker who 'combined fervent idealism and shrewd business calculation', ultimately becoming minister for finance briefly in 1792-93. Of this type of individual, Heller writes, 'They identified this new regime with the free market'.[45] Similar views were unambiguously expressed following the Thermidorian coup of 1794. One member of the new ruling group, Paul-Augustin Lozeau, rejected the Jacobin ideal of universal property ownership and abolition of poverty: 'Even if it were possible how then, asked Lozeau, could the big farmers, the merchants, and the industrialists find the labour power that was indispensable to their enterprises?'[46]

The nature of post-revolutionary France

The orthodox view of post-revolutionary France, held by virtually everyone from Engels to the revisionists, is that a mass of peasant smallholders, left in secure possession of their holdings by the revolution, acted as a break on the development of capitalism. The assumption here is that only large capitalist farmers can be competitive, but this is not necessarily the case. The division of the land wou ld initially have retarded capitalist development: 'But under free market conditions it would have speeded primitive accumulation over the medium term by unleashing the path of small-scale commodity production in both town and country.' This position was actually theorised under the Directory from 1795 by the proponents of what James Livesey calls 'commercial republicanism', who saw it as a conscious alternative to the British path of 'enclosure, tenant farming and agricultural innovation'. The post-Thermidorian reaction refused the demands of the peasants for land and upheld the ownership and dominance of 'nobles, bourgeoisie and rich peasants'. We therefore may have to revise the traditional view of the agrarian settlement and consider whether it was not 'the persistence of large property and the burden of rent, not small peasant property, which inhibited a more rapid development of French capitalism'. In turn, this might suggest that 'the popular revolution based on the petty producers ought to be seen as an essential element of the capitalist dynamic characteristic of this upheaval'.[47]

Heller agrees with Livesey that 'revisionist attempts to measure the economic consequences of the revolution in terms of short-term costs and benefits is historiographically misconceived'.[48] This does not mean that there were no benefits. In particular, Heller questions the conventional view that British manufacturing was superior to the French in the immediate aftermath of the revolution. First, Britain was actually less mechanised during this period than was traditionally thought; it was only in the latter half of the 19th century that this became dominant. Second, mass production was not the only method of industrialisation: 'With its higher quality production, France inserted itself differently into the international division of labour…[growing] at a rate comparable to that of its neighbours but based its secondary sector on small craft and manufacturing enterprises'.[49]

The missing international dimension

No book can encompass every aspect of a subject, but the one key area where Heller's account is noticeably deficient is in its treatment of the international dimension. Clearly a major contributory factor to the territorial expansion of capitalism during the 19th century was the competitive pressure which the existing capitalist nation-states, including France, placed on the feudal and absolutist regimes, forcing those which were able to establish nation-state structures and capitalist economies. As the theory of uneven and combined development would lead us to expect, once the development of capitalism became a conscious process then obviously changes to the relations of production tended to accompany or even precede changes to the forces of production, precisely because the aspirant capitalists knew what they were trying to achieve, unlike their predecessors in the period when capitalism first emerged as a distinct mode of production.[50]

At one point Heller notes that the market is scarcely a spontaneous generation in any historical circumstances: 'The provision of a more or less trained and disciplined labour force, a reliable currency, law and order, and an infrastructure of roads and bridges is not provided directly through the market but requires state intervention.' But the main role of the revolutionary French state was in nurturing, not conceiving, French capitalism, a process 'made necessary by the ongoing weakness of the capitalist economy in France as compared to, and in competition with, England'.[51] As the last sentence suggests, Heller does not ignore the effect on France of competition with Britain. However, he neglects two other aspects of France's situation in the formative world market, one in the period leading up to the revolution, the other in the period flowing out of it.

The first is the extent of capitalist production outside France. Any account of the formative process of French capitalism must include the colonial economy, particularly the slave plantations of the Caribbean. These classically 'combined' forms were perhaps the most advanced under French ownership and bore the closest relationship to those of their British rivals. As Robin Blackburn notes, 'It would...be wrong to propose a sharp contrast between English 'bourgeois' colonisation and French 'feudal' colonisation, since the social forces involved in both—merchants and colonists—were comparable'.[52] As C L R James notes of the slaves, 'Working and living together in gangs of hundreds on the huge sugar factories which covered the North Plain [of San Domingo], they were closer to a modern proletariat than any group of workers in existence at the time'.[53] Extending his focus to the colonial world would have strengthened the argument Heller wants to make about the pre-revolutionary existence of French capitalism.

The second is the international impact of the revolution. Apart from the inspiration which it provided to revolutionaries in other countries, the most obvious aspect is the direct intervention of the French state in the territories which it conquered. Indeed, one of the proofs of the bourgeois nature of the revolution is precisely the way in which it acted to attack feudalism outside its own borders, even after the internal reaction began with Thermidor. Heller's main references are to the extent to which the manufactured commodities of the conquered territories grew or failed to grow under French rule. There are clearly more of the latter than the former (Heller mentions Belgium, the Rhineland, Bavaria, Saxony and Switzerland), but the issue is surely broader than this.[54] Like the New Model Army in Scotland between 1651 and 1660, the 'people's armies' attempted to crush the local nobility, abolish feudal tenures and jurisdictions and generally rationalise economy and society. Their failure to do so on a permanent basis—for which there are also parallels with the New Model Army in Scotland—was an important factor in determining why capitalist stabilisation had to take place on the conservative basis of a restored monarchy.

The extent to which the French were able to establish sister republics in conquered Europe depended on whether indigenous forces existed which were willing to be involved in the process of reform, but precisely because of their isolation, their minority status, they were not necessarily those with popular followings, as the Spanish rebellion against France and its local supporters after 1808 was to prove. Where there were social forces committed to republican politics, it tended to be in those areas, principally Holland, where bourgeois revolutions had already taken place and consequently where these forces were opposed to the imperial role of the French armies.[55] In Britain, the most advanced of all, the ruling class were violently opposed to France and prepared to ally with absolutist reaction to defeat it, partly because the British bourgeoisie feared—as they had the Dutch in the 1650s—a successful rival, and partly because the very violence of the revolution had acted as an inspiration to nascent working class forces in England and Scotland, and to bourgeois revolutionaries in Ireland. In some territories, like Hanover and Westphalia in 1807, the French abolished serfdom only for it to be restored after Napoleon withdrew in 1813. In other parts of the German lands, notably in the Rhineland, it proved impossible to restore seignorial rights, but these examples were too few to be the basis for a Europe of independent states on the French model.

Perhaps the most important long-term international effect of the French Revolution, however, was the way in which it acted as a stimulus for revolution from above. Even in the short term, French victories led to internal reform. For Prussia, defeat at the hands of the Napoleonic armies at Jena and Auerstadt in 1806, and the subsequent humiliation of the Peace of Tilsit in 1807, seemed to demonstrate the superiority of free peasants over serfs as a source of manpower, while the indemnities imposed by the victorious French demanded an increase in revenues which was unlikely to be produced as long as serfdom endured.[56] The triumph of bourgeois revolution in France now meant that capitalism took on an unstoppable economic force it had not possessed when Britain was the only capitalist power of any size. But the bourgeoisies of Europe were themselves increasing paralysed between the conflicting desire to bring about revolutions that would place them in power and fear of the mass mobilisations that seemed necessary to achieve it. Ironically, it was the very grandeur and ferocity of the popular interventions which characterised the French Revolution that ensured it would never be repeated. Other forces, often from sections of the old ruling class, would eventually act in their stead, particularly in Germany, Italy and Japan.

It is for this reason that I think we have to question some of the formulations which Heller uses here. His work enters a debate over two different if related questions. The first is the specific one of the French Revolution—what caused it, who was involved, what were their motivations, and so on. The other is the general one of whether it is possible to produce a theory of bourgeois revolution that can encompass the French example, but also the quite different experiences of countries as distinct as Scotland, Mexico or China. Heller has made a considerable contribution to the first, but tends to avoid the second. Indeed, Heller suggests that the French Revolution was bourgeois because it was led by the bourgeoisie.[57] This is certainly true of France, but if direct leadership is the main criterion there have been precious few other bourgeois revolutions. Heller is surely correct to write: 'In Marx's eyes the revolution in France alongside the English Revolution was the classic form of a bourgeois revolution.' 'Classic' does not, however, imply that it was typical or characteristic, still less that 'it was a model against which the ascent of the bourgeoisie to power elsewhere could be judged'.[58] At certain points in his book Heller appears to recognise this, writing of Marx, 'His view of the French Revolution as archetypical of bourgeois revolutions may...be questioned'.[59] Elsewhere, however, he echoes the conventional view of the failure to repeat the French road: 'We must acknowledge that transitions to capitalism occurred in Japan and Germany without such a rupture, albeit at an ultimately tragic historical cost in the form of fascism'.[60] The view that fascism arose because of the failure or unfulfilled character of the German bourgeois revolution has been subjected to searching Marxist criticism by David Blackbourn and, in particular, Geoff Eley, who have turned the entire argument on its head by arguing that the German Revolution was more authentically 'bourgeois' than either the English or French. The tragedy of fascism arose not because of the form taken by the German bourgeois revolution, but as the result of the crisis of the Weimar Republic in the years immediately preceding the Nazi seizure of power.[61]

Conclusion

In many ways Heller's work resembles that of the late Brian Manning, a writer who defended the bourgeois nature of English Revolution in his work as vigorously as Heller does that of the French Revolution here. Manning was, however, suspicious of Marxist reappraisals of the bourgeois revolution which downplayed the conscious role of the bourgeoisie, seeing this as moving away from notions of class struggle.[62] I think Manning was wrong about this, since the view that revolutions do not *have* to be carried out by the bourgeoisie does not commit one to the claim that they are *never* carried out by the bourgeoisie, as in their different ways both the English and French revolutions were. It seems quite possible to be able to defend a conception of bourgeois self-emancipation, as Heller so ably does here, while still holding that this was not the only or the most common route to capitalist domination.

It will be interesting to find out what further thoughts Heller has on the subject. For the moment, however, this work is indispensable for anyone interested in a serious Marxist view of the subject. It is a notable demonstration that, contrary to what is claimed by Furet and everyone else who wants to wave goodbye to what Heller calls 'the capital event of the modern age', the French Revolution is not yet over.[63]

NOTES

1: G Lukács, 'Towards a Methodology of the Problem of Organisation', in *History and Class Consciousness* (London, 1971), p308.

2: A Cobban (1955), 'The Myth of the French Revolution', in *Aspects of the French Revolution* (London, 1971), pp95-106. Cobban developed these arguments in *The Social Interpretation of the French Revolution* (Cambridge, 1964).

3: J L Talmon (1952), *The Origins of Totalitarian Democracy* (London, 1961), p80.

4: E J Hobsbawm, *Echoes of the Marseillaise: Two Centuries Look Back at the French Revolution* (London and New York, 1990), p109; A MacIntyre, 'The End of Ideology and the End of the End of Ideology', in *Against the Self-Images of the Age: Essays on Ideology and Philosophy* (London, 1971), p4.

5: The phrase sounds rather more elegant in the original French, ie, 'le dérapage de la révolution'. F Furet and D Richet (1965), *La Révolution française* (Revised Edition, Paris, 1970), p126.

6: F Furet, 'The French Revolution is Over', in *Interpreting the French Revolution*, translated by E Forster (Cambridge and Paris, 1981), pp5-6, 12.

7: N Davidson, 'How Revolutionary Were the Bourgeois Revolutions? (continued)', *Historical Materialism*, vol 13, no 4 (2005), pp8-21, 27-32.

8: B Teschke, 'Bourgeois Revolution, State Formation and the Absence of the International', *Historical Materialism*, vol 13, no 2 (2005), p5.

9: G C Comninel, *Rethinking the French Revolution: Marxism and the Revisionist Challenge* (London and New York, 1990), pp182, 193, 200, 202.

10: H Heller, *The Bourgeois Revolution in France, 1789-1815* (Oxford and New York, 2006), pviii.

11: H Heller, *The Conquest of Poverty: the Calvinist Revolt in Sixteenth Century France* (Leiden, 1986); *Iron and Blood: Civil Wars in Sixteenth Century France* (Montreal, 1991); *Labour, Science and Technology in France, 1500-1620* (Cambridge, 1996).

12: H Heller, *The Bourgeois Revolution in France*, as above, p1.

13: As above, p149.

14: As above, pp26-28.

15: A Soboul (1965), *A Short History of the French Revolution, 1789-1799*, translated by G Symcox (Berkeley, Los Angeles and London, 1977); P McGarr, 'The Great French Revolution', *International Socialism*, 43 (Summer 1989).

16: H Heller, *The Bourgeois Revolution in France*, as above, p22.

17: To be fair to Guérin, his conclusions about the prospects of working class power in the French Revolution were ultimately more realistic than those of his followers: 'The objective conditions of the time did not allow the [*sans-culotte*] vanguard to beat the bourgeoisie at their own game'—D Guerin (1946), *La Lutte de Classes sous la Première République*, Revised Edition, 2 volumes (Paris, 1968), vol 1, p405.

18: H Heller, *The Bourgeois Revolution in France*, as above, p23.

19: As above, pp89, 93.

20: As above, p23.

21: G Lefebvre (1951), *The French Revolution*, (2 volumes, London and New York, 1962-1964), vol 1, *From its Origins to 1793*, translated by E M Evanson; vol 2, *From 1793 to 1799*, translated by J H Stewart and J Friguglietti; A Soboul (1962), *The French Revolution, 1787-1799: from the Storming of the Bastille to Napoleon*, translated by A Forrest and C Jones (London, 1989).

22: H Heller, *The Bourgeois Revolution in*

France, as above, p23.

23: As above, p74.

24: As above, p150.

25: As above, p7.

26: As above, p31. And see, for example, I Wallerstein, *The Modern World System* (3 volumes, New York, 1974-1989), vol 2, *Mercantilism and the Consolidation of the European World-Economy, 1600-1750*, pp87-90.

27: As above, p34.

28: As above, p36.

29: As above, pp5-6, 36, 45-48.

30: As above, p51.

31: As above, pp37-38.

32: As above, p67.

33: See, in general, P Anderson, *Lineages of the Absolutist State* (London, 1974), pp19-20, and specifically in relation to France, R Brenner, 'The Agrarian Roots of European Capitalism', in T H Aston and C H E Philpin (eds), *The Brenner Debate: Agrarian Class Structure and Economic Development in Pre-Industrial Europe* (Cambridge, 1985), pp286-291.

34: See, in general, M Mann, *The Sources of Social Power* (2 volumes, Cambridge, 1986-1993), vol 1, *A History of Power from the Beginning to AD 1760*, pp475-483 and, specifically in relation to France, T Skocpol, *States and Social Revolutions: a Comparative Analysis of France, Russia and China* (Cambridge, 1979), pp52-54.

35: H Heller, *The Bourgeois Revolution in France*, as above, p66.

36: As above, p67.

37: As above, pp67-69, 70, 147.

38: As above, pp54-60.

39: B Teschke, 'Bourgeois Revolution, State Formation and the Absence of the International', as above, p12. See also E M Wood, *The Origin of Capitalism: a Longer View* (London and New York, 2002), p63.

40: H Heller, *The Bourgeois Revolution in France*, as above, p72. For Gramsci's original discussion of 'organic intellectuals', see A Gramsci, 'The Intellectuals', in *Selections from the Prison Notebooks*, edited and translated by Q Hoare and G Nowell Smith (London, 1971), pp14-21.

41: H Heller, *The Bourgeois Revolution in France*, as above, p86.

42: As above, pp88, 89.

43: As above, p91.

44: As above, pp96, 103, 119, 129.

45: As above, pp76, 77, 78.

46: As above, p110.

47: As above, pp94, 99-103.

48: As above, p113.

49: As above, p137.

50: See, for example, my discussion of the transition to capitalism in rural Scotland, 'The Scottish Path to Capitalist Agriculture 2: the Capitalist Offensive (1747-1815)', *Journal of Agrarian Change*, vol 4, no 4 (October 2004), pp415-416, 423-431.

51: H Heller, *The Bourgeois Revolution in France*, as above, p126.

52: R Blackburn, *The Making of New World Slavery: from the Baroque to the Modern, 1492-1800* (London and New York, 1997), pp300-301.

53: C L R James, *The Black Jacobins: Toussaint L'Ouverture and the San Domingo Revolution* (London, 1980), pp85-86.

54: H Heller, *The Bourgeois Revolution in France*, as above, p139.

55 : S Schama, *Patriots and Liberators: Revolution in the Netherlands, 1780-1813* (London, 1992), pp12-15.

56: J Blum, *The End of the Old Order in Rural Europe* (Princeton, 1978), pp362, 370; TJ Byres, *Capitalism from Above and Capitalism from Below* (Houndmills, 1996), pp27-8.

57: H Heller, *The Bourgeois Revolution in France*, as above, p7.

58: As above, p11.

59: As above, p149.

60: As above, p65.

61: G Eley, 'The British Model and the German Road: Rethinking the Course of German History Before 1914', in D Blackbourn and G Eley, *The Peculiarities of German History*, as above, pp85, 154. These conclusions are supported by most serious contemporary histories of Nazi Germany. See, for example, I Kershaw, *Hitler, 1889-1936: Hubris* (London, 1998), pp73-75 and R J Evans, *The Coming of the Third Reich* (London, 2003), pp2-21.

62: B Manning, 'The English Revolution: the Decline and Fall of Revisionism', *Socialist History*, 14 (1999), p46 and pp44-46 more generally.

63: H Heller, *The Bourgeois Revolution in France*, as above, pix.

Book reviews

Wet Blunkett

John Newsinger

A review of David Blunkett, ***The Blunkett Tapes*** *(Bloomsbury, 2006), £25*

With the publication of his supposed 'diaries', David Blunkett has achieved an impressive hat-trick: the former heads of the Metropolitan Police, the Prison Service and the Armed Forces have all publicly called him a liar. This is a remarkable achievement for any former home secretary, let alone one as right wing as Blunkett. Indeed nothing like it has ever happened before. While at one level this obviously reflects on Blunkett's honesty, or rather lack of it, more important is what it tells us about the culture of New Labour and the state of the Blairite project. First though, what about Blunkett?

Of particular interest in this regard is the tale that Martin Narey, the former Director-General of the Prison Service, had to tell. He was incensed by Blunkett's self-aggrandising account of his performance during the Lincoln prison riot of October 2002. In his 'diaries' Blunkett relates how he had to instruct Narey to stop 'dithering' and if necessary to call in the army to retake the prison. He was worried that the rioting might spread throughout the prison system, that 'we were within a whisker of having on our hands a total and utter catastrphe'. Blunkett emphasises that on this occasion he made a real difference, that his intervention staved off disaster. He acted decisively to strengthen 'the arm of those who were prepared to act' and made it clear that he was 'prepared to override those who were dithering'. He modestly concludes that his performance on this occasion proved that he was one of the 'best' of Tony Blair's ministers and that he had prevented a 'firestorm' engulfing the prisons.[1]

Narey tells a somewhat different story. He observes that Blunkett's diary entry 'was clearly not written at the time because he refers to me as being in overall charge of corrections (prisons and probation), a position not invented at the time of the riot and one I was not to take up until 2003'. He, on the other hand, was so disturbed by Blunkett's behaviour that he did keep contemporaneous notes. According to these, a hysterical Blunkett phoned Narey to demand that the prison be retaken, no matter what the consequences:

'He directed me, without delay, to order staff back into the prison. I told him that we did not, at that time, have enough in the prison to contemplate such a move, but that many more staff were on their way from other prisons. I insisted, however, that although I was determined to take the prison back as quickly as possible, I could not, and would not, risk staff or prisoners' lives in attempting to do so. He shrieked at me that he didn't care about lives, and told me to call in the army and "machine-gun" the prisoners. He then ordered me to take the prison back immediately. I refused. One of the prison governors who overheard the exchanges remarked incredulously, "Did he really say he didn't care about lives?"'[2]

This episode reveals a great deal about New Labour and the state of the Labour Party. Blunkett was actually urging a prison massacre, something that shocked his officials, in order, it seems clear, to protect his political career. He feared that the rioting would spread to other prisons and that his carefully constructed image as a hardline reactionary would be destroyed. If this happened, his popularity with the right wing press would be at an end and his usefulness to Tony Blair would be over.

It is easy to forget the extent to which it is historically unprecedented for a Labour Home Secretary to find himself so far to the right of his prison officials, but then this government has produced many such surprises. It is a new development for a man of Blunkett's character and reactionary opinions to be a senior figure in the Labour Party, for such a man, before his (first) resignation in December 2004, to be seriously considered as Blair's possible successor, and indeed for him to remain a Labour MP at all. Once upon a time someone like Blunkett would have inevitably defected to the Conservatives. Clearly the Labour Party is not what it used to be. It would once have been inconceivable that a member of a Catholic right wing secret society (Ruth Kelly) could have become Secretary of State for Education or that the husband of a health minister (Tessa Jowell) could be regarded as an unfriendly witness by the Italian police in a case involving the illegal sale of contaminated blood products.[3] Today anything is possible with New Labour. One can only look forward, at the time of writing, to Blair becoming the first prime minister ever to be interviewed by the police over the sale of peerages! All this is really unprecedented, but we have got used to it. It is testimony to how far the Blairites have pulled the Labour Party to the right, the extent to which they have corrupted it and left it rotten to the core.

How has this sorry state of affairs come about? How is it that David Blunkett, once a young radical Labour councillor in Sheffield, later the leader of the so-called 'Socialist Republic of South Yorkshire', has ended up a discredited reactionary, a man regarded as a serious threat to civil liberties, one of the most right wing members of the New Labour government?

Blunkett, as is well-known, had a very hard childhood. After the death of his father in a horrendous industrial accident[4] the family was poverty-stricken and, of course, Blunkett was blind. He had enormous difficulties to overcome, but nevertheless succeeded, against considerable odds, in securing a university education and eventually becoming a Labour councillor, positioning himself on the left of the party. As Blunkett wrote in his autobiography, *On A Clear Day*:

'I had already learned sufficient history to appreciate that through the ages there has been a constant struggle not only between right and wrong, but also between those with power and wealth and those with neither'.[5]

He marched against the Springboks tour and was on the massive demonstration against the Industrial Relations Act in 1972. He made his name, however, as a champion of subsidised public transport. By 1980 he was the leader of Sheffield Council. According to his biographer, Stephen Pollard, Blunkett always took care to appear more left wing than he really was. He was, at this time, 'riding the left horse' as a career strategy. He was 'a master at playing the left gallery'. Pollard quotes one of Blunkett's friends on this left pose:

'Take the red flag flying over Sheffield; it was all gesture politics. It was all to make the left think that he was one of them. But he did not really believe in it. What he really wanted was office for himself and for the Labour Party'.[6]

He was far from alone in this adoption of a left pose at this point in time. The 1980s saw the rise of Bennism inside the Labour Party, and to secure a parliamentary seat, Blunkett had to establish his Bennite credentials. Given that his leftism was always exaggerated, it is worth making the point that at this time even the right of the Labour Party would have recoiled in horror from the politics of Blairism, from what would have been seen then as a kind of ultra-Thatcherism.

What began Blunkett's shift to the right was apparently Thatcher's defeat of the municipal left over rate capping and the defeat of the miners' strike in 1985. This began his trajectory from Tony Benn to Tony Blair via Neil Kinnock. What is interesting, of course, is that the miners' strike was one of those dramatic demonstrations of the 'constant struggle between those with wealth and power and those with neither'. The conclusions Blunkett drew from this particular episode in the struggle led to him eventually changing sides.

Which brings us, at last, to *The Blunkett Tapes*–surely one of the biggest publishing disasters of the decade. The publishers, Bloomsbury, paid £400,000 for this interminable 850-page exercise in self-justification and self-pity, for a book that is really without any redeeming features and that contributes nothing whatsoever to our political or historical understanding of the times we live in. Despite a massive publicity blitz on radio, television and in the press, *The Blunkett Tapes* sold only 769 copies in its first week on the shelves, something that will seriously affect the size of the advances paid to other Labour ministers for their memoirs.

What does Blunkett actually have to say? He is very much concerned to establish his own cleverness and decisiveness, to condemn 'human rights fanatics', 'woolly-minded liberals' and even 'the Socialist Workers Party and its hangers-on' and, of course, to sing the praises of Tony Blair ('absolutely superb...a real world leader'). Interestingly, he takes every opportunity he can to put the knife into Roy Hattersley, the former deputy leader of the Labour Party, who has watched Blunkett effortlessly pass from his left to his right with ill-disguised distaste. On occasions Blunkett's dislike for asylum seekers comes out. His infamous use of the word 'swamped' with regard to asylum seekers seems not so much a cynical playing of the racist card as something he felt quite genuinely. His resentment at asylum seekers turning up at his constituency surgeries is almost visceral, and on one occasion they were actually accompanied by 'a white woman, a real do-gooder'. This is all pretty unsavoury.

One problem with Blunkett's diaries concerns their reliability. Martin Narey, as we have already seen, effectively exposed his account of the Lincoln prison riot as fictional, and one suspects that the same is true for much of the rest of the diaries. His entries regarding the war in Iraq, for example, do not inspire the slightest confidence. It seems absolutely clear that the diary has been rewritten in light of the furore over the failure to find weapons of mass destruction.

While Blair and Co never seriously believed that they were going to find such weapons, they were confident that in the euphoria of victory such details would be easily forgotten. Blunkett's diaries show every sign of being written in the knowledge that this was not to be, that the failure to find WMD would come to haunt them, and that some other pretext for the invasion would be necessary. He writes that it was his belief that the question of WMD was always secondary because UN Resolution 1441 provided adequate justification for attacking Iraq. Britain and the United States were merely enforcing a UN resolution.

These are just not credible as contemporaneous diary entries. Similarly, his entry explaining away Clare Short's embarrassing revelations that the government had been listening in on the UN Secretary-General Kofi Annan's phone calls: she must have found the transcripts on a website. This was clearly made up after the event. Even with regard to his recent boast that during the war he had urged the bombing of Al Jazeera, one cannot possibly take his word for it without other confirmation. He might just be trying to demonstrate his reactionary credentials to the likes of Rupert Murdoch!

What do ring true, however, are his concerns about the impact of the anti-war movement. 'How do you count a march like the one in London?' Blunkett asked himself of the great 15 February 2003 anti-war demonstration. 'This is not going to be an easy time', he observed, with some understatement. 'We have got an uphill struggle on our hands.' And when the invasion finally began, he complained that 'we are getting demos all over the place'. A year later he was still writing about 'the backlash on Iraq'.[7]

It is necessary to put Blunkett's trajectory from 'soft' left to 'hard' right in context. Labour MPs, even former ministers, have often completed such a transformation. It is an established feature of Labour Party history. Indeed one only has to think of Ramsay MacDonald, the leader of the party for many years and twice prime minister, defecting to the Conservatives in 1931. An even more extreme example is provided by Oswald Mosley, a former Labour junior minister, establishing the British Union of Fascists in 1932.

What is new today is that under Blair the Labour Party as a whole has defected to the right, not just its leader or individual MPs. This reflects the shift in the balance of class forces in Britain that began under Thatcher and has continued under Blair. Big business and the rich are so powerful today that Labour ministers actually see themselves as being there to serve their interests, and indeed aspire to join their ranks. When the Labour Party was first established, whatever criticisms one might have of its reformism, it was committed to fight against the injustices and inequalities in British society. New Labour, however, has enthusiastically embraced them.

A key figure in the transformation of the Labour Party has been Rupert Murdoch, not just in helping bring it about, but also in indicating exactly how far the process has gone. It would have been absolutely unthinkable before Blair for any senior Labour politician to openly court a union buster and right wing media boss of the calibre of Murdoch. Even Kinnock drew the line there. Today it is regarded in Labour ranks as unexceptional, as routine, as an inevitable part of the contemporary political process. Indeed Lance Price, a senior Labour spin doctor, has actually described Murdoch as a de facto member of the cabinet, as one of its most important members along with Gordon Brown and John Prescott.[8] Attempts under the Freedom of Information Act to find out how often Blair and Murdoch have communicated predictably failed, the reason being, of course, that they are so regular as to constitute a scandal. And there is every expectation that when Blair finally retires from politics he will be rewarded with an extremely lucrative post at the top of Murdoch's News International. Some cynics would argue that he has, in fact, been working for Murdoch for years. What the Murdoch connection does, however, is personalise New Labour's intimate connection with the British capitalist class. It is indicative of the relationships that Blair *and* Brown have successfully established with big business and the rich.

Blunkett himself has benefited from Murdoch's generosity. He found the man 'perfectly decent to deal with—very reasonable'. One has to remind oneself that this is the same man who in 1986 recruited scab labour, sacked his entire workforce and fought a year-long lockout to break the print unions, one of the bitterest industrial battles of the period. Murdoch inflicted tremendous hardship on thousands of workers and their families, and dealt the whole labour movement a serious blow. This is of no concern at all to the New Labour leadership. When Blunkett found himself in serious trouble, with his political career collapsing around him, he wrote in his diary, 'Thank God the Sun is totally with me. At least one newspaper is trying to tell the truth.' This verges on the obscene. And when he finally had to resign from the government for a second time in November 2005, he immediately went to Wapping for 'a pleasant drink' with Murdoch, who offered him a regular column in the Sun.[9] He was to be paid £150,000 a year for this. The man who had first appeared on TV in 1967 to complain about nudity and who in 1983 walked out of a play in protest against nudity on the stage apparently has no problem with Page 3.

NOTES

1: D Blunkett, *The Blunkett Tapes* (London, 2006), pp404-406.

2: *Times*, 17 October 2006.

3: For a transcript of the BBC *Panorama* programme on David Mills see the BBC website.

4: In his autobiography Blunkett wrote of how when he was 12 his father had met 'a dreadful agonising end' after falling into 'a giant vat of boiling water'. He had stayed on working for the Gas Board after retirement age at their invitation. They used his age to try and avoid paying compensation. See *On A Clear Day* (London, 2002), p43.

5: As above, p56.

6: S Pollard, *David Blunkett* (London, 2005), pp104, 105, 127. Blunkett and his suitably right wing biographer subsequently fell out when Blunkett tried to blame him for his contemptuous remarks about fellow cabinet members and others. Pollard is now among those who dismiss Blunkett as an inveterate liar.

7: *The Blunkett Tapes*, as above, pp278, 293, 295, 308, 449, 450, 454, 461, 711.

8: L Price, 'Rupert Murdoch is Effectively a Member of Blair's Cabinet', *Guardian*, 1 July 2006.

9: *The Blunkett Tapes*, as above, pp360, 725, 853-854.

Important signpost

Andrew Murray

A review of John Rees, Imperialism and Resistance (Routledge, 2006), £14.99

Imperialism has entered the public political discourse over the last five years in a way which would have seemed highly improbable for most of the preceding generation or more. It has leapt out of the history books and the realm of jargon back to the centre of public debate.

This is a consequence of the policies of George Bush and Tony Blair in the first instance—but also of the nature of the movement of resistance to them, which in Britain (and to some degree more widely) is identified above all with the Stop the War Coalition.

John Rees is, of course, well known to readers of *International Socialism*. However, he has become known far more widely (including to the reviewer) through his central part in the creation and development of StWC, the most important political mass movement in Britain for generations.

It is therefore more than appropriate that he should have written this popular and accessible book addressing the main issues in contemporary world politics—imperialism and the resistance to its expression, and above all that misnamed 'war on terror' which has already left an ineradicable scar on the life of this century.

With this volume Rees has performed a further service to the movement, including to those who will not share all of his assessments and conclusions. His aim is to present the present struggle in historical context, to outline the main economic and political forces shaping the world today and to address the issues confronting the anti-imperialist and anti-capitalist movements.

His analysis of the role of oil in shaping the politics of modern imperialism, and of the rampant inequalities exacerbated by globalisation are among the strongest sections of the book and will help deepen understanding of those factors which impel imperialism, and above all the US, towards war.

Such an analysis is important because too often the Marxist left is content with repeating the undoubted truth that imperialism generates war without probing the specific reasons why that is occurring at any one conjuncture (and not another). Certainly many on the broader left have been astonished that the end of the Cold War has not led to the reign of universal peace which was promised at the time.

An assessment of the crisis factors underlying the post-1991 world capitalist economy, the re-emergence of anti-imperialist rivalry as a leading factor in international politics, and the competition to ensure control over the resources vital to growth and profit, while at the same time endeavouring to maintain a pan-imperialist unity in response to any threats to the 'new world order'—these are the building blocks of ruling class politics today, and they are well-detailed in *Imperialism and Resistance*.

However, I think that we could with profit—at least in terms of political understanding in the broader movement—dig deeper, even in a book aimed at a general readership. In particular, it is important to address the basis of imperialism as a phase in the world capitalist economy and how that has been modified post-1991.

One of the simplest—and most useful—Marxist definitions of imperialism was given by the British historian Victor Kiernan: 'Imperialism today may be said to display itself in coercion exerted abroad, by one means or another, to extort profits above what simple commercial exchange can procure.' This definition has the merit of both indicating the taproot of imperialism, rather than concentrating on its expression in the development of monopoly capitalism and the export of capital, and laying stress on the political aspect of imperialism as a system of world domination—its coercive aspect.

In 1916 Lenin described imperialism as a system based on monopoly capitalism and the export of capital. He showed how important spheres of the world economy (for example, the oil industry) had been centralised under the control of a handful of large transnational monopolies based in the most advanced capitalist countries. In addition, he showed how the export of capital from these countries to exploit natural resources and cheap labour had become an essential source of super-profits to sustain the capitalist system. Today monopoly capital remains at the foundation of the world socio-economic system—but it is important for us to address what is new in the drive for super-profits.

For example, the annexation of millions—perhaps billions—of people anew to the system of capitalist exploitation of labour affects the working class everywhere directly and intimately. Less than ever is imperialism something happening to other people in other places.

Take the position of labour in the US itself. The intensification of exploitation is proceeding at a staggering pace. In the last 25 years the average US worker has been compelled to increase his/her working week by 40 percent. A worker working 40 hours a week in 1980 will therefore be working 56 hours today. At the same time there has been a general stagnation in real wage rates, a factor now causing concern to even bourgeois economists in the US. The increase in the rate of production of surplus value can easily be imagined. This circumstance, which can only be destructive to the family life, spiritual development and physical health of the US worker, can surely not be divorced from the tremendous pressure on wage rates exerted by capitalist competition as it moves jobs and investment to countries where super-profits can be extracted.

The result of this is as one would expect. The *Financial Times* recently reported that the great US monopolies were now enjoying the longest period of double-digit profits growth since records began (January 2006).

Many factors have powered this increase in exploitation—the removal of barriers to the movement of capital, the introduction of new production and communications technology able to materially affect the organic composition of capital, as well as the systemic changes, effected by different means, everywhere from Berlin to Beijing. Millions of people across the whole world are being drawn into capitalist exploitation as wage labour for the first time.

Consider the scale of what is occurring. The recently-retired chairman of the US Federal Reserve, Alan Greenspan, perhaps the single leading figure in US monopoly capital over the past generation, told Congress that 'the addition of more than 100 million educated workers from former Soviet countries, large segments of China's 750 million strong workforce, and workers from India 'would approximately double the overall supply of labour once all these workers become fully competitive in world markets'. This, he added 'has restrained the rise of unit labour costs in much of the world' (*Wall Street Journal*, 4 November 2005). Greenspan spelt out the obvious fact that this process is restraining the wages of manufacturing workers—those whose jobs can most easily be shifted to the former Socialist countries, to Asia, etc.

The result? According to Greenspan's own statistics, managers and supervisors are enjoying wage increases of 10 percent a year on average, while production workers' pay is barely keeping up with inflation. This benign situation for capitalism will, Greenspan said, 'persist for some time'.

It is this exponential expansion in the employment of wage-labour, driven by 'globalisation' which is the big story of imperialism on the economic side in the last 20 years, the counterpart to the US-led drive for a 'new world order' with its attendant wars. It will ultimately reach its limit, not when every sentient being is drawn into the system of wage labour, but rather when that system no longer has the ability to realise its surplus value—surplus value which does not exist in money form but rather as production and consumer goods for which there is no market—hence an immense crisis of overproduction.

In the short term this huge increase in the mass of surplus value being produced has helped abate symptoms of crisis within the world system by counteracting the tendency for the rate of profit to fall, but already the struggles over trade, access to markets and other forms of inter-imperialist rivalry are becoming sharper once more. A little further down the road this struggle is likely to get more acute, in Asia in particular, and mark the passage from neocolonial wars to great power conflict. In my view, *Imperialism and Resistance* could have benefited from a more detailed exploration of these themes, although some of the points sketched out here are touched upon.

I have to enter one further point of reservation, beyond recording the fact that John and I come from different traditions within the Marxist left, something reflected of course in his handling of the Soviet Union and, to some extent, the Labour Party—the two questions which divided the left from the far left in the 20th century. Rees notes that the post-1991 situation has at least created the possibility of overcoming some of these differences, or of addressing them in a less adversarial context. This is one factor which has made the success of the Stop the War Coalition possible.

The point that needs comprehending in the context of the present book is the ways in which the collapse of the USSR and the associated states has had a dramatic impact on the shape of anti-imperialist politics in the world.

It seems to me undeniable that, in however a vacillating and sometimes self-serving way, the Soviet government did extend considerable military, diplomatic and practical support to a range of secular anti-imperialist movements around the world throughout the post-war period. The absence of that support after the late 1980s has had a range of consequences: it created the possibility for the First Gulf War; opened the space for the rapid development of anti-imperialist (and sometimes anti-democratic too) movements in the Middle East drawing their inspiration from religion; and made it more likely that the imperialist powers themselves would feel able to pursue different agendas in competition with each other.

This point is paradoxically highlighted by the two examples John cites of 'democratic revolutions' at the start of the book—the fall of the Berlin Wall in 1989 and the overthrow of Suharto in Indonesia in 1998. In passing, this juxtaposition highlights the limitations of the 'democratic revolution' analysis, since in the latter case the ruling elite was reorganised, while in the former the entire political and economic power structure was swept away. The main point here, however, is the differential impact on world politics. The change of regime in Indonesia, while a half-step forward for the Indonesian people, had little impact on politics at a world level. The GDR had, however, taken a lead (doubtless at the instigation of the Soviet government) in providing support to national liberation struggles in Africa. It was deeply involved in assistance of all kinds to the ANC, SWAPO and, a little earlier, ZAPU in Zimbabwe, as well as to the post-colonial governments in Angola and Mozambique. The incorporation of the GDR into the Federal Republic had an enormous and negative impact on the struggle in Africa. Of course, the African people can and will find their own ways of overcoming these difficulties without European support, but the political strengthening of imperialism as a result of the collapse of the Soviet systems is, in the short term, undeniable.

A variation on the same story could be told with respect to the Middle East and the decline of secular resistance to imperialism at the expense of the rise of those drawing Islamic inspiration. At any event, not all 'democratic revolutions' have impacted on the development of world politics in the same fashion.

This analytical lacuna does not cast a very long shadow over the central thrust of the book, however. The mass movement can only benefit from drawing on the analysis in the concluding chapter, which addresses many of the issues of principle and tactic which have arisen in the development of anti-imperialist politics since 2001.

In particular, the treatment of the Muslim mobilisation in the anti-war movement, and the related issue of Islamophobia is masterly, and serves as a more general example as to how the working class and the socialist left should approach the question of alliances against imperialism today, when the forces mobilised against the depredations of the US-led world order are more diverse than at any equivalent preceding stage.

The emphasis placed on the right to self-determination for peoples and nations in the world today is also vital. This principle is no more an absolute for all times and places than any other is, but it is the key to unblocking the road to social advance at present and, I would guess, for some time to come. Departing from it certainly leads incrementally to support for the Bush-Blair world agenda.

Rees's analysis here is all of a piece with his contribution to the leadership of the Stop the War Coalition, in particular in ensuring that the movement's requirement to be as broad as possible 'did not preclude a radical approach', and maintaining the focus on the US and British governments as the main enemy.

As he writes, 'While not being anti-imperialist in declaration, a strong anti-imperialist current of opinion, often commanding majority agreement, was always present. This was not just a question of intellectual argument by anti-imperialists within the broader coalition, although this was vital as well. Crucially the agenda of the imperial powers themselves and the instinctive reactions of tens of thousands of activists drove the movement in that direction.'

It is true that events are themselves driving masses of people to exactly that understanding of the world, in the process creating a political crisis within the Labour Party and leaving behind entirely the once-powerful (just think of the Yugoslav war) voices of the pro-war and pro-imperialist 'left'. But nor should the role of political leadership be neglected. This book will, I hope, extend the political understanding that its author has shown in practice to many more people as we build a still stronger movement—more united, more radical—for the battles ahead.

When Reason was revolt

Chris Harman

*A review of Jonathan I Israel, **Enlightenment Contested** (Oxford, 2006), £30*

This is a long (871 pages of text), often repetitive, occasionally confusing, and very important book. It continues the challenge to the conventional view of the Enlightenment made by Israel five years ago in his *The Radical Enlightenment.*

The conventional view, as Israel describes it, sees the Enlightenment as an essentially 18th century current, starting with the physics of Newton, passing through Locke and Hume, and finding its most vocal expression in the writings of Voltaire, Montesquieu, Gibbon and the Scots Adam Ferguson, Smith John Millar and Lord Kames. This was, for instance, the view that very much influenced me when I wrote my *A People's History of the World.*

Israel sees things very differently. He sees the driving force being a much more radical current that starts in the Netherlands in 1660s with the atheistic philosophy of Spinoza (in which 'god' becomes just a way of referring to the material universe) continues there with the writings of the exiled French Huguenot Bayle, wins the allegiance of small, often persecuted, circles of thinkers across Europe (including Vico in Italy) and then forms the decisive influence on Diderot when he produces the Enlightenment's most significant embodiment, the *Encyclopédie*, in the 1750s.

The 'moderate' current of Newton and Locke through to Voltaire, he shows, was at pains to try to reconcile the advance of scientific knowledge with religious ideology and the established social structure. Newton and Locke accepted Christianity in its entirety, even if there were sometimes qualms about the validity of some miracles, while Voltaire insisted there had to be a 'supreme being'.

In Newton's case his apocalyptic religious beliefs were not, as usually presented, just a weird aberration from an essentially mechanical, materialist view of the universe. The intervention of god, he insisted, was necessary to explain why the planets circle round the Sun instead of moving away in a straight line as his physics dictated. Israel suggests that the criticisms of Newton's views by Leibniz as well as Spinoza's followers were not as crazy as how they are often presented. Although often based on scientific and mathematical mistakes, they in some ways foreshadowed the insights of relativity theory in the 20th century.

The softness towards existing religious dogma was not just a ploy to conceal their ideas from censors by the moderate current. Its adherents waged continual philosophical warfare against what they called 'Spinozism' to such an extent that their efforts to reconcile religion and science won the support of key elements of the Calvinist, Lutheran and Catholic establishments from the 1720s to the late 1740s. Voltaire even had the backing of one of the popes for a period. The attempt at conciliation with religious orthodoxy was matched by endorsement of hierarchical notions of society and opposition to any form of radical democratism or republicanism. The ideal was the post-1688 English set up, where a hereditary monarchy shared power with representatives of a landed elite, so protecting property and the market from both despotism above and the masses below. Defence of property was identified with the rights of the individual—but in such a way as to endorse privilege, including hereditary privilege and in Locke's case slavery (in which he had a direct financial interest). Not surprisingly, there was acceptance, at least in part, of the developing racist ideology by some of this current (Voltaire and Hume, for example).

It is these trends within the moderate current that have provided postmodernist and postcolonial writers to depict the whole Enlightenment as permeated through and through with 'Eurocentrism', 'Orientalism' and racism.

But, as Israel shows decisively, the approach of the radical 'Spinozists' led in a very different direction. Their starting point was a fundamental break with the old intellectual orthodoxies. They criticised strongly both the tradition of Renaissance 'humanism' that provided distorted readings of ancient Greek philosophy to justify the teachings of the Churches and the conciliatory approach of the Newton-Locke tradition. Their materialism led them to assert the fundamental unity of humanity, seeing the lower classes as having the same potential for intellectual development as their rulers, even if 'education' was needed to bring this out, and rejecting the notion that some peoples were intrinsically inferior to others. And they drew republican, democratic conclusions, even if they often felt these could not be put fully into effect until the mass of people had been educated away from the superstitious and obscurantist influences. So while Voltaire and Hume accepted some racist notion, Diderot rejected racism and not only opposed slavery and colonialism, but supported the rights of the slaves of the colonial oppressed to fight for their own liberation.

Not surprisingly, the proponents of the radical Enlightenment received a very different response from established society to the moderates. They faced recurrent bouts of repression, and were forced to either to disguise some of their ideas in print or to publish abroad under pseudonyms if they were not to face imprisonment or exile.

Events, however, forced the two currents together in the 1750s (just as the first volumes of the *Encyclopédie* were being published). By this time, both currents were centred in France. But French Catholicism was divided down the middle. As well as the relatively sophisticated Jesuit wing, prepared to accept some modern scientific notions in order to win people to the faith, there was the mystical Jansenist wing which relied on ecstatic 'miracles' for its mass following and therefore opposed both wings of the Enlightenment. It was able in 1750 to create what we would today call a 'moral panic' about the impact of supposedly Spinozist texts, forcing the Jesuits and the Royal Court to turn against not just the radical Enlightenment but the Voltairians as well. The *Encyclopédie* was briefly banned and Diderot got a short spell in prison, and even Voltaire no longer felt safe. It was in this period that he turned his magnificent polemical skills against the counter-Enlightenment, with his slogan '*Ecrasez l'infame*' (wipe out the infamy, ie organised superstitious religion) and, in 1758, the publication of his brilliant and subversive satirical novel *Candide*. In the process the fundamental differences between the two wings of the Enlightenment could easily disappear from view, opening the way for them to be overlooked ever since and for the Radical current to be virtually written out of intellectual history.

It is this which allows pro-war, Eurocentric and Islamophobic liberals to claim to embody the Enlightenment tradition today, identifying it with the Locke-Voltaire wing (although Locke did not extend his notions of toleration to atheists and he backed slavery). It is this also which enables postmodernist and postcolonial thinkers to present the Enlightenment as a whole as a negative intellectual trend

In fact, even the moderate Enlightenment was not uniformly Eurocentric, 'Orientalist' or racist. Locke endorsed slavery, but tried to justify it on non-racist grounds, while Hume accepted racist ideas but regarded slavery as 'barbarous'. In a fascinating chapter Israel provides an account of arguments between the Radical Enlightenment on the one side and Christian ideologists and the Moderate Enlightenment on the other. They all agreed that China was an exemplary society, if anything superior to any to be found in Europe, surviving as it had for over 2,000 years. The Radicals claimed this as proof that atheism could form the basis of the most moral of societies. The Christian thinkers and the Moderates argued that Confucianism rested on a belief in god, which proved the necessity of religion for morality. Both sides might have been ignorant of the realities of Chinese society, but it was by no means an 'Orientalist' ignorance.

Even more fascinating is the account of the Radicals' attitude towards Islam. They were far from seeing it as do the B52 liberals who claim to be the heirs of the Enlightenment today. As Israel says, in 'radical texts' the 'image of Islam' was of 'a pure monotheism of high moral calibre which was also a revolutionary force for positive change and one which proved from the outset to be both more rational and less bound to the miraculous than Christianity or Judaism'. The Radicals' 'sharp criticism of post-medieval Islam' was 'for lapsing from its early intellectual openness and love of philosophy and science, as well as its former commitment to tolerance'. Israel also notes that Voltaire was favourable to Islam, as exemplifying his notion of a pure 'natural religion' based on a supreme being without superstition and miracles. 'Voltaire...gave currency to the... conception of Mohammed as a great leader, legislator and rational reformer rather than a religious visionary and wonder-worker.'

Bayle, for the Radicals, emphasised the central role of Islamic thinkers from the 8th to the 12th centuries in transmitting and developing the rationalist materialist notions to be found in Greek philosophers. The Andalusian Islamic thinker Averroes (Ibn Rushd) in particular is 'held up as the man who had the courage single-handedly to combat the bigotry, credulity and crassness of his time'.

Israel provides a devastating refutation in these chapters of those who uncritically interpret Edward Said's book *Orientalism* as proving a seamless trend of prejudiced 'Orientalism' dominating European thought for millennia and encompassing 'Aeschylus...Victor Hugo, Dante and Karl Marx.' Significantly, Said's book never mentioned (according to its index) Spinoza or Bayle, and only referred to Diderot and Voltaire in passing (in reading *Candide*, Said does not seem to have noticed that the hero eventually found tranquility 'cultivating his garden' in the Islamic Ottoman empire). Eurocentrism, racism and 'Orientalism' were far from being an endemic feature of western Enlightenment thought, but a product of the ability of west European states to dominate the world, something which only really began to happen from the second half of the 18th century onwards. So although traces of them can be found (although not uniformly) in the Moderate Enlightenment, they did not become all-dominant until the counterrevolutionary hysteria which swept Europe's ruling classes in the aftermath of the French Revolution brought the Enlightenment to an end.

What is more, the way in which the Radical Enlightenment could see their intellectual forebears as being in Confucian China or the Islamic empires as well as in Graeco-Roman and Renaissance worlds shows how mistaken it is, as the B52 liberals and the postcolonials alike claim, to see the Enlightenment as an exclusively 'western' product. As Israel puts it, 'There is no reason one should search only in the western philosophical traditions to find the intellectual roots of, or cultural basis for, personal liberty, comprehensive toleration, equality sexual and racial, and a secular morality of equity...'

I should say that, despite the wonders of this book, Israel is not a Marxist, but rather someone who takes the egalitarian, democratic goals of the Radical Enlightenment seriously in a way that contradicts much of what capitalism today offers. In the introduction to the book he presents a view of political change—especially the French Revolution—which counterpoises the development of ideas to social changes, and stresses the autonomous role played by the history of ideas. This approach has some advantages over a crude mechanical version of Marxism which sees ideas as a mere reflection of processes taking place independently of them (and therefore of human action). For that version implies simply sitting back and waiting for society to change without our intervention and forgetting Marx's adage that ideas that gain mass support themselves become a 'material force'. But Israel's approach fails to ask why this can happen at certain points in history and not others, why radical thought can guide human practice sometimes and yet radical thinkers spend decades or even generations apparently getting nowhere. The point is that human beings become open to new ideas when their old ways of seeing things no longer fit their situation. But they can only turn to such ideas if there are people already propagating them. And these people are themselves transmitting ideas that are a product of previous periods of social turmoil. So the Enlightenment arose out of attempts to come to terms with the political, social and intellectual upheavals of the 17th century. It then in turn fed into the great political upheavals at the end of the 18th century in North America and continental Europe, especially France.

The book is long and not always an easy read, it lacks a glossary to explain the scores of thinkers and events it refers to, and most people will not have the time to tackle the over 800 pages of each of Israel's two volumes. But what it says is very important, and let us hope that at some point the author produces a potted popular version which can rescue the Enlightenment from its false friends and its detractors alike.

Not just opium

Paul Blackledge

A review of Scott Mann, ***Heart of a Heartless World: Religion as Ideology*** *(Black Rose Books, 1999), £13.99*

How should socialists relate to social movements whose aims are informed by religious ideas? A moment's consideration of this problem is enough to suggest that a simple answer is precluded by the very diversity of such movements.

The recent emergence in the West of a powerful current of Islamophobia which has been used to justify war abroad and authoritarianism at home, and of a strong Islamicist reaction to this current, has posed the danger that socialists might use crude atheist critiques of Islam to justify siding with imperialism. Nevertheless, the reactionary content of many religious ideas means that socialists must avoid the opposite danger of painting Islamic opponents of imperialism red. Given the complexity of this political context, it is essential that socialists have access to some rudder by which they can steer a course between either tailing fundamentalism or capitulating to imperialism.

An obvious prerequisite for any serious socialist engagement with such movements must be that we make concrete analyses of concrete situations: the particular social content of any religious movement must be the keystone by which we judge it.

With respect to the relationship between Islamicism and imperialism noted above, it is obvious that the main enemy is globalising imperialism. On a more mundane level, when I sat with members of a local church group on the train to last year's demonstration against the G8 in Edinburgh, the fact that their presence on the demo was informed by the belief that we are all equal in the eyes of god meant that to have opened our conversation with an atheistic denunciation of the idea of god would have been childishly sectarian. Rather than take this approach, our conversation centred on the problem of how best to build a movement to overcome global poverty, and I noticed a definite radicalisation of their opinion on the way home after they had experienced their first mass demo.

Needless to say, it is not beyond the realms of the possible that I might be forced to confront this couple again in less propitious circumstances—on opposite sides of the abortion debate for instance—where the reactionary side of their religious beliefs might come to place us on opposite sides of the barricades. This example is enough to recognise that how socialists would relate to this couple specifically, and religious movements more generally, is dependent on the concrete content of the movements informed by religious ideas. However, while examples such as this reflect the power of a simple intuitive approach to such movements, it remains the case that we need to go beyond intuition if we are to provide a compelling alternative to other perspectives.

For instance, in his *The God Delusion*, Richard Dawkins lends his own scientific authority to the contemporary demonisation of that dreaded beast 'fundamentalism' when he argues that religious thought is the main enemy of contemporary enlightened opinion. If socialists are to go beyond this type of one-dimensional denunciation of religion, they need to outline an alternative framework by which religion is to be explained.

This is exactly the task taken up by Scott Mann in his *Heart of a Heartless World: Religion as Ideology*. The starting point of Mann's analysis, as is evident from the title of his book, is Marx's critique of religion. Famous for arguing that religion was the 'opium of the people', a line which when taken out of context was used by Stalin to justify his very own 'war on drugs', Marx actually outlined a much more nuanced analysis of religion.

Whereas Enlightenment thinkers had first pointed to both the falsity of religious beliefs and their role in propping up reactionary regimes, and following from this had, Dawkins-like (first time with grandeur, second time as farce!), aimed at overthrowing such superstitions with the power of argument, Marx was more interested in the social basis of religious belief. The full quotation, taken from Marx's *Introduction to the Critique of Hegel's Philosophy of Right*, from which both the above line and the title of Mann's book are taken, reads thus:

'Religion...is the *fantastic realisation* of the human essence since the *human essence* has not acquired any true reality. The struggle against religion is, therefore, indirectly the struggle *against that world* whose spiritual *aroma* is religion. *Religious* suffering is, at one and the same time, the *expression* of real suffering and a *protest* against real suffering. Religion is the sigh of the oppressed creature, the heart of a heartless world, and the soul of soulless conditions. It is the *opium* of the people. The abolition of religion as the *illusory* happiness of the people is the demand for their *real* happiness. To call on them to give up their illusions about their condition is to call on them to *give up a condition that requires illusions*. The criticism of religion is, therefore, *in embryo, the criticism of that vale of tears* of which religion is the *halo*.'

Thus Marx, as Mann shows with admirable clarity, argued that to struggle against religion in the manner of Dawkins is at best to tilt at windmills. For if the source of religious belief is real human suffering, then to imagine overcoming the former without dealing with the latter is to lapse into a state of illusion every bit as incoherent as the belief in god itself. For socialists this would be no mere intellectual error. Rather it is precisely because those at the bottom of society tend to suffer most that they are most likely to embrace religion. To create a barrier between these people and revolutionary parties by insisting that they discard their beliefs before they join would thus be political suicide: fine for the proud sectarians who are happy with life in the political wilderness, but disastrous for serious socialist organisations that hope to win mass support.

It was precisely for this reason that Lenin was against making atheism a condition of membership of the Bolshevik Party: he realised that religious ideas would only wither away slowly after their sources in human suffering had disappeared. More generally, Marx's approach provides socialists with a framework from which they are able to keep their independence from religious ideas, while refusing to reify these ideas as the key problem in the modern world. In a capitalist system marked by exploitation, inequality and war, socialists recognise that religion, like other ideologies, can reflect the critique of these barbarities or become an apologist for them, and often can do both at the same time. We therefore engage with religious movements not primarily as the embodiment of abstractly false ideas, but in the light of how they relate to these the real key problems of our age, fighting alongside those who hold these beliefs in so far as they confront these problems, and criticising them in so far as they do not.

Mann's analysis does not stop with Marx. He attempts to synthesise these insights with others taken from Darwin and, especially, Freud. If Darwin overthrew religious explanations of the emergence of life, and Marx provides a social explanation of why after Darwin many continue to hold religious beliefs, Mann argues that Freud provides the basis for an explanation of how individuals come to embrace the view of an all-powerful god, and indeed manage to square the belief in god's love with a recognition of 'evil' in the world. He suggests that these beliefs are a form of fantasy wish-fulfilment in adults that operate as unconscious defence mechanisms, the source of which can be traced back to earlier childhood relations with their parents.

Indeed he attempts to synthesise Marx and Freud by arguing that human conscience can be shown to be no subliminal link to god because what is considered to be right and wrong changes over time. Rather conscience is best understood as a reflection in the child's eye view of parental authority, and as such is historical: as the image of parental authority evolves over time so too do ideas of right and wrong and the image of god.

Mann's book includes fascinating discussions of how the image of god changed through history; from the worship of the goddess in pre-class societies in Europe to the overthrow of this religion and its replacement by male gods following the emergence of class societies after the last ice age. He also has interesting things to say about the rise of Catholicism and Protestantism, and even an entertaining, if speculative, discussion of Jesus.

While it is unfortunate that he does not discuss Islam, the theoretical strengths of the book ensure that it should act as an important starting point, complementing books such as Paul Siegel's *The Meek and the Militant* and Michael Lowy's *The War of Gods*, for anyone wanting a materialist understanding of religion. My only regret is having not noticed its existence earlier. Indeed, because it was published in 1999 there is a good chance that your local bookshop will not have a copy. Fear not, it is still in print and Bookmarks can order a copy for you.

The state of revolutions

Joseph Choonara

A review of D L Raby, ***Democracy and Revolution: Latin America and Socialism Today*** *(Pluto, 2006), £15, Tariq Ali,* ***Pirates of the Caribbean—Axis of Hope*** *(Verso, 2006), £14.99 and Michael Lebowitz,* ***Build it Now: Socialism for the 21st Century*** *(Monthly Review Press, 2006), £10.95*

These three books take seriously the challenge, laid down by Venezuelan president Hugo Chavez at the 2005 World Social Forum, to reinvent socialism for the 21st century. Each of the books attempts to do this with reference to recent struggles in Latin America, in particular the unfolding 'Bolivarian Revolution' in Venezuela.

D L Raby's book draws on the author's deep understanding of the region's movements. This is put to good effect in two long chapters on Venezuela and Cuba, which contain useful historical material and insights. However, the main function of these chapters is to help support a highly controversial argument developed elsewhere in the book. For Raby, socialism today means 'a state of revolutionary popular power in permanent tension with capitalism and imperialism' (p262). Such inherently unstable regimes, and Raby has in mind both Cuba and Venezuela, must hold out until 'such time (still remote) as revolution and popular power/Socialism spreads through most of the world' (p65).

A number of problems with this vision of socialism rapidly emerge. In the chapter on Venezuela, Raby describes the work of the 'missions' dealing with problems of health, literacy and so on. These are not simply social programmes, but include important elements of participation by local communities. However, there are limits to the extent of this democratisation: 'It is precisely at the level of more formal political structures that popular participation falls off, and this remains one of the weaknesses of the Bolivarian Revolution' (p192).

This is quite a serious weakness. Chavez himself frequently bemoans the existence within the Venezuelan state of an 'old bureaucracy', a hangover from the previous elites who ruled the country, and a 'new bureaucracy' composed of Chavistas who want to limit change. Raby does not deal with the continued power held by this state machine which, although increasingly fragmented and disorganised, is still essentially a hierarchical body designed to ensure the smooth functioning of capitalism and the rule of an elite. At times Raby seems to suggest that Chavez's direct relationship with the Venezuelan masses is enough to bypass the state altogether, and at others she seems to suggest that the whole state supports the process of transformation.

A second issue in Venezuela is the continued existence of a capitalist elite: 'Capitalists may still be able to make handsome profits, but they do so under conditions dictated by the Venezuelan state and not just as they please,' writes Raby (p195). Currently Venezuela's old elite is enjoying an unprecedented boom time, reflected, for example, in vast sales of luxury cars. The same oil income that fuels the missions also allows the rich to line their pockets. So the oil boom can, for a time, soften class tensions, especially given the nervousness of an elite that has suffered major setbacks when it has tried to topple Chavez. But I find Raby's confidence that this question can be postponed indefinitely, while socialism spreads through the globe, overly optimistic.

One way in which the problems could be resolved is if the struggle from below, which has helped keep Chavez in power so far, begins to create new organs of workers' power. This could form the basis for an alternative kind of state—a workers' state. The idea is briefly considered by Raby. Mass working class power, forged from below, was seen in the Paris Commune of 1871 and 'it would appear in the Russian soviets of 1905 and 1917 and would continue for two to three years after the Bolshevik Revolution, only to be stifled under the pressures of civil war and foreign invasion and the centralism imposed by the party' (p31). It would seem that understanding how Russia went from being the world's greatest experiment in mass democracy to a Stalinist dictatorship, which Raby rightly rejects as a model, is quite important. Unfortunately, she dismisses the two key theorists who could help make sense of this.

The 'Trotskyist thesis of the impossibility of "socialism in one country" is dangerously misleading', Raby argues (p65). Socialism in one country is possible, she claims, as long as it proceeds slowly, for example maintaining a 'socio-economic system' that is 'still predominantly capitalist'. The complicated holding operation she envisages leaves the question of state power and the transition to socialism unresolved until some point in the future when a second, unspecified, stage occurs. This is not so much 'skinning a tiger claw by claw' as plucking its individual hairs while a hoard of other tigers look on hungrily. The danger of progress being rolled back—by external aggression, the return to power of the old elite either by force or fraud, or the emergence of a Stalinist-style bureaucracy—seems extremely great.

Raby also explicitly rejects the theory of state capitalism, developed by Tony Cliff (here inaccurately referred to as 'the founder of the International Marxist Tendency'), which could help explain what went wrong in Russia. I don't believe Raby has really examined this theory. For example, she claims to reject it on the grounds that the Soviet Union's economy was not shaped by its 'external economic relations'. But for Cliff it was military competition with the West, not trade, that enforced capitalist accumulation in Russia. This is not merely a dogmatic question. The central reason why Cliff developed his theory was to defend what he saw as the core of Marxism—that the emancipation of the working class must be the act of the working class itself. While in Russia the successful revolution had been followed by Stalinist counter-revolution, the state capitalist regimes in Eastern Europe and elsewhere were installed without workers' revolutions, often imposed by military might. They were never socialist or democratic regimes.

This is highly relevant for Raby's other case study, that of Cuba. Here Raby points out that the exodus of the island's capitalists to Florida and the hostility of the US in the wake of the 1959 revolution helped push Fidel Castro into the Communist camp. Raby charts Castro's miraculous conversion from his position in the wake of the revolution: 'I want to make it clear now that I am not a Communist' (22 January 1959) to his revelation: 'I am a Marxist-Leninist and will remain so until the end of my days' (2 December 1961). But this retrospectively Communist seizure of power makes a mockery of the notion that Communism is, as Marx argued, the 'self-conscious movement of the immense majority'.

Raby claims there was mass participation in the revolution: 'Some Trotskyists and other leftist writers, while expressing admiration for the Cuban Revolution, lament what they describe as a lack of working class or popular involvement or initiative, implying that everything was done by fiat of Fidel and a few other comandantes. Nothing could be further from the truth: despite the crucial leadership role of Fidel and the M26-7 [Castro's guerrilla army] commanders, there was enormous mass mobilisation throughout the country. The hundreds of thousands, even millions, who came to listen to Fidel's speeches did so spontaneously, and they came not only to listen but to shout and to answer back and to give their opinions' (p99). The popularity of the revolution is not in question, but Raby makes a serious mistake when she confuses popular acclaim with revolutionary self-emancipation.

The lack of self-activity in the revolution itself, which was carried through by a few hundred guerillas, has implications for the kind of democracy that flows from the revolution. Because there were no organs of workers' power, Castro substituted the highly centralised and authoritarian guerrilla command structure. Raby, with typical honesty, gives a detailed account of how Cuban democracy actually functions. Elected municipal delegates are responsible for 'all local affairs' but only within 'parameters laid down at national level' (p124). How are these parameters determined? Through the election of a national assembly, elected with one candidate for each position. 'The election is more like a popular ratification of a pre-selected list of candidates' (p127). Real power is held by a ruling Council of State, its decisions ratified by the assembly, which meets only twice a year and always votes unanimously. Raby concludes, 'At national level there is little doubt that basic policy is decided by the Communist Party leadership' (p129).

This is a book intimately concerned with democracy, which rightly lambasts Western liberal democracy. But it is hard to see how Cuba has an 'essentially democratic character' which goes beyond parliamentary democracy. Raby also defends a peculiar kind of radical populism that seems to preclude the need for revolutionary democracy. In one of the weakest sections of the book, she argues that after the revolution 'the greatest inspiration for thousands of militants throughout the country was the charisma and political genius of Fidel' (p112). 'The people felt their deepest desires were interpreted by Fidel,' so, 'democracy—the power of the people—meant the absolute power of the movement which had overthrown Batista's tyranny and which expressed popular hopes and dreams after decades of frustration' (p113).

Raby wants to extend this formula to Venezuela. Here 'the Venezuelan people acquired a collective identity and were constituted as a political subject through the actions of Hugo Chavez and the Bolivarian movement' (p233). The connection between a 'charismatic leader' and 'the people' is key to Raby's notion of a revolutionary process. Raby does not seem to acknowledge any unevenness or tensions between 'the people', composed of different classes with different interests and modes of struggle. Even within the working class there will be different strategies—and a battle for ideas within the revolutionary process.

These weaknesses come out in an interesting discussion of Salvador Allende's Chilean government, overthrown in 1973 by the coup led by Augusto Pinochet. Raby quite rightly points to 'elements of popular power developing in the callampas [shanty towns] and working class areas around Santiago and other main cities' (p202). In particular the workers' 'cordones industriales' and 'comandos comunales' provided real examples of the kind of organs of democratic control that emerge in revolutionary processes. 'But neither UP [Allende's Popular Unity] n or Allende personally chose to encourage this popular revolutionary energy,' writes Raby (p203).

It is as if the process comes crashing down because of the 'decidedly uncharismatic' Allende. But the possibility existed of turning these workers' organs into an alternative workers' state, built from below. That would have required a mass revolutionary organisation, rooted in the day to day struggles of the working class, its members trusted as leaders, coordinated nationally and capable of drawing together the different sectional struggles. Raby rejects the idea of a 'self-proclaimed' vanguard party, but in doing so she also rejects the real Leninist tradition, one that is based on providing rather than assuming leadership.

While Raby makes a sophisticated attempt to engage with the movements in Latin America, Tariq Ali's book, *Pirates of the Caribbean*, seems far more superficial. The tone is set with a silly, geographically inaccurate title. The first two chapters are a dull read and seem largely concerned with lashing out at various figures from Ali's past who have deserted the cause of socialism. However, the author's literary flair is more apparent in the later chapters on Venezuela, Bolivia and Cuba. In the first two cases, Ali provides engaging historical accounts of the rise of Chavez and Bolivia's president Evo Morales. But while Raby paints Chavez as a kind of unconscious populist revolutionary, Ali tends to paint him as a traditional social democrat.

He writes of Venezuela: 'democratic and republican institutions will have to be rebuilt, strengthened and developed as a real alternative to neoliberal democracy, while simultaneously continent-wide structures need to be created as an alternative to the networks of the Northern global market and corruption consistently challenged' (p76). Ali offers no serious account of the class struggles that have fuelled the revolutionary process, the tensions within the state or the challenges that lie ahead.

Similarly the chapter on Bolivia ends with the election of Morales in December 2005, seen as the logical result of the waves of mass struggle. Ali suggests that 'what is being proposed in Bolivia is...a form of radical social democracy' (p96). Again there is no serious analysis of two periods, in 2003 and 2005, when mass popular assemblies, especially in the huge indigenous city of El Alto, posed the possibility of the emergence of a revolutionary democracy. The 2005 wave of struggle, arguably the high tide of anti-capitalist struggle in the past two decades, is not even mentioned.

The chapter on Cuba breaks with the historical presentation used in the previous two cases. Ali instead presents a diary of his recent trip to the island—which I was surprised to read was his first visit. The format means he does not consider the rise of Castro or the nature of the Cuban Revolution, but he does make some interesting, critical comments.

He writes, 'I have always been of the view that revolutions can enhance democracy in a way that is (especially in today's world) forbidden in the capitalist world. Public debate, criticism, the exchange of conflicting opinions will strengthen Cuba and empower and arm its citizens, already among the best educated in the world. This is now a political necessity and should not be indefinitely delayed' (p121).

Build it Now, by Caracas-based Marxist

Michael Lebowitz, is a more satisfying read. It brings together seven brief, accessible essays. While it lacks the level of detail in Raby's book, it would be a good work to recommend to someone inspired by developments in Venezuela to find out more about socialism. It begins with an admirably lucid summary of Marx's analysis of capitalism and works through ever more concrete discussions of the problems of socialism and democracy. It ends with an extremely concrete chapter on Venezuela today.

Lebowitz's Marxism is based on the concept of human needs. 'Look to what working people are doing, Marx argued. Through their own struggles to satisfy their needs (which, for Marx, reflect all aspects of their existence as human beings within society and nature), they reveal that the battle for a new society is conducted by struggling within capitalism rather than looking outside. In those struggles workers come to recognise their common interests, they come to understand the necessity to join together against capital' (p58).

Lebowitz's clear emphasis on 'socialism from below' immediately marks his work out as an advance from those of Raby and Ali. 'Socialism is not populism,' he argues. 'A society in which people look to the state to provide them with resources and with the answers to all their problems does not foster the development of human capacities' (p71). He is keenly aware of the different phases of mass struggle that have shaped events in Venezuela and also of the tensions within the state. He warns of those 'Chavist leaders' who wish to create 'Chavez without socialism'. He also raises important arguments about the limits of workers' control, particularly within what most of those in the government regard as 'strategic industries'.

At times Lebowitz seems to overstate the extent to which workers' co-management of industry and the formation of co-operatives can break with the logic of capitalism. There is a danger of seeing the political formation of a workers' state as an end result of a sweeping economic transformation within capitalism through the formation of a 'non-capitalist sector'. The potential to do this within a capitalist society, presided over by a capitalist state, is limited. Workers' organisation has to be focused far more on political tasks, forging a democratic workers' state from below, rather than attempting to run industry in a non-capitalist way.

A second weakness, linked to this, is over the question of state power. At one point Lebowitz draws on Marx's writings on the 1871 Paris Commune, arguing that the working class cannot simply use 'the ready-made state machinery for its own purposes' (p69) and arguing for a workers' state built from below. At other times he seems to argue that it is possible to take control of the state: 'The first step in Venezuela was to gain control of the existing state...that state is now being used to create the basis for new productive relations' (p110). I suspect that Lebowitz distinguishes between the Venezuelan state as it exists under Chavez, and a workers' state that could replace it, but this could have been clarified.

These concerns aside, Lebowitz puts forward powerful arguments. In particular he highlights the kind of institutions, the new Communal Councils along with organisation in workplaces, that could begin to create a new political power from below. He is also aware of the need for a 'political instrument that can bring together those fighting for protagonistic democracy in the workplace and the community' (p115). And whatever the debates provoked by the unfolding process, it is far better to have a world in which movements make these strategic questions of burning importance. Lebowitz's call for, 'Two, Three, Many Bolivarian Revolutions!' is spot on.

Dialectics of morality

Chris Harman

A review of Alex Callinicos, ***The Resources of Critique*** *(Polity, 2006), £16.99*

Alex Callinicos attempts to deal with important questions in this book. How is it possible for people conditioned by the structures of a certain society to go beyond these (a process Alex calls 'transcendence') to fight for a different society? How is it possible to find criteria of truth that escape social conditioning? And is it possible to lay down universally valid moral principles?

Alex approaches the issues by a critical appraisal of a number of recent philosophical and sociological works, by thinkers such as Badiou, Habermas, Zizek, Bidet and Negri. Readers should be warned that in doing so he adopts a style of writing much more difficult to follow than the lucid exposition of ideas he provides in the weekly columns he writes for *Socialist Worker*, and in works like *An Anticapialist Manifesto* and *The Revolutionary Ideas of Karl Marx*. In this book he confronts the thinkers he deals with in their own, often opaque, terms: it is as if, in taking on such opponents, he has been forced onto their own ground. I know experienced *International Socialism* readers who have struggled to get through the book, and a couple who have given up in the process. His endeavour is, however, a worthy one—even though I disagree with some of his conclusions.

His discussion on agency centres around the ideas of Badiou and Zizek, both of whom, according to him, see sudden revolutionary change as arising, in an almost mystical way, out of nothing. He argues that there are sudden 'leaps', when people begin to act in ways that break with their own conditioning, but that these can be understood as a reaction to contradictions in reality not immediately observable on the surface. He bases much of his argument on the 'realist' theory of science presented by philosopher Roy Bhaskar (before he moved towards notions of spirituality derived from Buddhism). This sees reality as operating at different levels, so what is happening at the surface does not tell us what is really happening and what can happen. Tensions below lead to sudden breaks at the surface level: 'strains within and between...structures...may well destabilise existing social relations and...motivate actors to seek change.'

These notions are not something particularly new discovered by Bhaskar. Marx pointed out in volume III of *Capital*, 'All science would be superfluous if the outward appearance was the essence of things.' Lukács stressed the distinction between different levels of reality in *History and Class Consciousness*, and much the same distinction exists in Engels' discussion on 'the real and the rational' in *Ludwig Feuerbach and the End of Classical German Philosophy*. But I do see some weaknesses in Alex's approach to these questions. Although he is prepared to accept elements of the materialist dialectic working as operating in nature, in a way in which he used not to, he still dismisses certain dialectical notions, reducing the dialectic just to the transformation of quantity into quality.

He does not see how the notion of the 'identity' or 'interpenetration' of opposites provides an insight into the endless, contradictory dynamic of change in nature and society, with the fixed forms correctly categorised using formal logic transmuting in ways which it cannot grasp. And by dismissing the 'negation of the negation' as 'idealistic', he misses out on something central. Living things are not merely the sum total of the conditions which act externally on them (their 'negation') but absorb these conditions and react back on them, creating something new ('negating' their 'negation'). Applied to humanity, it means that those who suffer passively from the conditions in which they find themselves have the potential of becoming conscious of the causes of their suffering and striving to master them. Alienation itself creates the possibility of the struggle against alienation ('A is for alienation that makes me the man that I am,' as the revolutionary folk singer of the late 1960s Alex Glasgow phrased it).

But not grasping these points fully, Alex weakens a generally correct approach to the question of agency and revolutionary change. Much less satisfactory, in my view, are his attempts to deal with the questions of objective knowledge and non-relativistic morality.

After spelling out the relativist case (in the version put by recent continental philosophers, although he could have done so using people who put the same ideas in a different form 40 or even 100 years ago), his own refutations seem a little feeble. On knowledge he seems to say that science has developed a set of procedures, and these enable us to get objective knowledge. But it is difficult see from his arguments what justifies these procedures.

Things are very much the same when it comes to morality. Alex claims that Marxism has suffered from a lack of an explicit morality in the past—'an ethical deficit'. But his own attempt to provide one rests on what seems an arbitrary procedure.

After recognising that different moral codes are shaped by different social circumstances, he then claims that it is possible to escape from relativism by adapting the 'liberal egalitarianism' of the America philosopher Rawls (which is itself derived from Kant's notion that asserting one's own humanity means recognising others as 'ends' and not 'means') so as to justify a moral code with equality as its core precept. As I read the book, I waited expectantly to arrive at the pages in which Alex provided some reason other than his own predilections (which I of course sympathise with) for this approach. But they do not exist. He has not solved the task he set himself.

My view is that the weaknesses of Alex's arguments come from his not taking seriously enough Marx's comment in his *Theses on Feurbach* 'that man must prove the truth, ie the reality and power, the this-worldliness of his thinking in practice. The dispute over the reality and non-reality of thinking which isolates itself from practice is a purely scholastic question'. It is this approach which is encapsulated in Gramsci's description of Marxism as 'the philosophy of practice'.

Knowledge and moral systems both arise out of human activity—and that activity has been socially organised ever since our ancestors descended from the trees (indeed, even before that, studies of our closest primate cousins suggest). Through 99.99 percent of history humans' interaction with each other and the world has been limited and so too necessarily has been their understanding of the world. In hunter-gatherer or peasant societies it is restricted to a very narrow geographic compass, with little knowledge of what is happening beyond the immediate region. So certainties about what is involved in the everyday tasks of making a livelihood are fitted into mythical accounts of the wider world.

In class societies knowledge is also limited by social factors. People do, of course, know what they themselves are doing. But the possibilities of fitting this into a wider framework of understanding are shaped socially. The leisure which provides opportunities to generalise about the world at large has generally been available only to the ruling classes and those who ingratiate themselves with them. But the practices of established ruling classes divorce them from much of the labour of interacting materially with nature ('work' is beneath them) and create a barrier to them seeing the world other than in their own narrow perspectives. And any established ruling class has to sanctify its rule with superstitions and irrational beliefs and is therefore frightened of developments of knowledge which undermine these. Meanwhile, the exploitation and oppression of the masses limits and distorts their understanding of reality in so far as they remain passive victims of class society.

But the fact that all knowledge is conditioned by social practice does not necessarily have to lead to relativism. For some forms of social practice cover a wider compass and so provide better insights into reality than others. A social class that is driven to confront the power of an existing ruling class has an interest in understanding the social process that produced that class's power—that is, in going to the root of things in a way the ruling class does not. Intellectuals who identify with its struggles are capable of going beyond the old levels of knowledge—of understanding both the standpoint of the intellectuals of the old ruling class and the limitations to that standpoint. The claim to deeper knowledge cannot, of course, come simply from claiming to represent a new class. It has to be validated by an ability to take on the most difficult of the arguments put in the past, but to show that doing so involves a different perspective from the old one. This is the process Marx undertakes in *Capital*, which is simultaneously a completion of the efforts of Smith, Ricardo and other classical political economists and a critique of their perspective. It is this also which George Lukács attempted to undertake in the central piece on philosophy in *History and Class Consciousness*.

But the method does not only apply to knowledge of the world. It also has implications for morality. Moral concepts are not arbitrary concepts made up by or imposed on individuals. They are social products. They assert a view of what human beings should do if a society is to continue functioning so as to satisfy the needs of its members. To be 'good' is to behave socially in certain ways (or at least not to 'misbehave'). In a stable, cohesive society which provides clear benefits to all its participants, what is involved is unproblematic. In, for instance, the foraging ('hunter-gathering') societies described by Richard Lee and Eleanor Leacock, people accepted unquestioningly that what was 'good' was fulfilment of their roles. They might have failed to do what they should, but would not then question that they had done 'wrong'.

But things change with the move from such primitive communist societies to class societies. Then contradictory notions of what is 'good' arise. People are torn between contradictory moral codes. This, for instance, is where the power of the ancient Greek tragedy comes from—to abide by an old code is to infringe a new one. In the process moral codes of any sort can come to seem arbitrary as different social groups counterpose their codes to each other. Yet the very fact that they can argue over what is 'good' means that they all recognise, implicitly, that some code is necessary for social living to continue. Arguments over what is 'good' rest on arguments about reality, even if they seem not too. 'Ought' does rely on arguments about what 'is'.

The central parameters within which these arguments take place are class ones. A class which fights to preserve existing society has one set of notions about what is necessary to keep society going, and attempts to impose on people the moral notions that correspond to this. It has to portray the values it propagates as the values necessary for society as a whole, what is good for itself as absolutely 'good'. By contrast, a class which feels its needs are not met and presses for society to be reconstituted on a different basis necessarily begins to advance different interpretations of moral notions. The contradictory interpretations become most intense when society enters deep economic and social crises, in which 'things cannot continue in the old way.'

Alex criticises as 'relativistic' what he sees as the traditional Marxist approach of denying that there can be any moral standpoint outside the context of a particular form of society. But the charge of relativism fails once you see the clash between rival moral codes as between those that try to preserve an old order which increasingly prevents society functioning on behalf of its members (threatening the reversion of 'civilisation' to 'barbarism' or the 'mutual destruction of the contending classes'), and others that point forward to a reconstitution of society on a new basis.

The successive 'modes of production' humanity has lived through since the rise of class society five or six thousand years ago have not only involved different economic organisation; they have also represented different stages of simultaneously developing and hindering the capacity of human society to fulfil the needs of its members. And with capitalism we have the stage of a mode of production that not merely rests on the exploitation of most of society's members, but which threatens the destruction of social living as such if it is allowed to persist. This is 'immoral' by any criteria of what is 'good'. By contrast the struggles of the main exploited class under this system do throw up the notions of solidarity, sharing and egalitarianism. These lay the basis for a new morality (or rather, the rebirth 'at a higher level' of the morality of primitive communism) which offers a way out of such destructive tendencies. This is what the young Marx meant when he spoke of the proletariat as a 'universal class'.

An approach that sees things in such terms provides a better basis for judging capitalism than the 'liberal egalitarianism' of Rawls.

Yet for all its problems this is a book which takes up important questions, even if it does not always provide answers.

Questioning post-Fordism

Paul Blackledge

A review of Bill Dunn, ***Global Restructuring and the Power of Labour*** *(Palgrave, 2004), £45*

Bill Dunn, whose edited collection on Trotsky was recently reviewed on these pages, has produced an excellent critique of the assumption, common across parts of the left, that changes in the conditions of labour over the last few decades have had disastrous consequences for the capacity of workers to mount collective struggles against capital.

Through a critical survey of the literature on both labour's situation in a number of key sectors of the world economy—automobiles, construction, semiconductors and finance—and the dominant explanations for that situation in terms of the emergence of a globalised economy and the shift to post-Fordist production techniques, Dunn offers an alternative basis for an explanation of the defeats suffered by labour and the hegemony of neoliberalism in recent decades. However, while Dunn breaks with the view that workers are merely passive victims of their social situation, he does not simply invert the fatalism associated with some accounts of globalisation and post-Fordism—according to which the objective situation of workers has become so bad as to condemn them to impotence before the power of capital—with an equally one-sided model of class struggle voluntarism.

With respect to globalisation theory, Dunn challenges the suggestion that the undoubted changes which have come to be bracketed under the umbrella term 'globalisation' have led to a fundamental weakening of either the power of states or the power of workers. He insists that states have not been so undermined as some would argue, and that in any case the power of labour should not be equated with state power. Drawing on the Marxist model of combined and uneven development, Dunn shows that globalisation has developed and continues to develop in an uneven manner, such that patterns of foreign direct investment, for instance, remain skewed towards the Triad economies of Europe, North America and Japan, and where there is investment beyond these economies it is highly localised.

Dunn therefore shows how the world remains an extremely unequal place, both between countries and within countries. For instance, enormous expansion in parts of China, India and other countries in what was once known as the Third World goes hand in hand with the continued existence of a sea of poverty and underdevelopment both within these countries and outside the triad more generally.

Whereas certain theorists of globalisation, and certainly those ideologues who have hyped up the idea to justify attacks on workers, have posited globalisation as a large-scale account of the recent decline of the power of labour, the suggestion that we have moved from a Fordist towards a Post-Fordist labour process in the post-war years has provided many with a small-scale model of the same. It has been argued, for instance, that the deepening of the division of labour within the working class has led to it becoming so fragmented that it is now politically powerless as a class, while the rise of consumer led production has undermined the basis for collective action across the working class. Dunn challenges both of these arguments, insisting that changes in the system have been overemphasised and continuities downplayed. Concretely, Dunn, in an overview of changes in the sectors noted above, suggests a more complex picture than that posited by theorists of post-Fordism. Thus, while he accepts that 'significant changes in the structure of capitalism occurred in the 20th century', he maintains that 'their social and spatial unevenness, complexity and differences of interpretation again suggest that the evidence is insufficiently conclusive to take labour's structural disempowerment as established' (p52).

As against those theorists of globalisation and post-Fordism who have tended to offer overly deterministic and consequently impressionistically pessimistic models of the decline of labour, Dunn proposes that the left would do better to analyse the defeats suffered by the working class from the mid-1970s not, mechanically, through accounts of the changing structures of either or both of the global economy and of the world of work, but rather through dialectical analyses of the relationship between these changes and changes in patterns of class struggles. Moreover, he argues that, while certain social processes have increased the tendencies towards the fragmentation of the working class over the last two or three decades, other processes have tended in the opposite direction, and this situation sets part of the context for class struggles without mechanically determining the outcome of those struggles. Indeed, against the simplistic view that changes in the labour process weakened the power of labour, he points out that, in the car industry for example, 'decisive defeats for labour preceded substantial restructuring and may have provided the basis for it, rather than simply being its consequence' (p202).

Dunn thus closes his book with a call for deeper analyses of the defeats experienced by the working class over the last few decades, with a view to pointing towards a way out of the crude economically deterministic models of the changes that have affected labour in that period. Moreover, he argues for bringing class struggle back into a sophisticated Marxist analysis of the defeats of the past, not out of simple academic interest in outlining a more powerful explanation of theses defeats, but, more importantly, as a means of offering a basis for a socialist strategy for labour in the 21st century. For, as he argues against the more pessimistic conclusions of certain theorists of globalisation and post-Fordism, a lot of evidence has confirmed the idea that 'workers' struggles continued, in practice, to make a difference' (p204).

Pick of the quarter

Political explosions are so frequent in Latin America these days that it is sometimes hard to keep up with them. The most surprising ones last year were in Mexico—first with the mass demonstrations in Mexico City against the rigging of the presidential election and then with the rising which developed out of the teachers' strike in Oaxaca (pronounced wa-haka).

Our website contains a report of the Oaxaca events, but for a fuller account of the background to what is happening there are contrasting articles by Dan La Botz in **Against the Current** (available on the web at www.solidarity-us.org/node/186) and by Al Giordano in the September-October **New Left Review** (www.newleftreview.org/?page=article&view=2633).

Also of interest in that issue of *New Left Review* is a fascinating piece by Mike Davis on Dubai (www.newleftreview.org/?page=article&view=2635), while *Against the Current* has at least two other articles worth a read. Sam Farber reviews Greg Grandin's *Empire's Workshop*—an account of how the neocons practised in Central America in the 1980s (against many Catholic populations) all the methods they are now justifying with Islamophobia in Iraq. And Au Loong-yu provides a very useful piece spelling out the interrelation of Chinese capitalism and the world system—in particular making the point that growth in China has been accompanied by the loss of 25 million jobs in the older sectors of manufacturing industry (www.solidarity-us.org/node/185).

There is another interesting piece on the Chinese economy by Phillip Anthony O'Hara in the summer issue of the **Review of Radical Political Economics** (which only those with access to certain university libraries are likely to able to get hold of), with attempts to calculate the Marxist categories of the rate of exploitation, the organic composition of capital and the rate of profit.

Even more interesting in that issue is a piece by Tim Koechlin, 'US Multinational Corporations and the Mobility of Productive Capital: a Sceptical View'. He analyses the figure for US investment and concludes that between 1991 and 2004 Foreign Direct Investment by US companies only amounted to 7.4 percent of total productive investment by those companies—and investment in 'developing countries' only 2.5 percent. He concludes that productive investment (eg in factories) is much less mobile than you would believe from the fashionable hype about globalisation meaning all production moving from the richer to the poorer countries—with its implication that workers have lost any capacity to fight back over wages and conditions. It is an article that deserves to be pirated and plagiarised (with recognition for its author) as a weapon of ideological struggle.

The opening piece in the November **Monthly Review** by Fred Magdoff also contains some interesting facts. He points out that, although the proportion of US national output going to arms is lower than it was 30 years ago, it still has a considerable economic effect, since 'official military expenditures for 2001-05 average 42 percent of gross non-residential private investment'.

Readers of the section on the events of 1956 in our last issue might want to read people's memories of that year in **Revolutionary History** and **History Workshop Journal** (again, unfortunately, only readily available at certain libraries). One recollection is of the university authorities issuing an official ban on students from taking trains to London on the day of the big Suez demonstration (presumably as part of the Cold War 'defence of democracy'). Especially fascinating are the minutes of the University Socialist Society committee, with Peter Sedgwick (later a founding editor of *International Socialism* but described by Jean McCrindle in another piece as a fervent admirer of Stalinism until the spring of 1956) arranging meetings to be addressed, among others, by John Saville (who had recently left the Communist Party to found the *New Reasoner*) and Mike Kidron (described in the minutes as recently at Balliol and into 'Trotskyism'). Delegated to meet speakers at the station was Irfan Habib—today one of India's foremost Marxist historians.

The contents of the latest issue (29) of **Socialist History** look interesting (I have not had a chance to read it yet) with articles by *International Socialism* contributor Christian Høgsbjerg (on trade unionism in Gibraltar), UCU union activist Steve Cushion on a miners' strike in Nazi-occupied France, and reviews by Ralph Darlington (challenging interpretations of the 2002-03 firefighters' and the 1984 miners' strikes) and Mike Haynes (on how Simon Schama treats history as a 'commodity').

Just arrived as we go to press is the latest issue of **Film International**, centred on cinema and realism. At first glance it looks like a treat. There is an excellent piece by Mike Wayne on realism, studies on realism in British cinema in the late 1940s, plus pieces on critical looks at the unification of Germany (including *Goodbye Lenin*), on John Sayles and on realism in South Asian cinema (by *International Socialism* contributor Talat Ahmed).

CH

Feedback: 1956 and Labour

Barry Conway

As a former pupil of Stan Newens in Hackney back in the 1960s, I now know why he gave me such good marks for a talk I gave on the Russian Revolution, despite the mess that I made of it. Given that it was the only time I ever got any good marks from him, I feel pleased I can now respond to his enlightening article on a British revolutionary's experience of the events in Hungary in 1956 with a fraternity utterly lacking in that grim Victorian classroom, save for that one brief moment.

Firstly, I would have to take issue with Stan that Gerry Healy's *Newsletter* group attracted former Communist Party members because Healy's group were better organised and resourced. More likely they were attracted to a political theory that said that Russia and Eastern Europe were still socialist despite the loss of political control by the working class. This answer as to why Russian tanks obliterated workers' struggle sat comfortably with people who had fought the bosses all their conscious lives. Accepting a theory of Russia as a degenerated workers' state, even though wrong, made their own struggles and sacrifices seem worthwhile.

Notwithstanding this disagreement, Stan has highlighted an aspect of shifting loyalties in the 1950s which is often forgotten in discussions today on the trajectory of New Labour thinking.

The Labour Party has always been short on theory. Much of its politics has been pragmatic and chameleon-like, hatched in committees with one eye on the share prices and the other on the polls. Nevertheless, the Communist Party (including its 1956 refugees who joined Labour) had an important influence in the 1960s and 1970s on the formative political education of some of today's leading Labour figures—John Reid, Charles Clarke, Jack Straw, not to mention Fife MP Gordon Brown, to name but a few. For these people, their initial flirtation with the promise of a workers' paradise by Stalinist diktat was always wedded to the more 'realistic' idea of state-run economies underpinned by productivity deals that would pay for the reforms they felt capitalism needed.

Their complete lack of understanding of the nature of the Russian state as a state capitalist economy exploiting and oppressing workers in order to compete globally, meant they could embrace nationalisation while condemning 'Communism' as some kind of Russian nightmare conjured up by Lenin which would never appeal to British workers. Draconian labour laws, camps for dissidents, lack of democracy, token trade unions, militarism, and a strong state manipulated by policemen and bureaucrats, accompanied by 'socialist' spin around peace and progress, were features rejected by Labour and trade union leaders. The idea that capitalism could take many forms, shaped by the vagaries of the world system, was simply not on their radar.

What is striking today is the way some of these New Labour leaders have reconfigured their early ideas and transformed them into something palatable for the City. Having given up challenging the private sector with the threat of planning, these people have turned their attention to the one area the Tories could never restructure—the welfare state.

New Labour's offensive against public sector workers—productivity deals underpinned with draconian leave, sickness, competency and capability policies, often rubber-stamped by trade union leaders, and delivered by tyrannical managers, would probably not have seemed out of place in turbulent Hungary. Neither would the utter contempt displayed by New Labour politicians and their creatures for working class people. Handing over control, as well as billions of pounds worth of the welfare state to capitalists through a myriad of legislation has come as a profound shock to millions of workers who, despite everything, still hold on to a kernel of resistance to a market-driven health and education service. Yet, under the guise of reform and progress, efficiency, initiative and partnership, this is precisely what is being done.

So what is happening? Is this straightforward privatisation when public service workers do not directly produce surplus value? But how do you maintain a nationalised health or education service while satisfying business demands to get their snouts in the trough? Do the billions of pounds ploughed into public services serve the same function as those fat military contracts did in the 1950s and 1960s and stabilise the system? Are today's Labour leaders following a path of deflected state capitalism with the logical result of imperialist war abroad and fear and terror at home?

It's a pity that Stan left the Socialist Review Group and subsequently became a Labour MP. Five years after giving that terrible talk in his classroom I joined the SRG's successor, the International Socialists. It was there that I learned that history-making events like the Hungarian Revolution provide both opportunities and dangers. The opportunities Stan has clearly pointed out (and socialists would not have missed the parallels with today challenges). But there's something in me that says that the dangers may well have been lying dormant in Stan's chosen party for the past 50 years.